Talking CBT with Parents and Children

A Guide for the Cognitive-Behavioral Therapist

DR. NAOMI EPEL

Talking CBT with Parents and Children
A Guide for the Cognitive-Behavioral Therapist
Dr. Naomi Epel

Senior Editors & Producers: ContentoNow
Translation: Zvi Chazanov
Assistant translator: Rina Tal
Editor: Tammy Kantor
Graphic: Oksana Kravtsova
Cover book: Benjie Herskowitz
Administration producer: Herela Hodaya Moise

Copyright © 2016 by Dr. Naomi Epel

ISBN: 978-965-550-594-8
International sole distributor: ContentoNow
3 Barzel St., Tel Aviv, 6671007, Israel
www.ContentoNow.com
netanel@contentonow.com

Talking CBT with Parents and Children

A Guide for the Cognitive-Behavioral Therapist

Dr. Naomi Epel

CONTENTO**NOW**

This book is dedicated in loving memory to
Professor Michael Rosenbaum
A pioneer of research and treatment in
Cognitive-Behavioral Therapy in Israel

Table of Contents

3 | A Parent's Gift to Their Children in Contemporary Times – Fostering Self-Esteem and Self-Efficacy

Acknowledgements

First and foremost, a thank you to Shmulik, the man who has stood by me for more than twenty-five years, and to my three children: Guy, Hadas, and Tal, all of whom have supported and encouraged me through every stage of writing this book, and who, together with me, celebrated the completion of composing each and every chapter.

A never-ending thank you to Talmor Zetler-Rom, my colleague at Shitot Institute, who collaborated in the writing of this book from its infancy and read all the material while commenting and enlightening with her wisdom and clarity of vision.

I would like to express my never ending gratitude to Rina Tal, my close colleague, for her sensitive and watchful eye during the translation of my book into English. She guided the process with an accuracy and thoroughness that is rare – allowing the reader to receive the exact spirit of my intentions and the processes detailed in this book.

A special thank you goes to my second family, the members of the Shitot Institute, who played a major role in the output of material that appears in this book. Additionally, they shared the practical application of tools, ideas, and methods, while observing and assessing the results of intervention. They were also the driving force behind the idea of writing this book.

This book has been made possible by the dozens of trainees and students I have had the honor to teach, who constantly asked me to publish what I practice. Thanks to all the wonderful people who inspired me and instilled in me the passion to write.

Lastly, I am especially indebted to my dear and cherished clients: the children, the parents, and the families whom I have treated over the past thirty years. We laughed and cried together and essentially never stopped learning together. Honestly, you have taught me the most. I learned about the uniqueness of each and every one of you, of your inner world and your world as a family, as a couple, as parents, and as children and about the bonds that connect between all of these. You have shown me more than any research I have ever read, about which things really work, which tools are more effective for you and which are less effective, what helped you to change behaviors, thoughts, and feelings, what helped you to feel better and progress towards your goals. Thank you for allowing me to write about scenes from your personal lives (under pseudonyms of course) and in this way assist many others to progress in the direction of their desired change.

During the writing of this book, I discovered, in contradiction to my initial expectations, that I have a tendency to write in a very personal style – a style which delves deeply into the therapeutic process. Perhaps this is not a coincidence. One of the complaints I hear about Cognitive-Behavioral Therapy is that it is too technical, lacking dimension and intricacy. It seems to me that readers of this book will discover otherwise. Many types of tools, techniques, and methods I have developed over the years are presented in this book, and yet each tool has a clear rationale, objective and function. We do not use a particular method in treatment because it's nice or because we've heard how effective it is; we use a certain tool only when it is clear what we intend to achieve by using it only when we fully understand the problem, the client, his needs, and the factors which caused him to seek assistance, and when we have a sound basis to assume a particular tool chosen will best serve our objectives.

Over the years, many field professionals have approached me with a request to write a clear and orderly list of protocols I have taught in professional courses, seminars, and workshops. Accordingly, the second part of this book deals with, among other topics, the protocols associated with the childhood years, based upon the children's books I have authored. These books were written essentially as therapy protocols, even though they are highly regarded as children's literature and deal with typical childhood problems: coping with anger and aggression, coping with childhood fears, and acquiring social skills for some various personality types.

This book is intended for experienced Cognitive-Behavioral clinicians. For clinicians who are just starting out and are interested in utilizing this book, it is advisable to fully acquaint yourselves with the basic concepts of the Cognitive-Behavioral approach. This is important because there are a number of concepts meant to be incorporated by clinicians, both theoretically and practically.

Dr. Naomi Epel

Why is Cognitive-Behavioral Therapy Special?

CBT is evidence based therapy. Cognitive-Behavioral Therapy has been widely researched since its inception, about one hundred years ago, and has continually developed over time, according to further empirical findings. Its principles have proven extremely effective in parent training and in child-direct therapy (Kendall, 2006; Lyneham & Rapee, 2005; Ronen, 2003).

Cognitive-Behavioral Therapy includes several important principles that allow the therapist to be accessible to his clients, while the client, whether a child or an adult, is an active partner in determining treatment goals and the manner in which these goals will be attained.

In contrast to other methods of therapy, there is an immediate endeavor on the side of the therapist to instill the client with a sense of security and to be understood by the client. The therapist works at the client's level: explaining, answering questions, involving the client in contemplations, the sharing of thoughts and uncertainties, and guiding the client toward achieving their goals, which are determined in collaboration with the client (Beck, 1995, 2011).

CBT therapists, even if working with a strict protocol, should have a fair measure of creativity and the ability to continually seek out solutions. The therapist must be flexible when choosing which tools are suitable for the client, and be able to keep the focus on the client's strengths and maintain positive thinking, while having the power to envision a better future for the client. The CBT therapist must advance slowly, step-by-step – and with small achievable steps – while constantly assessing the client's progress.

In comparison to other approaches, the CBT therapist does not interpret the client, but rather seeks the client's interpretations at each stage of therapy. In this respect, the therapist and the client, the adult and the child, work as a research team: together they investigate how the client thinks, feels, and behaves. Just as in research, they too are engaged in studying the connections between different variables, trying to predict reactions in accordance with those connections, arriving at conclusions and suggesting solutions.

The client in this type of treatment is meant to immediately feel understood, acknowledged, and secure. The client should feel that he has come to a professional – one who understands what he is doing and can guide him safely towards his goals.

The therapy process, which develops between therapist and client, in my view, is similar to a group excursion. Not an ordinary field trip, but similar to the excursions I experienced in my own childhood on the kibbutz where I was raised. Along with our group's teacher, we would go out into the fields, amazed by the redness of the poppies that greeted us. On the way, we met plants and animals and together we studied what we had found. We would take turns guessing, "that's got to be yellow-weed," or "that looks like a hedgehog," and our instructor would encourage us or refute our conjectures. These outings were always a constant stream of study and learning. We knew what sort of adventure to expect, where we wanted to go, and we also knew the route – but we were always excited about what we found along the way and when we ran into something really interesting, we tried to make sense of it together with our teacher.

Therapy is a kind of excursion, a type of journey. In Cognitive-Behavioral Therapy, the path must be a clear one. Where do we want to go? Which route do we take? What are the resources available to us, and when and how should we apply them? We should expect to find some surprises along the way, a few hurdles and possibly some hazards, so we will need much more than a map and a compass. We will require the capacity to be creative, to think with flexibility, and to be willing to alter our route according to the road conditions.

In a recent conversation I had with a dear colleague of mine, we spoke of our goals in the training of therapists, students of CBT therapy. He said something that stayed with me ever since and remained with me throughout the writing of this book, "It is imperative that therapists know what to do and not just do what they know." There is great wisdom in this statement and perhaps it represents the entire essence, especially when we are talking about psychological therapy, in particular, the treatment of families and moreover, children.

The CBT therapist needs to be sure of what he's doing. Regrettably, on occasion, we run into professionals working in the field of CBT who place too much emphasis on adhering to the treatment protocols, losing sight of the client along the way. This results in establishing a technical experience for the client: cold and lacking adequate acceptance and understanding.

Moreover, by complying too closely with the technical aspects of treatment, the therapist may not be able to identify the specific requirements of the client. Thus, it happens that behavioral therapists are often viewed as technocrats, who do what they know how to do instead of knowing what they are doing.

A certain dexterity is necessary in order to enable the therapist to safely maneuver between the contexts of therapy, which calls for a depth of knowledge of various different disorders and the effective methods applicable to each condition, along with therapy procedure. In this process, the client and the therapist are found in a unique meeting place, both intimate and matter-of-fact, one which demands the therapist to be attuned and attentive to the client at all times, all the while keeping in mind the treatment's common goals and objectives, which are decided upon during therapy.

Whenever I instruct professional therapists, I use the aid of management models in order to explain the flexibility required to maneuver between focusing on an objective and aspiring for interpersonal relations – the bond with the client. Borrowing examples from the field of management is not coincidental. In Cognitive-Behavioral Therapy, the therapist manages and leads the treatment in the direction of the client's goals. The therapist must do this in collaboration with the client, all the while explaining his intentions and methods of treatment. At the same time, the therapist is building a safe haven for the client, continually assessing progress towards the treatment's goals, along with monitoring the client's emotional experience during therapy.

We can graphically exhibit this in the following example:

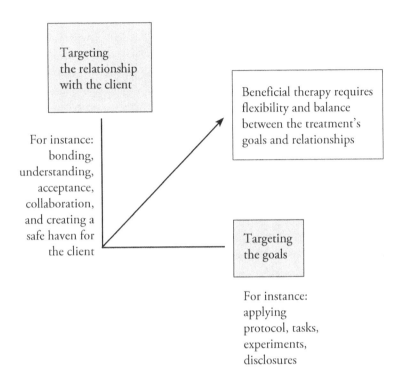

The goal of this book is to reinforce the methods and tools available to CBT therapists. In this book, the emphasis is not only on content, but also on the process of building trust, mutual understanding, and enhancing relationships with parents and children. The first section of this book deals with parent training, from the point of view that, except for extraordinary circumstances, every treatment of every child should take place with the parent's full cooperation and includes consistent counseling over the course of the entire therapy process.

Part A:

Parent Training

My childhood was spent on a kibbutz. One of the wonderful things about the kibbutz in those days was that children began working in the different branches of the kibbutz at an early age. In the fifth grade, we went to work in the children's farm: planting and tending the garden, taking care of the goats, rabbits, parrots, peacocks, ducks, and even bees! As time went on, we experienced working in the various branches of the kibbutz and could choose between them: the dairy farm, the field crops, landscaping, the chicken coops, or in the children's quarters taking care of the younger kibbutz children, from newborns until secondary school. Even though I chose to work in the dairy farm, I still had plenty of opportunities to experience childcare, from the youngest infants up to seventh graders, or thereabouts. Those experiences instilled in me a sense that I would be able to care for my own children one day in the future, that I would manage relatively easily to fulfill a parental role.

That theory was blown to bits after the birth of my first son. I was not aware just how difficult it would be to become a mother overnight. The desire to provide for all of the needs of this tiny and helpless baby, moment after moment, left me feeling quite helpless. How could it be that such a tiny creature would make me feel so powerless? After all, I am an adult, experienced, and I had already worked with children in the past. A baby's cry was nothing new to me and holding a baby was familiar to me. So why am I reacting with such intense emotions? Apart from the "hormonal hurricane" a woman goes through after giving birth, it's essentially an adventure – one that is like no other human adventure. This is a dialect; it involves the idea of giving birth to a new life, which creates strong and powerful emotions and great satisfaction. At the same time, the understanding that my husband and I are solely responsible for this newborn child and are absolutely attuned to his needs forces me to waive everything I previously knew. Essentially, this is a dialect of simultaneous giving and taking. I have given him life and my own life, the life I had known before then, has been put aside.

Being a parent is one of life's most complex roles, from an emotional aspect. Assuming the role of a parent requires many personal and interpersonal skills (for example, self-regulation and listening). The parent's role becomes even more complex when a couple's relationship enters the equation. A couple's relationship may lead to conflicts simply because two people have become a single unit, each one with different wants and needs. A lack of expertise in personal and communication skills can cause harm to one's own emotional welfare and result in genuine dilemmas for a spouse and affects the couple's ability to function as parents. A therapist who practices parent training and child direct therapy should have a comprehensive understanding of the systemic approach to family relationships, understanding the roots of conflicts in the couple's relationship and in their parenting system. This will enable the therapist to help navigate the family's ship to a safe harbor. Therapists who engage only in child direct therapy, without including parent training – which relates to the family system as a whole – may very well cause damage to the fragile family fabric.

This section will deal with the ability of the therapist to navigate between the parent's axis and the couple's axis in order to set clear therapy goals and enhance the personal welfare of the child and parents alike.

The task of parenting is diffused with endless disputes concerning the question of where to focus attention and invest energy. How much to respond to a child's ever changing needs as opposed to the parent's own needs? Am I allowed to focus on my needs when they conflict with my child's needs? What does it mean to be a good parent? If and how much should I demand from my child? If and how much should I intervene for my child's sake? What must I do in order to help him cope and achieve success in life?

Parents will try to solve these dilemmas in innumerable ways. They will develop coping strategies linked to the state of the parent-child relationship, their personality traits, the basic beliefs which guide them, their own personal value systems, their level of self-control, and the interpersonal communications skills they have acquired.

Additionally, in most cases, the parent has a partner or spouse and together they become a parental unit. This parental unit requires an entire system of coordination and balancing in order to care for their children. These questions, conflicts, and dilemmas become even more complex as the measure of stress intensifies when the parent experiences that caring for a child significantly increases parental frictions (Dattilio, 2010).

Therefore, in every parent training session, regardless of a child's specific problem, it is beneficial for the parents to understand their parenting style: what motivates them, what gaps exist in their unique parenting styles, where do they focus their parental attention and energy, and what can be done to improve the effectiveness of their roles on an individual level, as a couple, as parents, and as a family.

A working model of this sort will not only enable the parents to cope with the child's current problems, but will also allow them to function in a more effective manner as a parental unit in front of their other children. This will serve as a preventive mechanism for possible future issues at the family level.

Work with parents will relate to three central axes:

1) **The child's current problems, which brought the parents to treatment**. Generally, parents seek therapy for a child's acute problem (anxiety, misconduct, social rejection, etc.). At this point of intervention, we will want to understand the problem, assess it, give the parents an explanation of the problem and equip them with tools for resolving the issue. Sometimes we may discover the child doesn't actually have a problem at all and that the difficulty stems from the parent's panic over a developmental issue, one that is normal and sometimes even welcome. In this case, the intervention should be an explanation and a calming of the parents' fears.

2) **The factors that maintain the problem on the parental level.** Ineffective parental responses to the problems displayed by the child are related to the parents' perceptions, emotions, and behavior patterns, and the parent does not always grasp their significance. Practical work with the parents will address the identification of these elements along with the acquisition of appropriate tools designed to resolve the child's specific problem. Along this axis of intervention, we will also want to

understand the parenting style as well as the mechanisms which cause the parent to act in a certain manner. Together we will attempt to reveal the relationship and the chain of responses that maintain the child's problem and strive to modify these patterns at the cognitive, emotional, and behavioral levels.

3) **Building a joint parental vision.** Many parents perform their parental role while on automatic pilot, just trying to get through the day, responding to many tasks simultaneously.

They don't stop and ask themselves, what sort of child do I want to raise? What must I do in order to achieve this? How can I recruit my spouse to take part in achieving those goals that are important to me in raising our children? Many conflicts between parents stem from exactly these questions. Therefore, it is essential that parents address these issues, clarify their different points of view, and create a joint parental vision. This enhances their experience of control over the daily routine and keeps them focused on their long range goals as parents. From this it becomes apparent just how important it is to coordinate attitudes between parents, thereby allowing them to enhance their experience of control over the day-to-day routine as well as in future parental goals. Formulating a mutual parental vision creates a sense of understanding, empowerment, and motivation for cooperation when resolving problems. In this sense, the therapist assists the parents in weaving the fabric of communication within the family, alongside the family values and rules. By so doing. The therapist facilitates the parents in fostering higher self-efficacy and in believing in their ability as parents to progress towards those long-range goals, which are extremely important to them.

These three axes of therapeutic work with the parents are dynamic and modular. Despite the rational order between them, there may be situations when all three of the axes interchange position and priority. In order to initiate a process of significant change, the therapist must be mindful of these three axes and flexibly navigate between them according to the needs of the parents and the child. It is most worthwhile that these three axes become a beacon of light for the therapist and provide guidelines throughout the course of treatment sessions.

1

The First Session with the Parents

The telephone rings. "Hello," says the woman on the other end of the line. "I must see you right away, today even, if it's possible." "I hear the urgency, but let's make sure you've reached the right place," I answer.

The first interaction with the parents usually takes place on the telephone or by e-mail, and as therapists we can already sense the measure of urgency, understand the problem, and generally coordinate expectations. It is advisable to make a number of preliminary inquiries during the first telephone conversation in order to understand the reason and urgency for their initial contact with us, and to determine whether the therapist is trained and qualified to respond to their request for assistance.

During the course of the first session it is recommended to obtain as much information as possible, concerning the child's problem, his strengths, his role within the family, what suppositions the parents have relating to the development of the problem, what they already know about the problem and any attempts they have made to rectify the issue to date. It is advisable to employ leading questions such as these:

– What is the reason that led you to seek help?
– When did the problem begin?

- Do you have a theory why this problem developed?
- How do you perceive the problem? (Denoting the parent's cognitive capacity)
- If your child was here right now and I asked him about the problem, what would he say? (Denoting the child's cognitive capacity)
- If there was a camera set up in your house that documented what goes on, what would it record? (Denoting the behavioral aspects of the child and the parents)
- If it was up to you and only you, what would your child's life look like? What would your relationship look like? What is your ideal image of family life? (Examining parental visions and shared values)
- How have you attempted to resolve the problem?

After learning more details the therapist begins to form an idea about the child's problems and the parent's behavioral responses while coping with the problem. Throughout this process, the therapist considers the structure and set of problems, as well as the client's core beliefs and coping strategies. The therapist then determines therapy goals, working in collaboration with the parents, and explains the treatment plan, its potential outcome as well as possible difficulties. This becomes the treatment alliance.

At times, the first session with the parents will not include an extensive intake of information, but focus more on the parent's or the child's distress. This was the case when I first met with the woman referred to me when she was very agitated and frightened. In our initial telephone conversation, it became clear she was the mother of a twelve-year-old son who had suddenly been overwhelmed with extreme anxiety. I immediately arranged an appointment to meet with the parents.

My first objective as a therapist is to immediately imbue the clients with a sense of security in our relationship. It is my habit to come out of the therapy room to greet newcomers even if my current session with another client has not yet ended. "Hello Michal and Boaz, I'll be with you shortly and then you can come on in," I said with a smile. They smiled in return and waited patiently for their appointment with me. The nature of this sort of greeting, where the therapist comes out to personally welcome the client with a smile, allows the client, in return, to feel they have been expected, acknowledged, and that we are glad they have come. In that moment, a sense of security and positive expectations have been established.

After we made ourselves a cup of coffee, we spoke briefly about their drive over to my office ("It took an hour and a half..."), sat down, and I opened the conversation:

Therapist (T): I understand that it was very urgent we meet.

Michal: Yes, we are living inside a bizarre movie.

T: What does that mean?

Michal: Ever since the family trip, our life has turned upside down. Gil, our son, is afraid to leave the house or go to school. He's scared when we leave the house; he won't go to afterschool activities. It's hard for him to go to sleep, and he's exhausting us. He has simply stopped functioning.

(The mother starts to cry and the father takes up where she left off.)

Boaz: Look, we're devoted parents. We don't understand what's going on with our child. He's in terrible distress and we don't know what to do.

T: It sounds like Gil is experiencing anxiety. Did
        something happen on the trip? Do you have any ideas
        what may have triggered this?

Boaz: I think it's related to what happened in the middle of
        the hiking trail when we had to cross over a very high
        and narrow spot. Even though there was a fence, it
        was really scary, especially when I took the baby (two
        years old) and carried him on my shoulders.

Michal: I held Gil's hand. I was shaking with fear.

T: If I was a bird looking down on that scene, what
        would I see in each one of your reactions?

Michal: I was yelling at Boaz and shaking, and I was saying all
        the time, "Oh no, oh no…" Gil held my hand very
        tightly; he gripped my hand very hard and didn't say
        anything. After we passed the scary part, I kept on
        yelling at Boaz.

T: What were you yelling?

Michal: Are you crazy? Why did you bring us here? Have you
        gone completely insane?

T: And what were you feeling at the same time?

Michal: A lot of anger at Boaz and terribly frightened.

T: Boaz, what was going on with you at the same time?

Boaz: I was very tense; I felt like it was my responsibility. I
        went first and planned the route. It was only a short
        section, a few steps. Even though there was a rail, that
        part was really scary. I didn't expect it to be like that.
        There weren't any warning signs anywhere when I
        read about the trail route. I apologized to Michal a
        hundred times.

T: Then you were angry at yourself when you understood
        what was happening?

Boaz:　Yes, very! Also I knew that Michal wanted to kill me!

T:　You had an intensely stressful family experience. Did you feel your lives were in danger?

Michal:　(crying) I don't know if it was life threatening. I'm not sure, but I felt deathly afraid. Even now I can't forgive him for that. How can I trust him? It's not the first time he's messed up...

Boaz:　Yah, I never do anything right, I'm already used to that...

At this point, the therapist may very well be in a dilemma of priorities. Should I focus on their experiences as parents and in particular on the event they told me about? Should I bring up the differences between them as a couple? Should I suggest a possible prognosis and give them a psychoeducational explanation about what happened to the family, in particular to Gil? Shall I tell them how cognitive-behavioral therapy can help them in these situations? Should I ask about Gil's fears over the years? Isn't that the reason they came here?

Above all, Gil's parents came to me out of a sense of helplessness, under great strain over their child's distress – is it the right time to make a deep analysis of Gil and his family already during the first session, or should I allow them more time to adjust after the troubling events that led them to seek help?

At this moment, I was aware of the need to create a strong therapeutic relationship with these parents, as resonated in Beck's words: Before me stood the objectives of creating a therapeutic relationship (Beck, 2011), to create a pleasant experience for the client and the therapist's aspiration to build a strong therapy alliance and mutual understanding from the onset.

That is to say, according to my professional approach, the therapist strives to create a safe haven for the client right from the start, and this can only happen when the client feels the therapist cares about him, understands him, and will securely lead him towards his goals. This is a clear analogy between a secure relationship and the sense of reaching safe shores. In my experience, the way to do this in the first session is linked to the nonverbal messages (smiling, open body language, attentiveness, etc.) and on the verbal level with the therapist endeavoring to understand the problems the client presents, to normalize those difficulties and validate the client's experiences. After gathering the relevant information, the therapist can then share his impressions with the client by conceptualizing the problems, by giving a possible explanation for those problems, and by mutually determining the treatment goals with the client.

When a couple arrives with such a clear sense of urgency, as in this instance, it is advisable in the first session to focus on the issues they bring up in order to create the experience of a safe haven (we came to the right place). In this way, a comprehensive analysis can be done in stages and not necessarily in the first session. In this case, it's important to clarify to the client, in advance, that this matter demands a more in-depth examination, which will take place in upcoming sessions, and for the moment, as a therapist, it is important to treat the present plight.

T: You have described an event that would cause any normal family to experience extreme stress, not to say traumatic, in the manner in which you felt great fear when faced with a potentially life threatening situation (normalization). People cope in various ways in situations like these. Together we will soon understand why Gil's reactions to this event are so severe. But for now, I would be glad if we could focus for a while on your feelings, after having told me what happened on the trip.

Michal: (Angrily) Tell me, how can I count on him after something like this?

Boaz: Do you think I did it on purpose? You know I wanted to kill myself afterwards and I apologized to you so many times. What more do you want?

T: If both of you are so angry, then you have a reason for it (validation). We should try to comprehend the anger. In most cases both members of the couple are justified and mistaken at the same time. Let's look at what's going on right now, later on it will help us understand what Gil is going through.

Quite often we are faced with a situation where a couple comes in for parent training, but in no time at all conflicts surface which are not directly related to the child's problem and/or to the problem they indicated when they came in for training. The therapist needs to be attentive to this and should traverse between the different elements of the parents' relationship, while he tries to explain what he sees and determines clear goals conjointly with the couple. The reason the couple had come in for treatment was to alleviate their son Gil's distress. In order to progress towards a psychoeducational explanation about what happened on the trip, it was important to me that they comprehend the "here and now," the links between thoughts, feelings, and behavior, according to Beck's model (Beck, 1967, 1976).

T: Boaz, when you hear Michal say that she can't count on you, what goes through your mind?

Boaz: It crushes me.

T: Because…

Boaz: (With tears in his eyes) Because I do all I can to make her happy…

T: With your permission, I'll go to the board and try to understand what's going on right here and now.

Situation	Automatic Thought	Emotion	Behavior
Michal says she doesn't trust me.	It crushes me, I do all I can to make her happy.	Hurt Offended	I apologize.

T: Michal, when you hear what Boaz thinks and feels, what goes through your head?

Event	Automatic Thought	Emotion	Behavior
Boaz says that it hurts him, that he doesn't succeed in making me happy.	It's always the same. He makes a lot of mistakes and then apologizes. Enough! He should be responsible. He's not three years old, and he's a father!	Anger	Attack and blame

T: Boaz, when you hear Michal, what happens to you?

Event	Automatic Thought	Emotion	Behavior
Michal accuses me of not being responsible.	I'm fed up with her. She wants me to be someone else. Whatever I do, I'll never be able to make her happy.	Futility Helplessness	Retreat inward

T: What we've done here on the board is called a **chain of responses**. In actuality, every behavior becomes the basis for the next interaction with your partner, their thoughts, feelings, and behavioral expressions. Quite often we form a conditioning in the chain of response. This is to say, we have automatic thoughts, automatic emotions, and automatic behaviors, that repeat themselves over and over and we find ourselves inside a permanent cycle of ineffective communication, which impacts relations between us. Let's take a closer look:

Event	Automatic Thought	Emotion	Behavior
Michal says she doesn't trust me.	It crushes me; I do everything to make her happy.	Hurt Offended	I retreat and apologize.
Boaz apologizes.	It's always the same. He makes a lot of mistakes and then apologizes. Enough! He should be responsible. He's not three years old, and he's a father!	Angry	Aggressive, blaming, yelling
Michal blames and attacks.	She's fed up with me. She wants me to be someone else. Whatever I do, it's impossible to please her.	Futility Helplessness	I retreat inward, break off contact, stop talking.

Identifying the various components in a chain of responses will give the couple a better understanding of their partner's behavior, thought processes, and the emotions that explain that behavior. Take, for example, the following: illustrating the chain of responses helped Michal to understand that she was only seeing part of the picture. She tends to interpret Boaz's behavior in a very negative manner and focuses on his mistakes and failures. She is inclined to ignore the positive things he does, his motivation to please her, and the feelings of futility he experiences. Michal understood that her automatic judgment of his mistakes created a generalization of Boaz's personality as someone who cannot be relied upon. Because of the increased expectations from a spouse and the intense emotions that accompany life as a couple, often, there exists a problem with the negative and hostile interpretation of the partners' behavior. This negative and hostile interpretation leads to a process of escalation of tension in their interactions and is accompanied by accusations, blame, and desperation (Beck, 1988).

Identifying their chain of responses enabled Michal and Boaz to understand that every behavioral response of theirs originated from the interpretation they had given to the other's behavior while the other partner was also interpreting their behavior and this cycle was repeated again and again. In practice, working with a chain of responses chart made it possible for them to recognize how the fabric of their relationship was being woven from moment to moment.

The use of **chain response charts for parent training** can be very effective, leaving the therapist in a neutral, non-judgmental position. There is no question here of who is right or wrong; the therapist responds by saying, "Both of you are right and wrong at the same time since your interactions are influenced by your interpretation of the current situation." As the training progresses, this process allows for the identification of faulty cognitions, patterns of behavior, and conditioned responses that occur automatically during their interactions. This intervention creates a new discourse between the couple since it develops a new insight: "What is our relationship?" In a similar manner, parents will be able to examine their relationships with their children and it will be possible to produce a fully detailed picture of family relationships. In this sense the therapist researches, in collaboration with the parents, the relations along the chain of responses and directs them to the conclusion that their behavior – and the behavior of the entire family – is directly influenced by the way they interpret the situation. The chain of response allows us to see how relationships are fashioned **moment after moment.** It strengthens the client's sense of control and understanding. It instills hope that it is within his power to make a change in this chain that has been formed.

When parents are in the session and tensions arise, working with chain responses provides an effective exit, which successfully disengages the conflict. My message to them as a therapist is: Both of you have good reason to be angry, but let's put things in order and then we can understand the anger. I try to guide the therapy and navigate it towards a discourse aiming to identify the chain of responses.

After we touched upon Michal and Boaz's relationship for a while and established a better understanding of what happened to them on the family's trip, we could then address Gil's experiences.

T: We can now understand that our behavior is linked to a preceding thought. Gil's recent behavior is also connected to his thoughts. Let's try and make sense of this.

I went over to the board and asked them what conjectures they had concerning Gil's interpretation of the stressful episode during the family trip.

Event	Automatic Thought	Emotion	Behavior
Gil is standing in the edge of a precipice. Mom is saying, "Oh no, oh no." Dad is helpless.	Mom: He thinks it's the end. He will fall and die. Dad: He also hears Michal screaming and sees she's frightened and that makes him even more afraid. Mom: He must have thought to himself that if we brought him there, then he can't trust us.	Gil felt extremely frightened.	He remained silent and held his mother's hand very tightly.

T: We've viewed the process on the board; what do you suppose Gil is going through now?

Boaz: He's definitely frightened it might happen again.

Michal: Maybe he thinks that he can't trust us.

T: Because...

Michal: Because we didn't handle the situation correctly.

T: It seems to me that both of you are right. When a traumatic event occurs, the mind makes connections between the many things that happen at the same time. What connection do you think was made during those moments?

Parents: A sense of terrible fear and Gil thinking he would die + the height + the trip + our tension (even hysterics) + our quarrel + Gil thinking he can't rely on us.

T: Let's now try to suppose what apparently happened (psychoeducational explanation). Gil has been through a traumatic experience where he may have felt his life was truly threatened. An experience like this instantly floods him with feelings of fear, terror, and helplessness. Everyone reacts differently in this sort of situation. Your reaction (your screaming for instance, Michal) was automatic, understandable, and normal, but Gil experienced it as another element of distress and as validation of his internal experience, which was indeed a very dangerous situation, even if, in reality, there was a railing and no actual danger to his life. That was an unbearably difficult experience, especially for children, who understand reality through parents' reactions. The expressions of trauma, especially with children, may appear several days after an event and that is why the connection was not obvious to you.

Michal: (Crying) Is the situation reversible?

T: Yes, by all means. Cognitive-behavior therapy will make it possible for Gil to understand what happened to him on the trip. How the systems in his body, his thoughts, and behavior operated in reaction to an extremely traumatic situation. We will try to restore his sense of control over all these levels and I estimate that within a few sessions we will begin to see an improvement in his condition. Both of you will also have a major role in the process. We will work as a team to help Gil. You and Gil will be given assignments to do at home between sessions, which will greatly speed up the change in a positive direction.

In the meantime, until our next session, I would like to give you an exercise to do at home. Since Gil appears to have gone through a very frightening experience and at the moment is not able to express this in words, I would be glad if you would talk to him in such a way as to let him know his reactions are normal for such an intensely traumatic situation. I would like you to validate his feelings and give him a sense of hope that things will change for the better. In order to anchor this process in your memory, we'll give it the initials **N-V-S:**

Normalize the Reaction – Your reaction is normal and many children go through similar things.

Validation – We realize this is not easy for you – that it isn't easy to cope in stressful situations like the one we went through.

Sharing – We're happy that you came and shared this with us. We will get through this together.

So that you know how to do this at home with Gil, we'll practice a role playing game now. One of you will pass along the message and the other will play the role of Gil. The exercise for delivering the message includes verbal and non-verbal segments along with possible responses to your message that you may hear from Gil. Role playing will provide us with better control when passing along the message and prepared responses suited to Gil's needs. In addition, the N-V-N message will offer an opportunity to speak to Gil about the possibility of his coming in for therapy.

The example of Michal and Boaz clarifies for us the importance of parent training before direct child therapy. If we had met only with the child, there is a good chance that we would never have understood the complex context or the intricate system in which he lives. Our observations as therapists must be systemic. This child has grown up within an environment that influences him and is influenced by him. The interaction between family members and the diversity between them gives rise to different requirements, expectations, beliefs, attitudes, and values that demand cognitive, emotional, and behavioral adjustment. This kind of adaptation necessitates the ability to recognize thinking processes, emotions, and behaviors, which assist in the learning process of skills such as cooperation and decision making (Dattilio, 2010).

Additional Techniques for Gathering Information and Creating a Safe Haven in the First Session with Parents

Our goal in the first session of therapy is to create the experience of "A Safe Haven" as quickly as is possible. Our ambition is that during the first session with parents, a number of important things will take place; they should feel comfortable in sharing their problems, uncertainties, and hardships. They should be saying to themselves, "We're in good hands" – that they have come to the right place and they will get the help they were expecting. They should feel they are not being judged and in addition are given direction and instruction, which will steer them towards their objectives. They should have a clear picture of the treatment session goals, what and how we want to achieve them, what is required of me and of them in our therapeutic alliance. According to Beck (2011), our goal as therapists is to build a therapeutic process where it is understood by the therapist and the client how together they can strive to provide the most beneficial treatment possible for the client. Beck remarks that most clients have a greater sense of ease when they know what to expect from therapy: when they clearly understand their realm of responsibility, along with the therapist's area of accountability, and when it is clear to them how the treatment will proceed during each session and for the entire length of the treatment.

When we talk about "making a connection" at the beginning of the therapeutic process, this means we are attempting to address all of those parameters. The first session is critical to therapy, and if for some reason we fail to provide the client with these experiences, there is a good chance they won't return for the next session.

When we receive both parents for treatment, forming the initial connection is much more complex. The sense of being in a safe haven for one parent does not necessarily constitute a safe haven for the other. When parents arrive agitated, accusatory and angry, they expect us to judge between them. For them, a safe haven is where they find validation and justification that they are in the right. This is a place where many therapists are liable to be dragged down and become ineffective for the parents and the process as a whole. As therapists, we are required to take precautions that will ensure an experience of sanctuary concurrently for both members of the couple.

In the following segment, we will present a number of techniques that can aid us in the first session to, create a sense of security for the parents and collect relevant data.

When Were We Wonderful?

A positive psychological approach involves identifying the areas of strength within the client and incorporating ways to nurture and preserve those strengths (Fredrickson, 2001; Seligman, 2010). According to this approach, considerable importance is placed on the manner in which we ask questions and on the focus of attention for both the therapist and the client. The way we ask a question influences the entire course of the session and can guide the client to focus on his strengths instead of on his problems. I generally ask parents in the first session, "When were you wonderful as parents?" The question is divided into a few sections, and I invite them to write down their answers:

When were we wonderful as parents?

When am I a wonderful parent?

When was my partner a wonderful parent?

What do I think my partner will write about in response to the question: When was I a wonderful parent?

What do I think my partner will write about me?

The sample I am showing has been worked into a table for easier reading. In practice, each of the parents writes their answers on a piece of note paper and afterwards they exchange notes.

The Question	Mother	Father
When were we wonderful parents?	When Yoni, our son, was in the hospital, we had a special way of arranging who did what. We succeeded in coping very well with the situation.	When Stav, our daughter, was at camp and she was having a difficult time, we bought her candy and went to visit her, sat with her, laughed together and then we drove home. Stav stayed at camp.
When was I a wonderful parent?	In my opinion, I'm a wonderful mother when I sit with each child in bed before they go to sleep; we summarize the past day and make a ritual of a kiss and a hug before sleep.	When I bike ride with Yoni. When I take the children to the beach.
When was my partner a wonderful parent?	When Avi (my husband) makes Friday night dinner for all of us with special dishes.	When Anat (my wife) listens to music and dances around and goes crazy with the kids.
What do I think my partner will write about in response to the question: When was I a wonderful parent?	I think Avi will write that he's a wonderful Dad when he helps the kids with their homework.	Anat will write that she's a wonderful Mom when she makes them fantastic sandwiches for school.
What do I think my partner will write about me?	Avi probably wrote about my sandwiches.	I suppose that Anat wrote that I'm wonderful when I take the kids to the beach because then she has time to herself.

A similar exercise is done in couples therapy where I combine questions about parenting with questions about the couple: When were we a wonderful couple?

This kind of intervention in the first session lets us establish a positive atmosphere, a note of laughter, and a hint of humor that will direct attention to the positive areas of the parental experiences of the couple and help to learn what works well between them in their parenting. This is crucial information that we generally do not have access to when we are focused solely on the parents' problems. Often, I ask the couple how they would rate, on a scale of one to ten, their measure of satisfaction from their life together. Each time, I am amazed by the responses. There was a couple that came to me for parent training and they didn't have a single point of agreement between them. In my mind, I pictured the endless conflicts at home and when I asked them what their general level of satisfaction was from the relationship, they both said, "eight" (from a possible ten). As a result of their reply, my attitude changed and therapy went in another direction in order to clarify the nature of their satisfaction in their relationship and the wide gap between the high level of satisfaction and the mutual complaints which arose in therapy. Focusing on the parents' strengths, what works well and what is effective, allows us to create the therapeutic dialogue which suits them specifically. In addition, the cyclical questions the parents are instructed to answer about one another (what he thinks I'm writing, what I think he's writing, and so on…), offer the opportunity to build a foundation for understanding one of the most common pitfalls of couples: mind reading. Working on faulty cognitions will be dealt with later in a following section and will combine identifying and understanding the chain responses which have developed between a couple and within the entire family unit.

When I work with the question, "When were we wonderful parents?" the couple receives a homework assignment wherein each day of the week they write down, "When was I a wonderful parent today?" and "When was my partner a wonderful parent today?" The next therapy session begins with a review of the homework assignment and each successive session starts with the questions, When was I wonderful this week and when was my partner wonderful this week? Responding frequently to these questions directs attention to absorbing positive information about one another, promptly allowing the creation of a more positive dialog between the couple. Moreover, when there is a problem with a child-parent relationship, mainly negative feelings of the parent towards the child (anger, frustration, etc.), I will assign the same assignment to the child. In this case, the parent must record each day when their child was wonderful and when the parent was a wonderful parental figure to the child. The word "wonderful" may not be suitable in every situation and you can search with the parents for more appropriate wording. For example, I am proud of myself today because…/I really did well when…/I was fantastic when…and so forth.

Focusing attention on "what works" is done in order to both strengthen the parental unit and bond the couple, but there are cases when parents are so fixated on their child's troubles, expecting the therapist to "repair" their child or his condition, that some may object to discussing parenting issues. In these cases, it is my professional opinion to first focus on the child's problems, as defined by the parents and only afterwards to suggest that the problems might be linked to additional factors, which are worth examining together. Generally, when parents are more reassured about the current dilemma, they are much more open to broader diagnostic processes.

The Note Game

Another technique for gathering information while continuing to build a safe haven is "The Note Game." In the first session with the parents, we strive to gather as much information as possible for the diagnostic process. The process of compiling data will be far more encompassing than the specific examination of the declared problem itself. As mentioned earlier, in this type of diagnostic process great importance is placed not only on examining the problems of the parents and the child, but also on revealing their strengths.

The "Note Game" enables a quick and effective assessment of problems and strengths by asking direct and circuitous questions, which broaden the observations of parent and family dynamics.

Each parent is instructed to fill out on a separate piece of note paper his answers to the questions written on the board or verbally presented. Afterwards, the notes are exchanged and then checked to see if the partner is surprised about what was written on the other's note, what they think about what was written on the note, and if they have any questions about what was written down.

The instruction to write down responses and not to respond verbally is intentional. When writing, a person pauses for inward reflection, he is less concerned with reactions from the immediate environment and more often than not, is able to more precisely formulate his messages. The writing technique is very helpful in the event there is an escalation of emotions during the first session with the couple, and thus enables the therapist to conduct the session more effectively.

Personally, I use the "Note Game" according to the information I want to receive, what fits the parents' personalities, and lastly, the kind of atmosphere in the room.

The first version: what works and doesn't work in the relationship

Me	My Partner
What works well in my relationship with our child? What works well in our parental relationship?	What do I suppose my partner will write for, "What works well?"
What does not work well in my relationship with our child? What does not work well in our parental relationship?	What do I suppose my partner will write for, "What does not work well?"

The second version: focusing on behavior and its influence on the relationship

Me	My Partner
Three of my partner's behaviors that make me feel happy/joyful. Three of my partner's behaviors that make me feel frustrated/upset.	What will my partner define as three behaviors of mine that make him happy and three behaviors that make him frustrated.
Three of my child's behaviors that make me feel happy/joyful. Three of my child's behaviors that make me feel frustrated/upset.	What will my partner define as three behaviors of my child that make me happy and three behaviors that make me frustrated.

In my experience, this type of intervention during the first session causes positive tension between the couple. They are curious to know what their partner has written; they cooperate quite willingly and most of the session revolves around what's been written on the notes. If there is no acute problem which the parents have presented, it is possible to dedicate more than one session to this activity. In this case, the assessment produces a broad map of issues and strengths and facilitates progressing on to the next stage, which is determining priorities and treatment goals.

The techniques suggested here do not replace broad questioning of the child's problems, strengths, his relationships with family members, and his parents' assessment of the root of the child's problems – what the parents know about the problems and how they've sought to resolve them so far. The more comprehensive the information, the easier it will be to conceptualize the case, to establish therapy goals and treatment methods that will be the most accurate. One of the most important questions that must be answered after we have gathered all of the information is, who is the client?

When speaking of young children, parent training is the most effective way to create change with the child. In these cases, we may never even see the child. At each step, the parents will receive explicit instructions on how to respond to their child, which messages to send to their child, and how they themselves should behave.

What are some of the reasons which lead to child-direct therapy? The first justification is a question of initiation; in most cases, children do not seek assistance of their own initiative. They will come to therapy as a result of the adult environment (parents, teachers) who have referred them. In cases where the child himself has directly or indirectly asked for help (for instance, if aid has been offered to him and he responds in the positive), we should receive the child for treatment. In this case, the treatment will be for the child in response to their need. The child's own motivation and cooperation will contribute significantly to the process of change. However, in extreme cases, when the child is at risk or he himself poses a risk (suicidal, victim or perpetrator of physical/sexual abuse, or harmful sexual behavior), it is abundantly clear that direct intervention with the child is necessary in order to examine his mental state and determine the appropriate treatment.

An additional reason is linked to the child's personal characteristics, his age, and his phase of development. The younger the child and the more dependent he is on his parents, the more appropriate it is to begin the treatment directly with the parents and later on to weigh the option of direct intervention with the child. Older children, and certainly teen-agers who are coping with the process of self-identity or their problem is an internal disorder (as in anxiety or depression), can participate significantly in individual treatment. Even so, in these situations it is advantageous to involve the parents in parent training, which will promote their child's process of change. It is worth noting the important observations made by Hodges et al., in conjunction with Ronen (1994), concerning child-direct therapy. Their prognosis states that adults tend to seek treatment for children with behavior issues because of the hardships within the environment and their helplessness in the face of harmful behavior. Children who suffer from emotional distress aimed at themselves (self-esteem, depression, anxiety, etc.), will rarely be referred for treatment due to the adults' difficulty in recognizing their child's ordeal. Not long ago, a forty-year-old therapy client of mine suffering from social anxieties said to me, "If my parents had understood I had a problem and had sent me for treatment when I was younger, I would have been spared many years of suffering." In this sense, introverted children lose out and we must endeavor to open our eyes to their possible predicament.

Another reason for child-direct treatment is linked to the child's environmental network. When parental capabilities are low or it is not possible to work directly with the parental unit (during a difficult divorce, for instance), we become aware of the importance of directly treating the child, in providing the child with a safe haven and equipping him with the tools to cope when faced with an unwelcome reality.

Who is the client, The Parents? The Child? The Parents and the Child? What is the desired setting for treatment and what is the correct direction for therapeutic intervention therapy? Answers to questions like these should be arrived at after a comprehensive examination and following the establishment of treatment goals.

Determining Treatment Goals

When a couple arrives for parent training, it's natural for them to exhibit both parental and spousal communication patterns. In the process of gathering information, it is highly important the therapist be able to address both of these two sub-systems and the interconnection between them. For instance, it might be that the couple present a problem concerning a child suffering from anxiety. Further examination reveals that the frequent arguments of the couple and threats from one spouse to leave the home markedly intensifies the child's anxiety. In cases like these, scheduling to treat only the child and his accompanying anxiety as a treatment goal would be an inaccurate goal and not a very effective one either. Even if there is no couple therapy, it would be advisable for the therapist to target the couples' communication patterns as an initial objective of treatment. In my humble opinion, a therapist who practices parent training should be well versed in the field of couples therapy intervention. This requires an understanding of the roots of conflict with couples. In the framework of therapy – and not at the psychoeducational level – and in doing so, making it possible to determine clear treatment goals linked to the child's welfare.

After we have conducted a general examination of problems and strengths by utilizing the methods recommended here, we can move on to a more exact clarification of the issues by means of a structured questionnaire, which is beneficial in determining priorities in the treatment. The questionnaire presented here relates to the level of difficulty for the parent and to the level of difficulty perceived by the other partner. It is intended to help us determine goals in relation to the intensity of the parents' distress. In this questionnaire, the parents are instructed to answer questions about each problem area by rating their degree of difficulty and what they suppose the degree of difficulty may be for their spouse. In an additional column, they are asked to list their conclusions regarding each therapy goal, what their uncertainties are, and to classify the problem area on the list of priorities for treatment.

Questionnaire: Degree of Difficulty in the Family

Problem Area	My degree of difficulty from 0 to 10 0 – No difficulty 10 – Extreme Difficulty	Estimate of spouse's degree of difficulty from 0 to 10 0 – No difficulty 10 – Extreme Difficulty	Conclusions about therapy goals
General atmosphere at home			
My relationship with: Child 1 Child 2 Child 3			
Specific problems with: Child 1 Child 2 Child 3			

Problem Area	My degree of difficulty from 0 to 10 0 – No difficulty 10 – Extreme Difficulty	Estimate of spouse's degree of difficulty from 0 to 10 0 – No difficulty 10 – Extreme Difficulty	Conclusions about therapy goals
Children's discipline: Child 1 Child 2 Child 3			
The relationships between the children: co-operation, games, competition, aggression			
Performing house-hold chores: helping with homework, shopping, driving			
Joint decision making about the children and agreeing on parental messages			
Private time for myself (as a couple and alone): hobbies, entertainment			
Open communication about the children: Doubts and uncertainties, cooperation, consulting on the way to raise the kids			
Family activities: Trips, restaurants, movies			
Additional area			

2

Diagnosing Parenting Styles and Their Resulting Conflicts

Most parents come for parent training due to an ongoing state of crisis – their own or their children's. They may respond automatically to such a crisis, and most of the time their reactions require a review of their attitudes and positions, as well as the effectiveness of their responses to these personal and family situations. A review of this sort requires an examination of the differences that characterize their contrasting parenting styles.

Although literature is replete with models and approaches concerning parenting styles, (Skinner, Johnson & Snyder, 2005), I find that the model developed by Diana Baumrind (Baumrind, 1966, 1967, 1971) is easier for parents to understand and identify with. In a clear and precise manner, Baumrind describes basic parental styles, the differences between these styles and where they may conflict, while offering an optimal parental style that can enhance child rearing in the family.

Baumrind cites two fundamental dimensions as the basis for parenting styles: **Parental Responsiveness** and **Parental Demandingness**.

Parental responsiveness refers to the extent parents purposefully encourage uniqueness and emphasize the "me" of the child by being supportive, affectionate, and adapting to the needs and demands of their children.

Parental demands relate to the entire range of demands on the child that parents express in order to assure that their children will integrate into the family system. These demands emphasize adult supervision of the child, efforts to discipline and to confront the child when he is disobedient.

As a first step, I ask the parents to mark on a scale where they are situated in relation to the two different parenting styles. Accordingly, I ask them to indicate where they think their partner appears on the scale. In some cases, I may also ask them to indicate where their own parents might appear on the same scale.

Please indicate where you are on the scale and where your parents were:

Responsive--Demanding

Yossi (above the line) and Dina (below the line) indicated themselves and their partner along the scale in the following manner:

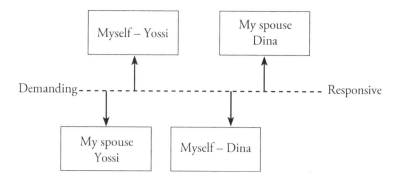

T: In general, you both agree that Dina tends to be responsive and you, Yossi, tend to be demanding. But there is a gap between your positions on the scale. Try to give an explanation for the gap between the two of you.

Yossi: Dina is always taking care of the kids; they're the center of her world and she is busy with them all the time. What she marked on the scale was far from the reality.

Dina: Honestly, I think Yossi exaggerates with the children and I moderate his unreasonable demands.

T: What are these unreasonable demands?

Dina: Does it seem all right to you to expect a six-year-old girl to clear the table, take out the garbage three times a week, and water the plants twice a week?

T: The logic can be found in your perceptions of each of your parenting styles. Let's try and understand what happens when there is no balance between responsiveness and demandingness and how this is expressed in your parenting style.

Psychoeducational Explanation:

We spoke earlier about the distinction Diana Baumrind makes between the two dimensions, parental responsiveness versus parental demandingness that are the foundation of parenting styles. Baumrind claims that various fluctuations between these two dimensions create three parenting styles.

A Permissive style – characterizes parents who are high in the dimension of responsiveness and low in the dimension of demandingness. The demands on the children are lessened and the parents allow the children to regulate their own activities, without setting clear boundaries. The children are the center of the parent's world and the parents are prepared to supply all the children's needs. The parent serves the child.

An Authoritarian style – characterizes parents who are high on expectations and demands from their children but low on the dimension of responsiveness. They act in a very inflexible manner, enforcing strict limits beyond the norm, applying punishments and sanctions in the case of disobedience. In this instance, the parent operates in a self-serving manner, for society and the environment, without considering the needs of the child.

Most parents have a tendency towards one style over the other. Quite often when one parent leans towards a particular style, the other parent tries to balance this by compensating with the other style. This can create a growing rift between parenting styles and cause severe conflict in child rearing and education of their children.

Yossi: That's exactly what happens with us. I think Dina is too lenient in the way she deals with the children. I saw how they were wrapping her around their little fingers and I couldn't stand it, even today I can't stand to see that.

Dina: I admit that I'm always taking care of them and it's important to me that they have everything they need. Sometimes I really feel frustrated with them; they act ungrateful and don't appreciate anything I do for them. I'm like their "slave." On the other hand, I see what goes on with them and Yossi. One of the children said to me, "I hate Dad." I can't bear to hear that. It's awful when a child hates his father.

T: The situation you are in is shared by many parents and can be changed.

The third parenting style, which Baumrind calls **Authoritative**, is characterized by the correct and effective balance of the two parenting styles mentioned above. This parenting style characterizes parents who balance responsiveness and demandingness. That is to say, they are strong both in the dimension of authority and in dimension of responsiveness. This parenting style is characterized by giving clear instructions to their children, by placing appropriate demands on them, and providing appropriate parental supervision. These types of parents mediate their distinct messages with warmth, affection, reason, flexibility, and discussion, which takes into consideration the child's perspective. They avoid power struggles and personal injury:

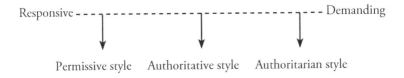

What is the price that each member of the family pays for their parenting style?

In the permissive parenting style, the child is at the center. Often, the price is the self-effacing of the parent. Dina, when you say that you are a "slave" to the children, this means you have lost your freedom. You have lost a little part of yourself within the parental role. This also has a negative effect on the children, and in actuality, you achieve exactly the opposite of your goal, to have the best for them. In her research, Baumrind (1966) found that the permissive parenting style – which does not set clear boundaries and lacks the element of parental

----

demand – significantly contributes to difficulties in children's emotional regulation, contributes to their rebellious and defiant behavior when faced with frustrating situations, and contributes to difficulties in being consistent when performing tasks and working towards goals.

Dina: Yes, I can see all of those things you mentioned at home… What can we do?

T: Learning to adopt a more authoritative parenting style is recommended. Let's look at the price Yossi and the family pay for his parenting style. With the authoritarian parenting style, the needs of the parent or the environment are central and sometimes there is invalidation of the child's needs. When it came up here in session that your son had said, "I hate Dad," perhaps it's because he feels his father does not understand or does not consider what he is going through, what he feels, and what he needs. In these situations, the child may develop a continuing antagonism towards the parent "who doesn't see him." The child is constantly busy avoiding criticism and perhaps even punishment, which may result in negative thinking towards himself or the environment. Children may feel they are not good enough, not worthy, and sometimes their motivation to do things, to initiate, to dare, and to develop, is relatively low (Baumrind, 1966).

T: This doesn't mean that this is what actually happens and what will happen with you, it only means that both of your parenting styles are not very effective.

Yossi: I never thought about it like that. It's ironic because one of the most important things in my mind is for

T: my children to have the courage to try new things and not be square like me. Now I understand I am causing the exact opposite…

T: It's good that you have come for some guidance. After we understand each of your parenting styles and what price each of you and your children pay for those styles, we can learn how to adopt an authoritative style where your needs as parents and the needs of your children are at the center. Do you agree that this should be the direction we work towards? You will have to work hard and consciously check your automatic responses. We will practice the new style here together, during our session, and you will receive exercises to do at home so that you can begin to adopt the authoritative style.

According to Baumrind's research (1966), the Authoritative parenting style substantially contributes to a rise in a child's self-esteem, to his happiness, and his belief that he can deal with all kinds of different situations. When comparing children of parents with the other two parenting styles, we find that the children of Authoritative parenting use more effective strategies for dealing with difficulties and have stronger academic performance, while exhibiting higher social and personal skills.

Dina and Yossi responded positively and eagerly to the new goal we established. They felt they could understand more clearly what had happened to them over the years, why there was a widening gap between them, why the children responded to each of them the way they did, and what their new goal should be. For homework, they were asked to monitor their interactions with their children and note expressions of their parenting style when and where their parenting style was expressed. Likewise, they were asked to record and describe any conflictual situations with their children. What thoughts were running through their minds during the situation? What feelings arose and how did they react (similar to what we saw in the tables of chain responses)? In our next session, we discussed in depth how their parenting style was expressed and how it influenced the attitudes and authority of each parent.

It's worth mentioning that part of defining goals is asking the question, **"What kind of child do I want to raise?"** I ask the parents to close their eyes and imagine their child in five years' time. How will he look? What will he be doing? How will he behave? How will he think? What is the greatest gift they would like to give him, from an emotional viewpoint, and how do they see his future life? The discussion about what they see in their mind's eye helps define the goals of the training sessions and assists in redefining the problem and its possible solution through a changing of the parenting style. More specifically, I ask, "Does the way you are handling things today, as parents, promote progress towards your goal, towards your parental vision?"

Developing Beneficial Authoritative Parenting

Parenting isn't taught in any school, but it does demand highly sophisticated skills at the personal and interpersonal levels. As parents, the processes we want to steer our children through are channeled in numerous directions. One part of us aspires to direct our children, guide them, allow them to develop and gain experience, and another part of us wants to protect them emotionally and physically. This side of us wants to safeguard them from suffering, to make life easier for them and to comfort them. The other side of us prefers they listen to us, be obedient, and appreciative. Yet a different part of us longs to just play with them and simply enjoy each moment together.

The dialog between our inner voices may very well cause internal conflict, and if that's not enough, there's an external system of pressures which influences us: the immediate needs of our children and our spouses, attempting to please them while at the same time heeding one's own personal needs, as parents and as a couple. The system of demands, which challenges a parent at almost every given moment, is liable to lead the parent into distress. The parent acts automatically in the face of these strains, and often this leads to having a negative effect on the parents themselves or those close to them. How can we assist the parents to safely traverse between all these adversities? How can we develop a consolidated parenting style, that allows us to simultaneously see our own needs as individuals as well as the needs of others? How can we develop that authoritative style which Baumrind speaks of, when we have so many inner voices – some of which respond automatically and in contradiction to our goals? One of the most effective ways to handle ourselves and our relationship with our children is by adopting an assertive manner. Assertiveness demands the skill of self-control and the ability to communicate our desires, feelings, and needs in a straightforward manner while being mindful of the needs of others (Wolpe & Lazarus, 1996).

Parental Assertiveness

Historically, the term assertiveness was integrated into the behavioral approach of the 1950s. Joseph Wolpe (1958) was the first researcher to use the term in an attempt to ease feelings of anxiety. He found that a person cannot experience two opposing emotions at a given moment in time; a person cannot be both relaxed and tense simultaneously. When a person is able to be assertive in stressful situations, he can lessen his anxiety and cope with the situation at a more feasible level (Wolpe, 1958). Since the 1950s to present day, there has been additional research supporting these ideas, particularly in neuro-psychological literature and research findings on the different sections of the brain, which are involved in situations of stress and of relaxation. In general, research points to increased activity of the amygdala during episodes of distress and anxiety that causes the heightening of physiological and emotional intensity, which is then calmed by the intervention of the cortex (the upper section of the brain), affecting a person's ability to self-regulate (Goleman, 2006).

When I explain this to parents, I use a metaphor of an elevator and talk about the necessity of "taking the elevator up" from the amygdala, which is situated at the base of the brain, up into the cerebral cortex, which is found in the upper region of the brain. When we succeed in "taking the elevator up" from the amygdala to the cortex, we are better able to cope with the situation we are facing, even in stressful conditions. When the amygdala takes command, we react automatically – in the survival mode – disabling any calming thought processes and our responses, for the most part, become ineffective. In order to run a family with all of its complexities, as well as the relationships with the children and the pressures being placed on us at all times, we need the assistance of calm thought processes – the rational and the functional. This requires a high level of self-control and the use of cognitive techniques, which make it possible to quickly maneuver from the amygdala to the cortex.

The assertive approach is based on a sophisticated system of identifying automatic processes and the ability to utilize cerebral cortex thinking processes. No one is born assertive. Assertive behavior is an acquired behavior and anyone can learn assertiveness. However, the mechanisms of assertiveness operate in contradiction to our automatic response mechanism, and therefore, it is difficult to apply assertive behavior.

In conflictual situations, our brain reacts as if we are under imminent threat. When our child screams because he's not received something, when our spouse is angry with us, when a client isn't pleased or the manager is disappointed – we react automatically in one of nature's three basic survival responses: fight, flight, or freeze. Even though this is not an actual, real-life threat, the brain perceives the situation as a psychological threat, therefore activating our survival warning system, which functions in the presence of dangerous circumstances. In conflictual situations, our automatic response system will express itself in two principle directions: one direction being to freeze and/or yield when faced by a threatening person while conceding our own desires, needs, and wishes due to a fear of confrontation with that person. By taking this route of response, we pay a heavy internal price in order to please the other person. The other direction of expression is attacking the other person in order to gain control over them or the situation. In this manner of response, we pay a high external-environmental price by distancing the other person from ourselves.

Maya and Dan are trying to cope with Yuval, their twelve-year-old son, who is constantly staging a power struggle. He defies them and does not comply with their requests, often screaming and ranting when faced with frustration. In an examination of the chain of responses, we observed the following process:

Situation	Automatic Thought	Emotion	Behavior
Yuval is screaming because he didn't get more chocolate.	Maya: He's spoiled. What is he thinking, that whatever he wants he gets? It's impossible to listen to his screaming; he'll have to be punished.	Angry at Yuval	Maya: Raises her voice and aggressively yells at Yuval, "You've gone too far! Stop that screaming and go to your room!"
Dan watches how Maya is coping with Yuval.	Poor little guy, if there's no chocolate I can run over to the supermarket and get him some. What's the big deal? Why is she yelling at him and telling him to go to his room?	Angry with Maya Afraid of Yuval's response	Dan: Makes a face, goes to Yuval's room and tries to calm him down. "Don't worry. I'll bring you some chocolate later on."

T: My dear Maya and Dan, your behavior was very natural but not very effective. Do you have any idea what Yuval learns from that kind of reaction and how it affects his behavior?

Maya: He learns that his Dad is a push-over, somebody who can't say no, who's scared of his reactions and that he can manipulate him any way he wants to…

T: Let's assume that all of that is correct. What do you think is the reason that caused this to happen?

Maya: I don't know. He (Dan) always has to be okay with the whole world; that softy routine drives me crazy.

T: Dan, do you agree with Maya?

Dan: It's true that I try to be all right, but that's not the reason. I can't stand to see the way Maya treats Yuval. She's always yelling at him, always blaming him, and punishing him. He's only a boy.

T: What's happening in your case happens in many homes (framing the experience as normal). We understand that each one of you interprets Yuval's screaming in a different manner. This influences your emotions and your reactions to them. Let's try to make a diagram of what happens to you in conflictual situations, not only with Yuval. For example, when your manager is angry at you or when your parents are mad at you.

(I asked each partner to write down where he is on the scale between passivity and aggression in different situations.)

Dan in confrontational situations:

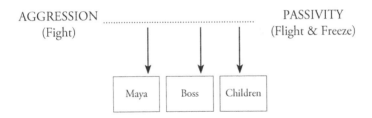

Maya in confrontational situations:

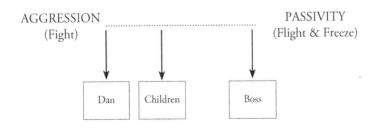

T: Does anything in this scale surprise you? Would you like to ask your spouse anything?

Dan: I don't understand. Why can't you be nicer at home, like you are at work?

Maya: It's not the same thing. At work I have to make an effort to be nice all the time. My house is my home and I don't have to prove myself. I am allowed to behave however I feel like and what's happening at home at the moment, isn't to my liking.

T: I want to repeat what you just said but slightly differently – outside of the house you activate self-control, which isn't used at home. Self-control is our ability to overcome internal and external stresses on the route to achieving our more important goal (Rosenbaum, 1990). Self-control requires effort; it acts in contradiction to our automatic responses. When you are at work, you invest effort in order to overcome various difficulties and to please your manager, and when you come home, you don't exert the same effort because you're at home, resting. Is that correct?

Maya: Partially. At work they wouldn't allow my aggressiveness. I have to plan my reactions and honestly, my manager is not an easy person to get along with, she's very aggressive herself. If I get into a confrontation with her, I'll lose my job.

T: You bring up an important point relating to the balance of power, which has a big influence on the choices the brain makes whether to attack or submit. The more we feel threatened by someone or something, the tendency is to run away or to submit. The more we

feel in control, the more we tend to attack when faced
with a threat.

Dan: What does that mean? Do I have to be more aggressive
with her so that she'll be nicer at home and stop
yelling?

T: That's one way of looking at the situation, but power
struggles at home are not beneficial. They will not lead
you to a sensible and progressive solution for all sides.
Instead of that, I suggest we learn how to communicate
more assertively so that we can get our messages across
in a clear manner and we can maintain good relations
without hurting one another. Assertiveness isn't found
on the chain of automatic responses for escaping or
attacking, it requires effort because it demands the
use of self-control, but the advantages are much more
substantial with this approach. It's an adjustment to
the dialogue with yourself, with each other, and also
with Yuval and the rest of the children. Your chances
of making a change in this case are really quite good,
but you will need to practice and work at it, because
these skills aren't found in your toolkit at the moment.
I advise we begin by working in this direction. Does
this sound sensible to you?

After getting Maya and Dan's agreement, we switched to the
psychoeducational element of the assertive approach, which is
critical to forming a joint vision and a clear path for the couple.
Where are we going and how do we get there? At the same time,
we strengthen their motivation for change and their desire to
co-operate in creating this kind of change.

Psychoeducational Explanation:

The assertive discourse is dialectic. On one hand, it deals with our ability to express our needs in a matter-of-fact, clear and succinct manner. On the other hand, it relates to our ability to understand and be mindful of the needs of others, while paying attention to their viewpoints and considering their concerns. This process is in direct contrast to our dichotomous, automatic survival responses: fight or flight.

The difficulty of being within this dialectical space is linked to the survival instinct system of "fight or flight," and is further connected to the adoption of erroneous thinking patterns. For instance, with the Submissive type of person, we can see attitudes such as, "If I give my opinion, they won't want to be friendly with me anymore," "I don't deserve this," and "He knows better than I what's good for me." With the Aggressive personality types, we can observe thinking patterns like these, "Who does he think he is?" "Nobody can tell me what to do," or "I'll get my way in the end."

Let's visualize for the moment that each one of us is a separate circle. In the event of a conflict, I may very well find myself reacting automatically with aggression or with passivity. In such cases, a situation is created whereby I "devour" my neighboring circle or otherwise am "devoured" by them. Let me explain. If I am concerned only with my own needs and don't see the needs of others, I am "devouring" them. I am essentially denying their needs, their desires and wishes. If I am busy trying to please the other side and do not pay attention to my own needs, then the other side essentially "devours" me, my needs, and my wishes.

T: Do you recognize this situation?

Dan: Yes, that's more or less the story of my life.

T: In a situation like this, like yours, Dan, we create a state of "internal pain," since we avoid conflict and by doing so give up our needs, not by freedom of choice, but rather from the fear of losing their love, of being blamed, and feeling guilty. Later, we will clarify the root of your fears. Many times we do things for the sake of others at our own expense, and then develop hostility, anger, and feelings of resentment towards those whom we actually wanted to please. In this long and ongoing process an "ulcer" is formed, on a psychological level. I am not gratifying myself or my wishes; my moods are oppressive, and I am under stress and sometimes, also anxiety. With some people, real damage to their self-esteem takes place and this weakens their ability to love who they are.

    In your case, Maya, the tendency is to be aggressive at home; the cause of the "ulcer" is found in the environment outside the home. You are not applying self-control at home, responding with a lot of anger, aggression, yelling, and criticism, and this behavior takes a heavy toll on your relationship with the people you love the most.

    Let's try to outline this on the board.

During therapy, I frequently utilize drawing charts and sketching graphs. I have learned that presenting things in graphic form helps the client to better understand and clarify matters. With people who have a stronger visual memory than an auditory memory, this is especially critical.

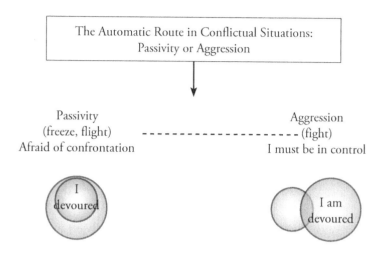

The goal here in therapy will be to construct a situation where I defend my own circle while safeguarding the circle of my counter-part. I don't want to "devour" or be "devoured." When we understand how important it is to speak our minds, express our opinions, and at the same time safeguard the circle of the person across from us – the chances for a healthy and effective relationship are much better.

In order to achieve this goal we work in stages.

We begin the first stage when we identify how we tend to respond to conflict, in different situations, on a behavioral level.

At this point, we examine the current stage and the thoughts you have during conflictual situations and then try to find ways to divert those thoughts in a more effective direction. In the next stage, we practice the art of communicating our messages in an assertive manner.

Investigating Automatic Thoughts in Conflict Situations and Finding a Self-Coping Statement (Self-Instruction)

The focus of Cognitive-Behavioral Therapy is on identifying the automatic thinking patterns that stem from the core beliefs and schemas a person has about himself, others, the world, and the future (Beck, 1976). Automatic thinking is characterized by the spontaneous flow of thoughts arising without control, without pondering or rational thinking. It's difficult for people to catch hold of these thoughts at the same moment they occur, and therefore, we are more aware of their accompanying emotions. Automatic thoughts pass through our minds in the blink of an eye and we tend to accept them as correct without actually examining them. Practicing to identify these thoughts will allow for higher self-awareness and a broader sense of control over the way we feel and act (Beck, 2011).

Our automatic thoughts are linked to schemas we have developed over the years. Schemas are the resulting structure of reactions, which have developed from experiences and memories and emerge in our thinking and reaction process, and hence, influence how we translate events and respond. Schemas encode information that is not accessible until observed and deciphered. The context and the organization of the schemas differ in individuals in accordance with his experiences (Barlow, 2008). Our schema will determine how we respond in conflictual situations. A negative schema may remain "dormant" during long periods of time when there is an absence of stress, but re-awaken in response to external/ environmental stress factors or internal factors of symbolic value. For instance, a young man is disappointed when his girlfriend cancels their date (external stress). As a result, his core beliefs are activated – beliefs that are linked to his lack of self-esteem and childhood memories of abandonment. When these schemas are activated, they awaken a complex system of negative thoughts, contributing to the negative interpretation in situations of social stress, which results and is characterized by erroneous thinking (Alford & Beck, 1997).

As a result, the aim of Cognitive-Behavioral Therapy, in general, is to increase the ability to create assertive communication in particular, and identify the client's core beliefs and schemas, which have evolved over the years. We can learn how these schemas are connected to the client's automatic thoughts, to his emotions and interactions with his surroundings. Much has been written about the methods of identifying automatic thoughts, the erroneous thinking that typifies them, and about techniques like the downward arrow for identifying a person's core beliefs and the technique of the Socratic questioning for disputing negative and irrational perceptions (Beck, 1976; Beck, 1995; Ellis, 1979; Padesky, 1993).

When working directly with parents, we should relate to two main channels on the cognitive level for identifying automatic thoughts: the channel of interpersonal communication between the couple and the channel of communication with the children. I will continue by describing the on-going work with Maya and Dan on the subject of identifying automatic thoughts connected to Yuval's behavior and how we can progress towards cognitive restructuring, which will, in the end, aid in implementing assertive communication with him.

T: Maya and Dan, in our previous session I asked you to describe, by using the chain of responses, at least one incident of conflict that happened with Yuval during the past week. I asked you to guess what Yuval's automatic thoughts and feelings were in order to understand the chain of responses. Before we touch on your notes and descriptions themselves, was there anything that surprised you at the time you were writing down the chain of response?

Maya: The exercise made me step into Yuval's shoes, and since I was so angry at him, I discovered that I wasn't at all noticing what was going on with him. I think this is the first time I understood what you said last time about the price of my aggression and the "ulcer" I cause in the people close to me.

T: That was definitely one of the goals of the assignment: to be able to step into the shoes of someone else for a moment, which isn't easy, especially for someone who has a tendency to attack. Let's see what you wrote down during the week.

Maya's Table:

Situation	Automatic Thoughts	Emotion	Behavior
I asked Yuval to take out the trash and he answers, "I don't feel like it."	Cheeky, not willing to give of himself, we do everything for him, ingrate	Angry at Yuval	Shouts aggressively at Yuval, "You are so ungrateful. Don't ask me for anything because I'm not doing it for you."
Mom says, "You're ungrateful. Don't ask me for anything because I won't do it for you."	Maya's guess about Yuval's thoughts: Mom hates me, doesn't matter what I do.	Angry at Mom	Yells at Mom, "Don't do me any favors; nobody asked you to."

T: How did the incident end?

Maya: We kept on yelling at each other. Then he went into his room and slammed the door so hard the whole house shook.

T: When you look back on that now, could you have acted differently?

Maya: I could have not asked him to take out the trash. But it's really important he does things around the house.

T: Our goal is not to retreat from confrontation, but rather to know how to handle it. There is no reason you should concede on the things that are important to you. The idea is to see in which way the messages are communicated effectively and assertively. To do this, let's think if there are any other additional interpretations that you might give to Yuval's reaction "I don't feel like it," and how they would affect your feelings and your behavior, which is to say, on the chain of responses. Dan, you are welcome to help us.

Situation	New Thoughts	Emotion	Behavior
I ask Yuval to take out the trash and he answers, "I don't feel like it."	Maybe he meant he didn't want to at the moment. Maybe he's angry with me and that's why he reacted like that. Maybe there's something positive in he said straight out what suits him. I can't expect people to always do what I want.	Understanding Calmness	A question instead of blaming: Are you mad at me? Did you mean you don't want to right now?
Question: Are you angry with me?	Maya's guess about Yuval's automatic thoughts: Mom gets me; she's sensitive to me.	Calmness	I'm not mad at you. I just don't feel like it right now. I'm doing something else.

T: These new thoughts broaden our view of the situation and let us take into account what's happening to the person we are interacting with.

Maya: It all sounds very nice, but in the moment of truth, when he says, "I don't feel like it," it doesn't seem as if I'll be able to tell myself all those thoughts.

T: You're right. It's very difficult to take the elevator up from the amygdala to the cortex in a stressful situation. Therefore, we'll learn to apply self-instruction. This allows the brain to easily make the jump from one of the "hot spots" in the brain to the "cooler" areas of the brain.

Self-instruction is an internal dialog, which repeats itself and influences our consciousness. Its goal is to create an internal dialog that strengthens our self-control (Meichenbaum, 1977). In stressful situations our brain becomes "hot" very quickly. If we could, we'd want to stop the process of thinking and ask a question such as, what's going on in my head right now? Is it beneficial? Is there another way to think about this situation? But sometimes it requires so much energy, we skip over that part and go back to the familiar automatic thoughts. The more impulsive we are the harder it is to stop the automatic thinking. Self-instruction acts like an electric switch in the brain, like turning on a light. The phrase that we choose for self-instruction is meant to immediately halt the "hot" process in the brain and activate "cool" thinking, the rational logic that is beneficial to us in any given situation.

The basis for finding the right self-instruction is hidden among the automatic thoughts, but the automatic thoughts are linked to an earlier basic belief. In order for the self-instruction phrase to be effective, it should relate to a basic tenet.

T: Let's examine your basic beliefs when you ask Yuval to do something and he doesn't do it.

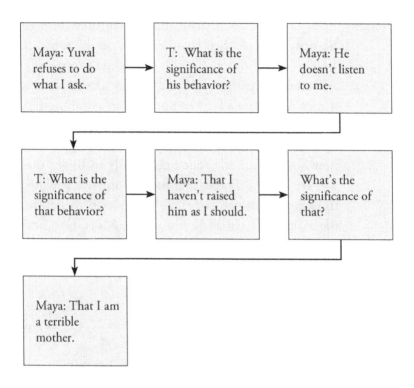

T: In actuality, Maya, every time Yuval doesn't do what
        you tell him to do, your initial automatic thoughts are
        directed at blaming Yuval; you are angry with him and
        attack him, but when we search deeper, we discover
        the basis for this is your fear or concern – or even
        belief – that you are not a good enough mother.

Maya: Exactly.

T: And the interesting thing is that the negative chain of
        response that has developed between the two of you
        actually strengthens that basic belief of yours that you
        are not a good mother. Can you tell me when you are
        a good mother?

Maya: Plenty of times. I sit with them when they do their
       homework, cook their favorite dishes on the Sabbath.
       I try to spend one hour with each child every week,
       separately; I pamper them and buy them clothes,
       games. We laugh a lot; I'm not such an awful mother.

T: When you are confronting Yuval, the brain doesn't
       remember all the good things you mentioned just
       now about yourself. Your brain tends to forget that
       you are a good mother and focuses on your negative
       thinking about yourself. Let's find a way to remind
       the brain. We'll try, all of us together (Maya, Dan, and
       I). Right now, we'll write on the board all the possible
       phrases that might help Maya when she has a conflict
       situation with Yuval.

Confrontation doesn't mean I'm a horrible mother.
I'm a good mother even when there's a conflict.
I learn to take a deep breath and not respond right away.
I will never be perfect; relax already.
I'm not frightened; I'm breathing.
I am managing the conflict; the conflict is not managing me.
Breathe and think.
I have the ability to change the chain of response.

At this point, I asked Maya to grade the phrases according to
their order of relevance:

    10 = a phrase which I can relate to and can help me; 1 = a
phrase that doesn't help me.

Maya graded them like this:

Confrontation doesn't mean I'm a horrible mother. = 7
I'm a good mother even when there's a conflict. = 8
I am learning to breathe deeply and not respond right away. = 9
I will never be perfect; relax already. = 9
I'm not frightened; I'm breathing. = 10
I am managing the conflict; the conflict is not managing me. = 9
Breathe and think. = 10
I have the ability to change the chain of responses. = 6

After rating the phrases we'll use guided imagery to choose exactly the right self-instruction phrase. We'll take the chosen phrases that received the highest scores and by a process of elimination, we'll choose the most appropriate phrase.

T: I'll ask you, Maya, to close your eyes and imagine a situation where Yuval says to you, "I don't feel like it." I want you to try and feel, as much as possible, the emotional and physical sensations accompanying your thoughts. If that scene doesn't spark your memory, we'll look for another dramatic situation. It's important to me that you try and experience, as much as possible, the negative reactions you usually experience in order to test more precisely which of the instructions succeeds in increasing your sense of control.

The exercise is done in several stages and by a process of elimination, we will choose your self-instruction phrase:

Close your eyes
Imagine a confrontation situation between yourself and Yuval.

Nod "yes' with your head when you are in that situation.

I will repeat each phrase twice (three phrases compete each time).

Check which of the phrases is best for you. There doesn't need to be an explanation, only in the sense that it works for you.

Beginning the process of choosing between the phrases:

– I am learning to breathe deeply and not respond right away.

– I will never be perfect; relax already.

– I'm not frightened; I'm breathing.

The phrase that was chosen: **I'm not frightened; I'm breathing**. In the next stage, the previously chosen phrase will compete against two additional new phrases:

– I'm not frightened; I'm breathing.

– I am managing the conflict; the conflict is not managing me.

– Breathe and think.

The phrase that was chosen: **Breathe and think.**

Sometimes, in the process of choosing a self-talk phrase, new and more concise phrases are created. Since the phrase itself includes an instruction to act (to breathe), during the exercise, we'll introduce the breathing along with the self-instruction. In Maya's case, she had to take one deep breath and say to herself the self-instructing phrase (Breath and think).

To test the effectiveness of the phrase it is advisable to challenge the self-instruction phrase.

Challenging Self-Instruction

The aim of this exercise is twofold, to test the effectiveness of the phrase that we practiced in guided imagery exercises that reflects our personal reality, and to internalize this phrase so that it can be used automatically in stressful situations. The choosing of a self-instructing phrase is a cognitive process. Nevertheless, in order for it to be effective for the client, there must be an emotional and sensory association. In most cases, if the self-instructing phrase does not help the client in distressful situations, this means it is not precise enough, that it does not touch on one's core beliefs and does not relate to their personal experience.

T: Maya, you've chosen a clear and concise self-instructing phrase so it has more potential to influence your ability to take control of your experiences and your responses. In order to use the phrase in stressful and conflictual situations with Yuval – and perhaps even for broader use in additional situations – we will challenge the instruction in this manner: You begin to say the self-instruction and then add a smile. The smile sends an immediate message to your brain that there is no reason to be frightened (Goleman, 2006). At the same time, I will say to you the negative thoughts that tend to pop up in your mind in those situations, as we saw in earlier stages. In effect, we are practicing going up on the "elevator." Practicing your ability to switch from automatic – hot and quick – at the base of the brain to the activation of the upper region of the brain, which is more calculating and regulated. We are doing this by exposing you to those difficult, intolerable thoughts.

Maya: (Begins to say the self-instruction phrase while smiling, again and again) "Breath and think."

T: (I begin to flood her with negative thoughts.) "I'm a bad mother," "I can't handle my children," "He hates me now," "How dare he say that to me?" "What a terrible mother I am. He won't even take out the trash." Maya, how did you feel during this trial exercise?

Maya: At first it was really hard for me, but then I tried to connect and concentrate on the phrase and at some point I heard your voice in the background and it didn't affect me.

T: Excellent, the phrase helped you to focus your attention on your goal and you succeeded in overcoming the negative voices in the background. Now, we will step up the pressure. I'll do the outside voices, like blaming. Dan will help me. The purpose is to increase your negative sensations, so that you can utilize the self-instruction phrase and focus on your goal, in spite of the accusations coming from the outside.

Dan: (smiling) I've wanted to do that for a long time.

Maya: (laughs)

Maya begins to say her phrase, over and over again without pausing, continuing smiling while Dan and I attack. "What kind of mother are you?" "You're yelling all the time," "You're a bad mother," and "You'll never be a good mother." At this point, Maya begins to cry.

T: If you're crying, it means we've touched exactly on a spot that hurts. Don't stop the exercise. Only check if you want to change the phrase or add something to the phrase.

Maya: Yes, I couldn't hold on to the part that I'm actually a good mother.

T: What would you change?

Maya: Breathe and think. I'm a great mother.

We repeated the exercise; we verbally barraged Maya and gradually added angrier and louder tones. Surprisingly, Dan, who is usually the type who avoids confrontation and is perceived as weaker, revealed his aggressive side.

T: Maya, how do you feel after that rather difficult exercise?

Maya: Yes, it was very difficult. Also, I was shocked from what came out of Dan. Why doesn't that side come out more with Yuval?

T: You have come upon a point connecting between parenting style and responses to threatening situations. My guess is that Dan tends to avoid conflict and instead he placates the children, among other reasons, because he is afraid to confront them. The more he sees your aggressiveness towards them, the more he feels a stronger need to protect them and tends to be more responsive to them. You see his responsiveness and it makes you angry because his reactions don't contain any element of demand. In our next session, we will work on the application of assertive communication, and then we will be able to break this cycle, but it's important for me to know what other feelings you had after the exercise we just did.

Maya: It was a tough exercise, but somehow, it seems to me, I'll be more resilient in conflicts with Yuval, whenever they happen.

T: If that's the case then, Maya, your homework will be to practice self-instruction in direct situations with Yuval, especially in conflictual situations. Next time, we'll work in the same manner and choose a self-instructing phrase for Dan. Then I'll ask you, Dan, to write down additional incidents with Yuval during the week that caused you to feel uncomfortable.

After both of you have found strong and effective self-instruction phrases, we can move on to the next stage: training in assertive communication.

Sometimes, in therapy, we affix the self-instruction phrase to a song or even a dance. This depends a large part on the nature of the therapeutic relationship, the trust that's been built, and the general atmosphere of the therapy.

Training in Assertive Communication

Training in assertive communication requires a gradual progressive effort in order to acquire new behaviors (Wolpe & Lazarus, 1996). For many people, it is a strain to express their opinion in a forthright manner; often they may not even know what their opinions are. These people tend to avoid confrontation, skirt possible conflict, are afraid of rejection and of other people being angry with them. Assertiveness training with these types of people will increase their belief in themselves, decrease negative provocations, and thus contribute to a lessening of tension and fear, allowing them to better control averse situations. With people who have a propensity to attack in cases of conflict, training in the assertive approach will improve their ability to relate to the needs of others and offer them the option of co-operation and finding possible solutions to the problem.

Assertive communication is aimed at resolving problems and requires interpersonal skills such as: attentiveness, self-control, and planned responses that balance between the individual's needs and the needs of others. For this purpose, it is best to divide the training into three parts:

Part One – Training in active listening.
Part Two – Training in identifying the individual's goals and needs, while identifying emotions that arise during conversations or conflicts.
Part Three – Training in communicating assertive messages.

Active Listening

The ability to listen to someone else is one of the cornerstones of creating effective interpersonal communication and is the first elementary step in active communication. It is best to differentiate between tolerant listening, which is hearing what the other says in a passive manner, and active listening, where the listener is an active partner in the desire to understand the other's message by way of showing interest, asking questions to clarify, and reflecting back the message that was conveyed. This is a very hard task, even though it seems to be quite taken for granted, and its application is even more difficult in conflict situations when we are reacting automatically from a survivalist standpoint. Active listening can be taught but requires frequent practice. Most of us feel a great sense of satisfaction when we are listened to and heard. Listening to what we say, and especially the ability to reflect back to us what was understood by the other listener, causes us to feel that our message was received exactly as we meant it to be understood, and thus builds an experience of trust and security in relationships (Hendrix, 1988).

In order to enable the efficient exchange of messages, we must actively listen to each other's words and focus on what is being said. In addition to the verbal content, we need to be aware of the non-verbal messages that are being expressed. This enables interested listening and appropriate, empathetic response to what is being said. Without even noticing, we actively use non-verbal gestures such as eye contact, leaning towards the speaker, nodding or shaking of the head, all of these broadcast a willingness to hear what the other has to say while exhibiting attentiveness to his words.

In addition to active listening, one needs to express empathy towards another person. This means the ability to put yourself in someone else's shoes and try to understand them. The empathetic experience begins with active listening. This is a skill, as we have said, that can be practiced and learned for use under conditions of strain and conflict, like any other behavior.

Active listening is comprised of several distinct abilities:

The ability to ask clarifying questions: for example, "What do you mean?"

"I didn't exactly understand… could you explain it to me again?"

The ability to reflect back to the other what you have heard: "If I understood/heard correctly, you said… Have I understood correctly?"

The ability to be an active partner and show genuine interest in another's messages and express that in words: "What do you say?" "I hadn't thought of that," and "That sounds very difficult."

Most of us tend to concentrate on the messages that we want to send out to others, without the capacity to be fully attentive to the other and without the ability to absorb the words of the sender (Hendrix, 1988). Developing the aptitude to listen to someone else demands self-control. This is even more challenging when we are engaged in a conflictual situation and we successfully manage to listen despite our natural tendency to give an automatic impulsive "hot" response. The first exercise in the skill of listening is not to respond immediately, but rather allow the other side to explain what they mean. People prone to impulsivity will find this very hard to do, even at this early stage; therefore, it is advisable to initially work with them on self-instruction, thus enabling them to delay their impulsive reaction and be able to listen to others. One of my clients chose the self-instruction phrase, "Shut up and Listen," a self-instruction that let her, for the first time in her life, according to her, listen to her children and spouse.

Active listening is a condition for effective management of conflicts and has two important purposes:

1. To give the other side a sense that his words are important to you even if you don't agree with him.
2. Active listening helps me to better understand the other side and plan my responses so they will be more effective in solving the conflict.

In practice, listening during a conflict is two-sided listening, internal and external. External listening involves active listening while also attempting to identify the messages, the needs, the feelings, and content that are being sent. However, at the same time, there is a necessity for introspective listening during a disagreement, which will enable me to recognize my own needs, wishes, emotions, and objectives, and help me manage them for myself and for my partner in the dialog. This is a very complex undertaking and requires much practice. One of the more effective methods for enabling a client to adapt assertive listening patterns is to train them at the behavioral level, which requires them to be in touch with feelings and cognitions at all times, while being able to simultaneously govern what is going on internally and externally.

Assertive Behavior Training Model

At the behavioral level, we will aspire to establish the assertive communication principles, verbal and non-verbal alike, by an explanation of the model, and afterwards, by rehearsing role playing exercises.

It is easier for clients to understand the practical steps of interpersonal communication after they have received a comprehensive explanation of what they are about to do. At this point, I usually present a simple and clear behavior model composed of three modules:

1. Connecting to the needs of others.
2. Sending out my message.
3. Invitation for co-operation.

Continuing the process of integrating assertive parenting, I began to work with Maya and Dan on the behavioral expression of assertive communication according to the aforementioned model.

T: Let's understand the model I showed you. The first stage of the model deals with safeguarding the other person's circle. We use active listening to try and find out what their message is, and attempt to relate to their needs – being empathetic even when we don't agree with a single word. Let's think of some phrases that might be suitable for giving the other person the sense that we have listened to them and that we care about them.

Dan: Maybe something like, "I understand what you're saying."

T: Very good. Sentences that begin with "I" lessen the

other person's feeling of being threatened. When we start with "You," there is a suggestion of blame, which in turn activates the survival system of flight/fight within the other person. Which is easier to connect with – flight or fight?

Maya: Flight.

T: Correct, the fleer is an expert at identifying the other's need, because he is always busy adapting himself to the needs of someone else and not to his own needs. It's no coincidence that Dan can easily find a sentence which relates to the needs of another person. Some other phrases for connecting with the needs of others might be: "I understand I made you angry," "I am trying to understand what you are saying to me," "I understand that it's important to you." Essentially, in this segment, we are safeguarding the "circle" of the other person participating in our dialog (the same circles we talked about in the psychoeducational explanation section).

In the second stage, we are concerned with sending our message in a clear, concise, and matter-of-fact fashion. For whom is this stage easier?

Dan: For Maya. That's a big thing with her and sometimes I envy her for it.

T: This stage is easier for those that have a predilection to attack. They are very centered on their own message. It's very clear to them what their message to someone else is, but on the non-verbal level they are sending their message aggressively. The fleers are more fragile in this stage, and sometimes they can't even define for themselves what the message they want to send is. There is good reason for you to envy Maya, Dan. She has a better ability to send clear messages. You can also learn to do that.

Dan: If I can do that, this session will be a lot more than parent training and treatment for the relationship with Yuval. I can finally ask for that salary raise and I'll be sharper in staff meetings at work. Sometimes there are things that get me so angry, but I don't say anything so that I don't start arguments, and afterwards, pay the price.

T: Excellent, shortly we will begin to rehearse with the model and you'll see it's not so complicated. It simply requires a lot of practice.

The second stage of the model relates to our "circle." We don't concede messages that are important to us to send out, rather we construct the message in a manner that will not hurt someone else. The third and final stage relates to both "circles" together. This is the stage where we deal with problem solving. An assertive person looks for a resolution and does so with the collaboration of his partner. The phrases that we should use at this stage have the style of an invitation for co-operation: "So, how can we solve this?" "What can we do?" "I think that… What do you say?" "What do you suggest?" or "Certainly we can solve this. Let's think of a solution." The third stage is critical for creating a sense of security and trust in the relationship. This stage lets us feel that even though we don't agree, our counterpart is concerned and has not "closed the door from the inside"; he shows a willingness to solve the problem and preserve good relations in spite of our conflict.

Now, after we have understood the model and what the role of each step is, we can begin to practice. For your homework assignment, I asked you to write about two conflict incidents that occurred during the week – one between the two of you and the other with Yuval, while trying to pinpoint the thoughts that went through your mind during the incidents and try to chart the chain of responses. Who's ready to start?

Dan: I'm ready. The incident took place last Saturday. Usually, on Saturday, I take the kids with me until the afternoon and let Maya have some free time to herself. But on Thursday, I got a call from a good friend who invited me and a few other friends to a "guy's day" at his place from ten o'clock until six o'clock. I told Maya that it was really important for me to go. Maya said that she had already planned lots of errands.

T: Okay, let's start from there, the chain of response, from the moment of that conflict between you, only this time try to examine the chain of response that went on inside of you.

Situation	Automatic Thought	Emotion	Behavior
I ask Maya to take the children so that I can go to my friend's place and she says: it's not convenient because she has lots of errands to do and asks me to go at two o'clock.	I never ask her for anything. If I ask, that means it's really important to me. All the time I'm considerate of her. Why can't she think of me once? The significance of the thought is, Maya doesn't see me. I'm not important to her.	Anger Helpless	I made a face, didn't say anything, and told my friend that I'd probably be late.
My behavior (I made a face, didn't say anything, and told my friend that I'd probably get there late).	What a loser I am. I should have told her that I don't care, I'm going anyway. It doesn't happen every day and it's important to me. She didn't care; she'd just tell me she was going and that's it.	Anger (at myself and Maya) Sadness	Made an angry face, disappointed. I was really bummed but I didn't say anything.

Dan: In the end, I got to my friend's place at one o'clock, but in a bad mood. It took me a long time to relax and enjoy myself; I started to have fun after about two hours.

T: That's the price we were talking about in our previous sessions: the very same "internal ulcer" that is caused when we run away from confrontation and internalize our negative feelings. Let's reconstruct your message to

Maya together according to the model we learned about.

1. Connecting to the needs of others – "I understand that you planned to run errands on Saturday and I know how important that time is for you."

2. Sending my message – "But it's very, very important to me to see my friend. This is something that doesn't happen very often…and it will be so great to get together with all the guys. I'd be truly happy if you'd make the effort for me this time."

3. Invitation for co-operation – "What do you say?"

Dan was a bit hesitant when I asked him to send this message to Maya in a role playing game, "I'm not good at that," he said. The more we progressed in the role playing game set around the incidents they had written down and Maya practiced her active listening – the more Dan began to feel freer and more confident in sending clear messages. He was surprised by Maya's reaction, "I like it when you say things clearly." The rest of the training exercise was spent on acquiring skills for managing conflicts with Yuval.

Conflict management with children proceeds a little differently and depends on their stage of development. At the younger ages, we don't always use the third element of inviting co-operation, particularly when it is not suitable to introduce negotiations of parental demands. For instance, when a child hits his brother in anger, we can say, "I realize you are angry, but hitting is not allowed." Even so, at a calmer time we can utilize all three of the elements: "I noticed that you were very angry earlier, but you know I don't allow any hitting, at all. Let's think about what you can do when you get so angry…"

The greatest advantage in using the third element of the model with children is that it can improve their skills for problem solving. More often than not, we tend to solve the children's problems for them, suggesting solutions and not allowing them to develop an inner belief in their ability to solve problems themselves. A child who knows how to form and provide solutions on his own is strengthening his personal and social abilities while nurturing his own mental well-being (Meyers, 2012). Asking questions such as, "What do you think you can do?" or "How can it be solved?" enables the child to broaden his observation of the problem, to view the variety of possible solutions at his disposal, and to develop positive self-efficacy in relation to himself and his ability to cope with life's challenges. This a true gift for any child, a gift for their personal and social growth.

In order to develop assertive communication with children, parents are required to be role models for them. The model that children learn is the model they observe when their parents manage conflicts with them and between themselves. In this way, the child learns assertive communication and can use it himself in conflict situations. Assertiveness is not only a way to cope with conflict – it is also a way of life. The ability to send clear messages about my needs ("I'm going to sleep now and I'm asking you not to make noise"), or my various feelings ("That really makes me happy"), instills the message that here is a parent who expresses his needs and respects the rights of others. This message is critical for the developing child to realize that his needs are legitimate, that he needs to attend to them when interacting with others. When this is done with a combination of verbal and non-verbal messages – "I'm on your side even if I don't agree with you" – the child learns to see the other individual and can be emphatic towards others.

Sometimes, parents are called upon to cope with an

impulsive child, one who experiences heightened fits of anger, and the parents are helpless to do anything, especially when the child loses control: becomes aggressive, destructive, throws things, gets into a rage, swears, screams, and hits. In this case, intervention is necessary. Intervention will be focused upon the parent's abilities, and/or the therapist's, to furnish effective tools for extreme situations.

The "BASIC" Model for Coping with a Child's Fits of Rage

Anat and Uzi are the parents of seven-year-old Nadav. They describe extreme outbursts of rage each time Nadav doesn't get what he wants, or every time things don't go the way he wants them to. Nadav was diagnosed with an attention disorder (ADHD); he is very impulsive, hyperactive, speaks non-stop, often becomes angry and irritated, and his parents feel exhausted. Moreover, they feel helpless whenever a fit of rage erupts – sometimes several times a day – accompanied by his throwing objects, smashing his fists into the walls, and even violent behavior against family members.

In such cases, I prefer to work with the parents alone and only in the event that no desired change has been achieved – I will then invite the child for direct intervention treatment. In the parent training session with Anat and Uzi, an intervention process similar to what was described earlier, took place: defining parenting styles, identifying automatic thoughts, finding a self-instruction phrase, and learning and training for assertive communication. According to the parent's reports, there was a significant lessening in the frequency of Nadav's fits of rage, from a number of outbursts a day down to once or twice a week. However, the intensity of the angry outbursts did not change.

T: I'm very proud of you and the progress you've made so far. You have done very well and we can see the evidence of this – Nadav's fits of rage are becoming less frequent. Do you have any ideas about why they are less frequent?

Anat: I think we are much clearer with him and we're calmer too. It's clear to us where we're headed and how we'll get there. In addition to the instruction we get here, we've been trying to send Nadav the message that we are on his side but we don't agree with his behavior. But still, we are genuinely powerless when the outbursts happen. They are so intense; it isn't normal.

T: Your sense of helplessness is quite understandable. It's not easy to stand by and watch explosions of anger, like the ones you describe, and therefore, we will focus, for the time being, on your understanding of Nadav's fits of anger and learn how to help him regulate them.

A Psychoeducational Explanation for the Parents

Anger is considered to be an emotion linked to our survival. The feeling of anger makes us understand that something in the situation isn't as it should be. Anger helps us fight for our lives and react to threats around us, and it varies in intensity from mild irritation to intense fury and rage (Spielberger et al., 1991). For most people, anger lasts for approximately ten minutes (Tyson, 1998). There are people whose anger continues for hours, days, and even weeks, and they are characterized with hyper-thinking (ruminating), which causes them to focus on their anger and plans of vengeance (Bushman, et al., 2005; Denson, Pederson & Miller, 2006).

Anger is an emotion possessing highly negative stimuli and

is directly connected to aggressive behavior (Berkowitz, 1990; Eisenberg & Epel, 2007; Fabes, 1992; Southam-Gerow & Kendall, 2002). Controlling anger is possible when the person is capable of identifying the emotional stimulus and interpreting this as anger: this includes understanding, defining the emotions as anger, determining the intensity of the anger, and how to express it appropriately. (Southam-Gerow & Kendall, 2002). Dodge and and his colleagues (Dodge et al., 2002) claim that children with problems in identifying and understanding emotions have a tendency to negatively and hostilely interpret the intentions of others and the stimulus of emotions that they experience as a result of the actions and behavior of others. These children have trouble adopting pro-social goals and they assume aggression in certain social situations is a suitable response as a result. In the therapy process, we will strive to nurture, together with the parents and children, the ability to identify, to understand, and express emotions without harming anyone.

The younger the child, the weaker the child's self-control skills are (Eisenberg, 2006; Ronen, 1994; Epel, 2007), and the parents fill a more central and critical role in the child's development of self-regulation (Cohen, 2006).

From a practical point of view, when a child is in the midst of a fit of rage, he is like a tornado in action and it's difficult to stop him. We should focus, then, on the child's ability to identify and regulate the anger before it reaches a peak, in order to decrease the aggressive behavior of the child towards himself and others in the child's immediate environment.

We can describe such anger in terms of a very rapidly rising wave, a wave that remains at its peak for ten minutes, after which it should descend slowly, returning to a state of calm.

Let's draw it on the board:

Process of Anger

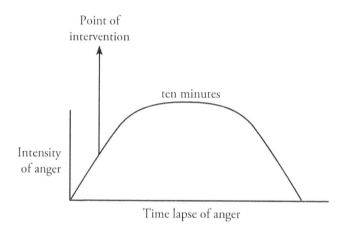

Point of intervention

ten minutes

Intensity of anger

Time lapse of anger

Our aim is to intervene at the time when the wave is on the rise. We will want to teach Nadav to recognize the warning signs of an approaching wave of anger and enable him to control it, by sort of "surfing the wave" in a stormy sea. The metaphor of surfing the waves helps both the parents and children alike. A seasoned surfer catches the wave as it begins to rise and stays with the wave, navigating its progress while surfing along with the wave. It's impossible to "catch" a wave at its peak, and even more importantly, if the surfer crests the uppermost edge of the wave, there's a very good chance he will fall (wipeout). Therefore, when coping with a wave of anger, we shall attempt to surf on it when it begins to take shape, when there are clear signs that the wave is on its way. When the wave is cresting, all that can be done is to lose control, just as a surfer loses his balance. So, in order to surf on a wave of anger – which is a natural and important emotion – we will use a model which is called the BASIC: 1. Breathe and signal; 2. Detach and increase deep breathing or release energy; 3. Calm down and talk.

How does the BASIC model work?
At the time of heightened emotional arousal, it is difficult for us to control our speech, which requires cortical activity. Each intervention model is based on physical expressions alone. Only when the system returns to a state of calm, words may be supplemented. We understand that anger increases negative reactions in the body. The first step will be to intervene on a physical level – lowering the degree of biological alterations by taking a long deep breath. While we are taking a long deep breath, we make a hand signal (agreed upon ahead of time), which means, "I take responsibility for my anger and I'm going to calm down now." In conflict situations, many of us have a habit of blaming someone else for our anger. The implication of signaling to someone is, "Let me have my space to calm down," and let us take responsibility for the anger, and at the same time let the other person know what is expected from him in the present situation.

There are people for whom the simple act of breathing helps them calm down and regulate their anger, while others find physical activity helps them self-regulate. Therefore, when you are describing the intervention to a child, it is recommended to explain that the time out phase (in the child's room, or a particular corner in the house), is an experiment to help him calm down. The child may try deep breathing while they are on a "time-out" or run in place as fast as they can for thirty seconds.

After fifteen minutes, when the child has calmed down, they can return to their previous activity. If you want to talk about what happened, you should wait a while – preferably, an hour or two before asking what happened or suggesting any possible solutions for the next time. Breathe and signal, then separate to another place. Increase Breathe or Release energy. After ten minutes, calm down and talk.

B	A	S	I	C
Breathe	And	Signal, then separate	Increase deep breathing or release energy	Calm down and talk

Parents who teach their children the BASIC model should do so only during calm periods. Anat and Uzi practiced with me in the treatment room on how to use the model, and we also did some role playing exercises for sending their message to Nadav. They decided to talk with Nadav together about the BASIC model and agreed that Anat would lead the conversation in light of her talent for sending clear and accurate messages. Accordingly, in the role playing, Anat played the role of herself and Uzi played the role of Nadav.

Anat: "Nadav honey, it's important for both of us to talk with you about what happens to you when you're very angry. Do you remember when you were really sorry after you got angry and broke things in the house? You lost out on that, too, since you broke the computer screen and don't have a computer now. Lately, we've seen an improvement in your ability to control your anger, but we would like to suggest another type of activity that will help you deal with situations when the anger goes up and up. The situation as it is today, can't go on any longer, and we need to try and solve the problem. We'll all benefit and it will be a lot nicer for all of us at home. Your father and I learned that anger is like an ocean wave, it rises up and then crashes down, and we can all feel when that happens – when the anger goes up. For instance, I feel a kind of heat in my body and then I know I'm inside a wave of anger. What do you feel when the anger rises? (The parents guess what Nadav would say.) So that we can control the wave of anger and not injure ourselves or others when we get mad, we wanted to tell you about a technique we learned, called "BASIC." It can help control our feelings of anger and prevent painful outbursts. When you feel the first signs that a wave of anger is on the way, take a deep breath and signal to us that you are going to take care of the anger. Which sign would you like to use, Nadav? (Uzi makes a sign like a fist.) Excellent, Nadav. Every time we see you make that sign, we will know that you are feeling a wave of anger approaching and that you're going to work it out. Let's think of somewhere that seems like a good place for you to go when you have to deal with the anger.

Uzi: I'll go into Dad's study. (Anat and Uzi laugh.)

(Nadav): "I don't want to think about what will happen to my study if he goes in there when he's angry."

T: If you are concerned, then negotiate about the place. You don't have to sacrifice the study. Instead, you might say to Nadav that if he manages to cope with the anger in a certain other place you agree on, the next time, you could allow him to use Dad's study. That way he will have an incentive and you can be reassured – he's already at a stage where he has improved his ability for self-control.

Anat: When you're in your space, Nadav, that's the time when you can "surf the wave." Don't be frightened by the feelings of anger, breath into those feelings. We all get angry. It's only natural – and important, too – it's a sign that "something's wrong," but we would prefer that instead of breaking and destroying things, you will eventually be able to tell us in words, "I'm angry." Until then, you can "surf the wave," or take deep breaths, or run in place as fast as you can. Come on, let's practice the options and together we can see which one helps you more, okay?

After the wave has passed and you feel calm again, you can come back and join us. When you do the BASIC and come back calmer, we'll toss you up in the air the way you like, because that means you surfed the anger wave really well.

Afterwards, in the next session, Anat and Uzi reported on Nadav's fantastic cooperation and that the hand signals for the anger wave were currents flowing through his hands, and that Nadav had chosen his bedroom as a place to calm down. Then they told of how he chose to run in place instead of the deep breathing, and how twice already Nadav had used the BASIC method quite remarkably well. Lastly, after each wave had passed, Uzi tossed Nadav up in the air the way he loves to be tossed.

It is very important at this stage to talk with the parents about the anticipated process of change whenever we teach new behaviors. Our learning curve is not necessarily linear and doesn't always proceed at a steady rate. We should expect regressions into automatic behaviors whenever adopting a new behavior. I showed Anat and Uzi the expected learning curve graph:

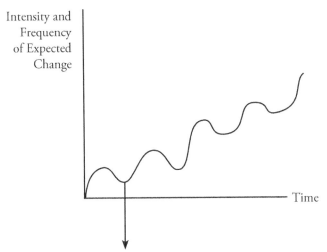

A sense of despair at this stage of regression will
lead to an interruption in the process
of positive change

We expect that with time, Nadav will progress towards a change in his fits of rage and will be able to better control his feelings of anger and the aggressive behavior resulting from that anger. Even so, we can expect some setbacks. Often at this stage, we may become despondent and say to ourselves, "Nothing is helping." This is a very problematic reaction, since the nature of our message is: there will never be any change. However, if we can foresee the setbacks and tell the child, "It's all right. That's the way it is when we learn something new. Never mind, let's keep on the way we planned," then we have permitted ourselves and our child to successfully continue onward in the direction of positive change. This lesson, according to which every process of learning includes the potential for failure and disappointment, is important for all learning processes and achieving change in our lives. Our message as parents and therapists is: We aren't afraid of possible failures and we don't give up when something doesn't work out. What will bring about success, learning, and change, is the capacity to try again and again.

When working with small children, we can use the BASIC model using terms such as, "putting the anger to sleep." Here the dialog will be more game-like and songs may be incorporated: songs that will aid the younger child to internalize the message. Here are some examples:

"I'm strong;
I'm big;
Cool the anger;
Yes, I will";

"When I'm angry;
I run wild like a horse;
Giddy-up, giddy-up;
Whoa! Then my anger slows down";

"When I'm angry like a dragon;
My nose flares with fire;
Then I breathe in lots of air;
And I'm brave like a knight";

"Here it comes.
I know you!
Hey, let's calm things down;
Give me a smile instead of a frown."

Playing a game with the child, even when time is short, is a very important parenting skill and contributes dramatically to inducing psychological resilience. The term "playfulness" relates to spontaneous behavior expressing pleasure, humor, curiosity, imagination, and is a variable full of substance and meaning, even in situations of extreme duress, as in wartime, for example (Cohen, Chazan, Lerner & Maimon, 2010).

When we are speaking of very young children, even toddlers, who often exhibit anger, and especially those whose behavior is replete with fits of rage, the playful part is crucial for their ability to self-regulate. Take for example, the parents of a four-year-old child with terrible fits of anger, who taught him to wave his fisted hands in the air whenever he felt angry and roar like a lion, "I'm an angry lion!" The capacity to recognize the feeling of anger and translate it into words aids the child's aptitude for regulation.

When we are working with the parents of young children, we should remember to adopt age appropriate therapy tools according to the age and stage of development of each child. We will be able to assist the parents in composing clear messages for the children and help foster full collaboration between the parents in the sending of those messages. Practicing the application of each new therapy implement with the parents in the treatment room is required before they attempt to apply the tool with the child. We cannot expect parents who have not practiced the application of a new instrument to succeed in utilizing that tool in real-life circumstances, when they themselves are experiencing an episode of stress and lack of control.

We will also develop and train the parents in the art of playfulness by simply being able to experience play between the parents and by reconnecting with the pleasure of playing a game.

A few years ago, I met the parents of a five-year-old boy whom the kindergarten teacher had referred to us for parent training, "because the boy looks sad all day long." The parents said that most of the child's playtime was spent putting together puzzles. When I asked them whether or not they laughed together, the parents answered that their house is mostly orderly and serious. Both parents are professional orchestra musicians and it's important for them to raise their child amid structure and discipline. "How much do you think your child enjoys his childhood?" I asked them. "We haven't thought about that," they replied. I told them of the importance of spontaneous play between parents and children and then we played the "Face Game"; they were asked to sit across from each other, and in unison, make the funniest faces they could. It was difficult for them at the beginning, but after I showed each of them how to do the faces, they succeeded in making funny faces to one another. "We haven't laughed so much in ages," they said. Later on, we played children's games (tag, hide-and-seek, ball games). They were asked to play one of the games they had learned with their son every week. The emphasis was on having fun and not on the "work" or "task." The results were soon apparent. After a few weeks, the kindergarten teacher reported a definite improvement in the child's mood. It should be noted that this child was a sort of "thermostat" of the home's atmosphere. There is a high probability that a child who grows up in a cold home atmosphere – demanding and serious minded without laughter or spontaneous game playing – will be an unhappy child.

Preventing Family Conflicts

In addition to intervention focused on acute problems, there are many exercises for training parents that help to lessen unnecessary conflicts and contribute to a positive family climate. Further along in the book, these varieties of games will be presented, though specifically for the matter of preventing family conflicts, I have chosen to exhibit one instrument whose purpose is to resolve situations with a high potential for creating conflict. We're talking about a situation we are all familiar with: arriving home after a day at work. An entrance such as this is often accompanied by high tensions centered around the expectations placed on the member of the couple who has just returned home and is expected to help alleviate the mounting pressures of childcare. The method presented here is simple to operate and its results are quite effective when applied diligently and consistently. "Hugging at the Door" is aimed at strengthening couple/parental communication and the prevention of conflicts upon the arriving home of one member of the parental couple.

A Hug at the Door

Hugging at the door is a simple tool with enormous power whose purpose is to change the conditioned negative chain of responses. Entering the home triggers a chain of responses by the creation of a new stimulus in the environment. Many of the parents who have come to me for therapy over the years reported on tensions that began with the partner's entrance into the home after returning from a day at work. In most cases, one member of the couple remains at home and deals with the demands of daily multi-tasking (preparing dinner, bathing the children, helping with schoolwork, getting ready for bedtime, and so on).

They often experience frustration when they don't have help in coping with all the many different jobs of parenting. On the opposite side, the other parent who has just come home from a day at work, sometimes exhausted, experiences frustration when they are greeted at the door with demands to do chores and tasks around the house, without the ability to fulfill his own needs, which are perceived as basic (short rest, food, etc.). The arrival of the partner after a day at work inherently contains potential for conflict, which activates a negative chain of responses, harms the family mood, introduces tension, which may last for many long minutes and overshadows the family evening, to say the least. The home, which is supposed to be the heart and haven of security for its dwellers, in the blink of an eye turns into a battlefield of demands, tasks, and opposing expectations. The hug-at-the-door exercise is intended to prevent the igniting of anticipated conflict when one of the parents comes home after a day at work.

Instructions for the Exercise:
For the instruction of the exercise, we will place the father in the role of the parent who is entering the home and the mother as the partner who remains at home.

When Dad enters the house he announces his arrival, "Hi, I'm home." If Mom can reach the door, so much the better, if not, Dad looks for Mom and the first connection that takes place between them is a long hug. From this moment on, any exchange of words is done from inside that hug. Within the hug Dad asks, in a whisper to Mom's ear, "How are you?" Mom updates Dad with a few words about what went on at home until he arrived, and thus ushers him into the family situation upon arriving home. Dad tells Mom how it was at work that day and asks, "What can I do right now to make things easier for you?" Mom requests, clearly and precisely (shower the kids...get the little one into bed...or, tidy up the kitchen, and so forth). Dad, who just this moment got home from work, and has to balance between his needs and the needs of the family, replies, "No problem. I'll do it in (X) minutes. I want to drink/ eat something and then I'll happily take care of it." The couple practices the "hug at the door" with the therapist through a role playing game. The therapists takes the role of the children in the game in order to present as many situations as possible – the children are nearby, the children are yelling, the spouse who stays at home is in the middle of a hurricane, and so forth.

Couples who practiced the "hug at the door" and later applied it over a length of time at home, reported a significant improvement in the running of the house in the evenings: the coordination of immediate expectations, the sense of belonging felt by the partner who has just entered the house thanks to the update about goings-on at home, the straightforward request for specific assistance, and the sense of collaboration in running the home, especially apparent with the spouse who spends most of the day with the children, and positive change in general within their family life.

The sense of partnership, belonging and closeness, lessen the levels of conflict within the family and prepares the groundwork for two of parenting's greatest gifts in the modern era: nurturing self-esteem and self-efficacy in your children.

3

A Parent's Gift to Their Children in Contemporary Times – Fostering Self-Esteem and Self-Efficacy

A few years ago, at the conclusion of a lecture of mine to an audience of parents, one of the parents came up to me and asked, "What is the most important thing I can do for the sake of my children?" On the trip home from the lecture, that question stuck in my mind. What are the things that we, as parents, can do to best benefit our children?

Parenthood is a journey. It has its ups and downs, happiness and hurt, pleasures and burdens. As in every journey, we need to pack a knapsack suited to the terrain. The world we live in is a world of change, not always clear-cut and not always secure, a world replete with competition, achievements, expectations, a flow of information at our fingertips, and a world of many psychological hazards, which require us, as parents, to deal with these hurdles in full view of our children.

Who is a good parent? What are the most important roles

for parents in the modern world? What are the things we can do to best benefit our children? Beyond the parents' ability to manage their family in an assertive manner, which combines the hand that holds, firmly guiding, with the hand that caresses, offering empathy and encouragement, there are in my opinion two more "Life Gifts" that parents can give to their children – a full measure of self-esteem and a fair portion of self-efficacy. As we will see in part three of this section, these are two gifts that a child cannot acquire on his own; a child is dependent upon his environment to provide these for them. A child who succeeds, with the help of his parents, in attaining these two gifts, is a happier and more successful child in a broader range of areas in his life, than a child who, unfortunately, does not receive these endowments.

Time after time, research shows how a person's level of self-esteem and their degree of self-efficacy is a major influence on their mental well-being (Bandura, 1997; Judge & Bono, 2001; Kuster, Orth & Meier, 2012). Self-esteem and self-efficacy are corresponding concepts but not identical. There is a conspicuous connection between them but the existence of one does not necessarily predict the existence of the other (Uzonwanne & Uzonwanne, 2014).

The term "self-esteem" relates to the question – how much does a person love himself and to what degree does that person perceive his own sense of worth? Whereas the term "self-efficacy" relates to the question – how much a person believes in their ability to lead themselves towards their goals in different areas of their lives (Bandura, 1997).

In this chapter, we will examine in depth the two concepts and present ways to intervene and provide parents with assistance in fostering both of these qualities in their children.

A: Self Esteem
Fostering a Child's Self-Esteem

It's seven o'clock in the evening and I'm scheduled to meet her for the first time. I had already met with her parents, who didn't really understand why it was so important that she come in for therapy. Opening the door to greet her, I am astonished by her beauty; from her long waist-length wavy blonde hair, her almond shaped eyes which are staring at me, and all I can do is, say, "Wow, how beautiful you are." Her almond shaped eyes fill with moisture and heavy teardrops begin to fall from them. "What are the tears saying?" I ask myself, and therapy begins even before I've introduced myself.

Hadar is sixteen years old, an honor student, a guide in a youth movement, has a boyfriend, is surrounded by friends, according to her parents and Hadar herself. "So why have you come?" I ask her. "Because I don't like who I am," she replies.

Hadar's words blend seamlessly with Bandura's definition (Bandura, 1997) of self-esteem. Self-esteem is defined in emotional terms as self-love – the degree to which a person loves himself just the way he is. There are some who define self-esteem in terms of the consistent self-perception one has of one's self (Hamlyn, 1983), or in a more general view, a person's total perception of themselves (Baumeister, 1999). In simpler terms, we can say that self-esteem is connected to questions such as, Do I love who I am, as I am? Do I feel I am worthy? Do I feel deserving?

The ability to live in harmony with ourselves is one of the key factors for experiencing human happiness. A child who learns to love who he is, is a happier child, a healthier child, more resistant to stressful situations and social rejection, to failures, disappointments, and psychological distress (Butler, Hokanson & Flynn, 1994; Christie-Mizell, Ida & Keith, 2010; Donnellan et al., 2005; Leary et al., 1995; Nezlek et al., 1997). Likewise, a connection was found between low self-esteem and the sense of social rejection (Leary, et al., 1995; Nezlek et al., 1997), academic achievement (Lane, Lane & Kyprianou, 2004), behavioral issues, criminality, anti-social behavior (Baumeister, Bushman & Campbell, 2000; Donnellan et al., 2005), mental disorders such as depression (Beck, 1967; Kuster, Orth & Meier, 2012), eating disorders (Vohs et al., 1999), and more recently there are testimonies on connections between self-esteem and physical malaise (Christie-Mizell, Ida & Keith, 2010; Martensa et al., 2010). Therefore, it is possible to perceive self-esteem as a factor that aids a person in coping with life's challenges in an effective and beneficial manner.

In contrast, there is evidence showing that exaggerated self-esteem is liable to cause negative results and even harm to others (Baumeister, Smart & Boden, 1996).

Much knowledge has been compiled over the years on the subject of high self-esteem (but not exaggerated) as an indicator of resilience, an influence on one's sense of bliss, of one's satisfaction with social connections, of intimate relationships, and of the capacity to succeed academically and in employment (Judge & Bono, 2001). The significance is that there is a great importance on ensuring the development of self-esteem from a very early age. Therefore, one of the greatest gifts a parent can give his children is to teach them to love themselves and to accept themselves as they are.

How can we aid parents in nurturing the self-esteem of their children and guide them towards a balanced self-love and the psychological well-being that results from it?

Positive self-esteem is produced as a result of repetitive positive messages a person receives for their behavior, attributes, even for their mere existence in the world. The personal experiences of an individual's life are the principle sources for developing self-esteem. The positive or negative experiences of life that a person encounters create a cognitive blueprint of the "self." A positive approach can be applied, which will lead to healthy feelings of self-esteem, while a negative approach may very well create negative feelings of self-esteem. In the early years of childhood, parents are the strongest source of positive or negative experiences the child will know. Those basic experiences are processed and translated later on in other areas of the child's life and influence future levels of self-esteem (Brown, 2011; Hewitt, 2009). Essentially, we are saying that self-esteem is built as the result of consistent positive messages from the child's immediate environment. These messages are internalized and established within the child and allow the child to bolster himself. In turn, this self-reinforcement significantly contributes to the increase of his self-esteem.

Research shows that high self-esteem, but not exaggerated, is a major contributor to one's ability to cope with life's myriad situations.

High self-esteem creates a kind of emotional resilience, which enables a child to better cope with stressful situations, rejection, and failure (Brown & Dutton, 1995).

Environmental Reinforcement

Self-reinforcement

Increase in Self-Esteem

Virginia Satir (Satir, 1985) equates the self-esteem, which is taking shape in a child from the day of his birth, to a large kettle. When the child's kettle is neglected, it is empty, which means there is an injury to the child's self-esteem and to their future as an adult. Our role as parents, or principle caretakers, according to Satir, is to watch over the child's kettle of self-esteem as we would when cooking: to stir, to check the taste, and so forth. In terms of Satir's metaphor, we can say the more a person's kettle of self-esteem is filled, the more he is psychologically safeguarded.

The image of the metaphor can aid us as therapists to illustrate for the parents one of the most important missions in parenting – keeping the child's kettle full.

The Self-Esteem Kettle: A Model for Working with Parents

Satir's wonderful metaphor can be of great assistance to us in our therapy work. If we take the idea of the kettle for self-esteem and we try to monitor the measure of a person's self-esteem, we can form an integration of those experiences linked to the self-esteem that has been formed and the causes of those same experiences. Inside the kettle, we draw a graph from zero to ten, which expresses the amount of worth that an individual allots to himself. The graph is also linked to the degree of external influences on his indicated value. The lower the person's self-esteem, thus the environmental influences are greater upon the measure of self-esteem he has allocated himself. The higher the self-esteem, the more inoculated he will be when facing adverse stimuli in his environment (which are liable to lessen his self-esteem), hence the environmental influence on self-esteem is lower.

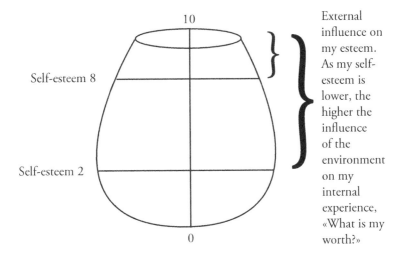

Self-esteem 8

Self-esteem 2

10

0

External influence on my esteem. As my self-esteem is lower, the higher the influence of the environment on my internal experience, «What is my worth?»

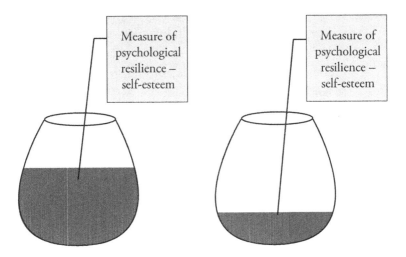

Measure of psychological resilience – self-esteem

Measure of psychological resilience – self-esteem

So that parents may understand the metaphorical idea of the vessel and be able to master the array of tools offered to them as treatment continues for the fostering of their children's self-esteem, it's advisable to work with the parents on their own personal vessel. In my professional experience, when parents understand their own vessel – how and by whom it was formed and how it was filled or emptied over the years – it will be easier for them to find the motivation for change in their children's vessel. They will absorb more easily the tools afforded to them and will then apply them in a more consistent manner, which is required for the nurturing of their children's self-esteem.

That's how it was with Arnon and Tamar, the parents of eight-year-old Shelly, who came for treatment because of their concern that Shelly might become a victim of sexual harassment. "What caused this concern?" I asked.

Arnon: She's very weak. She does everything she's asked, and she's a "giver" – she can't say "no."

Tamar: She's like a feather floating on a breeze. We try to tell her to stand up for herself, but every time we criticize her or get angry with her, she immediately starts to cry, so we leave her alone, so as not to hurt her feelings. It's hard enough for her anyway.

T: This sounds like you are trying to protect her all the time.

Arnon: Yes, we are worried about her. We know what sort of people are out there who might exploit her weakness. Even more because of her wanting to please everybody, even the girls in her class turned her into a kind of "slave." They exploit her and hurt her. We can't bear to watch it.

T: It's quite natural to want to protect her. If you could give her one gift, what would it be?

Parents: That she would be stronger.

T: How do you imagine her to be as a strong girl?

Tamar: She'll know when to say, "no." She will value herself more. Now it's as if she doesn't exist.

Arnon: She'll be able to stand up to the girls in her class and not be their "servant." She'll feel worthy and not be a door mat. She'll understand the dangers out there and know how to defend herself.

T: Your ability to see clearly what you want to happen is very important. In essence, you've described a work schedule which sets for us our goal to strengthen Shelly's ability to stand up for herself, to feel her self-worth, and her capability to create within herself an internal resilience in social situations. To do this, treatment will begin with the focus on the two of you and only if it's necessary, we'll bring Shelly in for therapy. You have a lot of work to do. You are the key to the inner resilience Shelly will form and this is why it's good that you came to us for assistance. In the first stage, we will work on fostering Shelly's self-esteem, and afterwards, on her assertiveness skills. It seems to me it's best to begin with the task of strengthening Shelly's self-esteem. Does that sound reasonable to you?

After receiving Tamar and Arnon's agreement on the goals of therapy and the path we will take to reach them, we began working on their vessels of self-esteem.

T: Working on Shelly's self-esteem will demand our deep understanding of the concept, self-esteem. There are many definitions of the concept, yet the definition I have adopted is the definition formulated by a very eminent researcher by the name of Bandura. He relates to self-esteem in terms of self-love: how much I love who I am. If I ask you right now, how much do you love yourselves the way you are on a scale of one to ten, what would be your response?

Tamar: For many years I was a two or a three, in recent years it's gone up to five.

Arnon: I'd say around seven to eight.

T: Let's try to understand your replies. Virginia Satir, who is considered to be one of the most influential family therapists, wrote an inspirational book, *The Modern Family* (1985). You can read it if you like. In the chapter, "The Kettle of Self-Esteem – The Kettle No One Tends," Virginia Satir makes a comparison between self-esteem and a kettle in which a slow-cooking stew is simmering over a span of years. In order for the stew to turn out delicious, someone must keep an eye on it. Whoever is in charge of cooking the kettle must make sure to stir it, taste it, adjust the seasoning, and add liquids and such. The stew cannot do this for itself, only someone outside the kettle can tend to its quality. And the same is true for our self-esteem. It is not built by itself; it's built from external messages – messages that we receive about who we are. Let's take a look at how each of your kettles evolved.

I asked each one of the parents to sketch their kettle (how much do I love who I am, from zero to ten), according to two parameters: chronologically, the change in the kettle over the years, and circumstantially, in the presence of certain people or in different situations.

Arnon's Kettle:

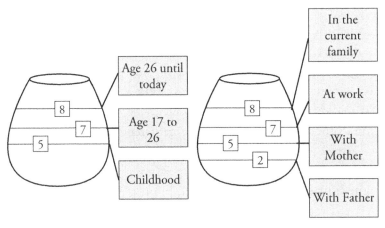

In the process of working with Arnon, it became apparent that his father was a very strict and critical man, while his mother was a more compassionate image, more understanding and accepting. Criticism and negative reinforcement from parents causes children to adopt a negative perception of themselves and lessens their self-esteem (Brown, 2011). Arnon had his first girlfriend at age seventeen, began to workout at the gym, and felt better about himself. After that, he met Tamar, a sort of pillar for him, who allowed him to love who he was. In answer to my question, "How does she do that?" Arnon replied that she simply accepts him the way he is. She doesn't try to change him. She doesn't criticize him, and she appreciates him and regularly sends him positive messages of her love for him. By means of the kettle metaphor, Arnon could see the changes in the level of his kettle over his lifetime and how positive messages from the external environment help the level in the kettle to rise. To my question, what needs to happen so that his kettle will rise to a nine, Arnon answered, "If I knew that my father respected me, I think I'd reach a ten."

Consistent positive messaging from the person who is considered to be a "**critical exponent**" can fundamentally change the very way a person feels about himself. According to Emler (2001), self-esteem is linked to a person's aspirations, in the standards he sets for himself – not only for material or social gains – but for the quality and the kind of person he is. Estimation of our own value is based on a judgement of how we think others value us. This judgement relies on characteristics we attribute to others. Someone who is seen as essential and/ or as "successful," we will judge them more highly, as reaching something that is harder to attain. In other words, what shapes our self-esteem is not an objective goal or achievements, rather who are the assessors and what is their message about us (Ramsey, 1994). So, it is very important to make clear to parents that they are the crucial assessors for their children, and just as Arnon longs for the day he will receive validation from his father for his self-worth, Arnon's children will look to Arnon and Tamar to define for them what their self-value will be.

T: Arnon, your father is a critical assessor for you and his voice remains with you even today as an adult. You too will be an inner voice that accompanies Shelly during her lifetime. Our goal is not to push her up to a level of ten in the kettle, but rather to reach the position where there will be interaction between herself and her surroundings in relation to her self-esteem. I will explain what I just said. A mark of ten or a mark of one are both negative points on the kettle scale from the point of view of self-esteem. The "0" point means the kettle is empty, that is to say, when a person does not love himself at all. This is a situation which endangers a person's psychological health and a distinct factor for the development of depression (Beck, 1967). In contrast, an overly full kettle is also problematic. A mark of "10" in the kettle does not leave room for outside influence on our esteem. This means that I feel omnipotent, like superman, have exaggerated self-love, arrogance, and may even injure others to aggrandize myself on someone else's account and aim to enhance my self-worth in my own eyes and in the eyes of the people around me.

There exists a direct connection between exaggerated self-esteem, narcissism, and hurting others (Baumeister, et al., 2003; Baumeister, Smart & Boden, 1996). A person with exaggerated self-esteem is liable to think he is superior, to be overly sensitive to offenses and threats, and react violently in an attempt to bolster his own superiority. This is in direct opposition to the accepted assumption that only low self-esteem leads to depression and aggression (Baumeister, et al., 2003). Baumeister and his colleagues (Baumeister, Smart & Boden, 1996) relate to this along egoistical lines, narcissistic behavior, according to which others are present only to satisfy their personal needs. The superiority and arrogance, which is often times accompanied by a lack of empathy for others, enables the rationalization for injuring others inferior to themselves. This subject is interesting in terms of the kettle metaphor. If we take for example, a man characterized by narcissist traits, then we can essentially say that at level ten the kettle is simply a false pretense, since the narcissist is constantly coping with his self-esteem, in seeking self-glorification and validation from external factors for measuring his worth. In effect, we can assume that his genuine self-esteem is much lower than the recorded level in the kettle because of the influence of the external environment upon his self-esteem.

In a case like this, it is worth examining the level in the kettle when in situations of failure. How much did he love himself when things didn't go as well as he hoped they would?

T: So, Arnon, even though you said that you would reach a ten only if your father would respect you more, it's important to understand that our goal isn't to make Shelly a 10 in her kettle, but rather to cause a rise in the level of her kettle, which will enable on the one hand, mental well-being and create a constant dialog between self-esteem and the reality surrounding her.

Arnon: So, I am in a good place then.

T: True enough, your kettle has filled over the years and I hope it continues to be full. So much depends on your ability to strengthen yourself in successes and also when you are coping with difficulties.

Tamar: I wish my kettle was like Arnon's kettle. I know I would be happier and that it would be easier for me to deal with the children.

T: Now's a good time to get to know your kettle, Tamar.

Tamar's Kettle:

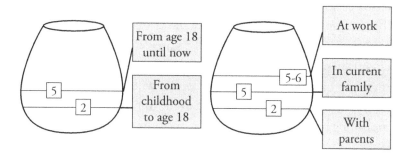

T: Tamar, what do you think the explanation is for the two in the kettle?

Tamar: I never felt my parents loved me. They love my brother more and he always succeeds at everything. I was a shy, quiet girl, lacking self-confidence; even socially it was difficult for me. I felt like I was a burden to my parents.

T: What did they do to make you feel this way?

Tamar: With my brother, they would smile a lot more, hug him more often, and compliment him more. I mostly remember the different look on their faces, the worried expression towards me, and the proud expressions for my brother. It was unmistakable.

T: In a moment, we will talk about this important point you've brought up, but before that I would like to ask how you explain the rise in the kettle to five?

Tamar: While I was completing my service in the army at age eighteen, I had a close friend and I also met Arnon. I felt more confident.

T: How did they behave towards you and cause you to feel better?

Tamar: I felt they liked me just as I was. They were warm and affectionate to me. Arnon gave me compliments and made me feel more confident.

T: So, we understand that your kettle rose because of the significant people around you who treated you with warmth and made you feel like an equal. This is exactly the way the self-esteem kettle works, yours and your children's. One of the greatest gifts that you can give to Shelly is to raise the level of her kettle.

Arnon: We're trying to do that all the time…

T: When you're trying to do that, what sort of expression does Shelly see on your faces: the worried face or the proud expressions?

Arnon: I get your point…

T: In order to help you be more effective in your goal to foster Shelly's self-esteem, we will need to work on the way you look at her, because just as Tamar picked up on the expressions from her parents, Shelly notices your own facial expressions. To help you with this, I want to show you a work model that we will practice on together in therapy, and afterwards, you can apply it at home with Shelly.

In order to raise the self-esteem of a child, the parent's role is to send a message of unconditional love and acceptance (Brown, 2011). This is not always clear to us in practice. What does it mean to accept the child unconditionally? Is it even possible?

The "Warm" Model that I will illustrate for you will help us understand how to apply this in practice.

The "Warm" Model for Fostering a Child's Sense of Self-Esteem

One of the ways we can assist our children in raising their sense of self-esteem is to implement The "Warm" Model (Epel, 2013). This model has been applied for many years at the institute where I practice, by dozens of therapists who have received training in its use. The clinical results are impressive according to reports from parents and children in relation to the sense of self-esteem, feelings of belonging, and positive changes in behavior that occur with the use of this model. The model is usually implemented by the parents when coping with a variety of children's problems and is especially effective in increasing the child's self esteem.

The first two elements of the model – smile and touch – are the non-verbal components which allow the child to feel a sense of security. The second two elements of the model – encouragement and compliment – combine verbal and nonverbal messages and enable the child to reinforce positive behavior, feel good about that behavior, and over time to feel better about themselves.

Parents fulfill a crucial role in building the self-esteem of their children. Parents should receive instruction about the importance of building a child's self-esteem and their decisive role in this mission (Brown, 2011). The "Warm" Model is presented as a theoretical and practical method for the parents to fulfill their crucial roles.

How does the model work?

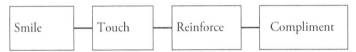

SMILE
Why smile? Because a smile quenches the spirit's thirst.
A smile is the most important non-verbal component of interpersonal relationships. A smile creates a stimulus response between changes in facial expression and a sense of security while causing the brain to secrete endorphins, a substance that lessens feelings of physical and mental pain and generates a sense of well-being (Oster, 1978). When the smile suits the situation, it enables the establishment of positive agreement with those around us. When a smile is not suited to the situation, it induces a sense of confusion and discomfort.

Parent's Homework Assignment: The parents must smile appropriately to the child in three situations with the potential to influence the chain of responses established in the family. It's best if the smile is as consistent as possible in these three circumstances: when the child or the parent enters the home, when the parent addresses the child ("Sweetie, please pass me the salt"), and when the child addresses the parent ("Mom, where are my blue pants?" – "In the laundry basket, honey").

While working with Arnon and Tamar, the exercises in using the appropriate smile in these situations helped them to change their facial expressions in front of Shelly from looks of concern and worry into messages of affection. A smile helps the child feel his parents are supportive of him. Even if conflicts arise, ultimately the prevailing attitudes that the child experiences with his parents will determine his readiness to love who he is.

TOUCH
Why touch? Because touch provides a sense of affection and protection.
Gentle touching of the skin also release endorphins – peptides, which block pain and are secreted by the body when pain occurs – and which are similarly released in times of pleasurable physical activity, when jogging for instance. A pleasant touch can bring us a sense of security and serenity. Ailing children who received medical treatment accompanied by touch were observed to have lower levels of anxiety and cortisol – a hormone secreted by the body during stress (Field, 1998).

Parent's Homework Assignment: To stroke the back of the child's shoulders once a day unrelated to his behavior. For example, when the child is watching television or playing a computer game. The message sent is, "I see you," "You are part of my world even when we're not talking." The idea is to stroke in a circular movement once or twice and then to break contact. This sends a message via indication. Of course this doesn't contradict other forms of touch such as hugs, kisses, or any other agreeable contact appropriate to the relationship. The opposite is true: the more touching – the better.

Tamar and Arnon began to employ the touch exercises only after they had already applied the smile training. Our aim is to combine all four components in stages. The parents try out each different aspect of the model, by order: smile, touch, reinforcement, and compliment. When they have mastered the practice of sending positive messages according to the model, the parents are requested to report on how they used it and how it influenced the chain of responses with the children.

REINFORCEMNT
Why reinforcement? Because reinforcement guides us along our path.

Reinforcement is aimed at causing certain behaviors to be repeated. If we want to help a child adopt a certain behavior, then we must reinforce that behavior in the desired direction. Reinforcement utilizes a bond forming stimulation between a particular action and its ensuing results (Meyers, 2012). The "Warm" Model focuses on symbolic verbal reinforcement ("Good for you for helping a friend") and nonverbal reinforcement (smile, touch, wink, etc..), given by a central figure in the child's environment – parents, teachers, and family members. This kind of reinforcement has a positive influence on the child's sense of self-worth and at the same time teaches the child the desired behavior. Therefore, over time, the child learns to reinforce himself as a result of the same desired behavior ("Good for me that I helped a friend").

Parent's Homework Assignment: In order to create the desired conditions for consistent reinforcement, we should combine reinforcement with the activities of the "Good for me" game before going to sleep at night. This game is accompanied by a smile and a touch for the child, thereby promoting a positive bond between the child, the parent, and the tools learned in the game. The game has four aims:

1. Self-reinforcement and external reinforcement.
2. Modeling for self-reinforcement and external reinforcement.
3. Directing attention to the positive comprehensions.
4. Enhancing a sense of belonging (secret code).

In the first stage, one of the parents sits across from the child and says, "I want to teach you the 'Good for Me' game, and if you like it, we'll play it every evening before you go to sleep. I'll tell you, 'Good for You,' for something you did today, and afterwards, I'll say, 'Good for Me,' for something I did today. Then you tell me, 'Good for You,' for something I did today, and at the end, you tell yourself, 'Good for Me,' for something you did today."

Example of Mom: "Good for you for taking out the trash bin in your room. I'm proud of you and I think that's very grown-up behavior," "Good for me that I prepared your favorite omelet for dinner this evening, even though I was very tired."

Example of Child: "Good for you, Mommy, that you drove me to soccer practice." Mom doesn't remain indifferent, but instead reinforces what the child has said, "Thanks honey, that's nice to hear." The child: "Good for me that I did my arithmetic homework because I really didn't feel like doing it, and I don't like arithmetic."

Mom responds: "That's true. You really deserve a 'Good for you.' I love to see when you're doing something that's a little difficult. It shows how strong you are."

At the conclusion of the game, there is an additional stage that is meant to strengthen the connection and the sense of belonging between a child and his parents. This is the stage of the "Secret Code." Mother: "Now we'll choose a code that will be just yours and mine, a code that makes us feel powerful. For instance, 'We're the winning team,' or 'We smile and the whole world wins.'"

It is important that the code is centered on "we" and not on "I" so the sense of belonging is boosted. Likewise, it would be worthwhile to combine the secret slogan with a physical gesture such as, clapping hands or holding hands and so forth. After a period of time playing the game regularly, the slogan can be used in additional places and situations and empower the child in times of hardship, perhaps social rejection, separation difficulties, and more.

It is important that the parents practice the "Good for Me" game in the therapy room before they play it with their child at home. Practice will be done by role playing the game beginning with one of the parents and the therapist and following that, the couple should practice with one another. Parents learn two distinct advantages in rehearsing with any new tool. The first is getting a clear picture of how to use the tools at home, and the second advantage is recognizing difficulties, perhaps things we hadn't thought of earlier. For instance, the parent's awkwardness when reinforcing the child, any unspoken messages that do not reflect the words, or what happens if the child doesn't find reinforcement for himself and so forth.

Positive reinforcement has a dramatic effect on a person's self-esteem. At this point, we should bring up the matter of the difference between trait self-esteem and state self-esteem, which often show up in literature. Trait self-esteem expresses the permanent level of security and affection people have for their qualities and characteristics that define them, over time. This measurement relates to the total judgement a person has of themselves. Do I love who I am the way that I am? Research reveals that this index is very consistent and indicates a distinct connection between a person's high self-esteem and his psychological well-being (Rosenberg, et al., 1995). State self-esteem relates to the momentary variable of esteem, how people feel about themselves when found in different situations and circumstances (Crocker & Wolfe, 2001). This variable indicates the way in which I perceive myself according to my worth in a certain field. For instance, I am worthy only if I look good or I am worthy only when I win a competition.

Crocker & Wolfe's Contingencies of Self-Worth model (2001) is based on the premise that self-worth is dependent upon successes and failures in different areas, upon which a person bases his self-esteem: external validation, appearance, religious identity, family support, academic achievement, competition, and moral validity. These fields are reliant on culture and we are reliant on success in these fields. If a person experiences success in a particular field, he will also gain positive reinforcement from the environment, which will be a significant contribution to his state self-esteem in that field. If a person experiences failure and/or criticism from the environment, the state self-esteem will decrease. The more our self-esteem is reliant on more numerous fields, separate and independent, so our esteem will thrive and our failures will fade when one of those areas is in decline. Therefore, reinforcement in different arenas enables an eventual increase in the trait self-esteem and provides the power to cope with undesirable realities.

Returning to the kettle, we will address the personal experience of the kettle, in a dialog between the invariable kettle and the variable kettle. Which kettle accompanies a person? When does the kettle empty and when does it overflow? How do different situations alter the kettle experience and at what level does it tend to stabilize? It is important to explain all this to the parents before implementing the "Good for Me" game. In addition, we would like the parents to broaden, as much as possible, the areas of reinforcement for their child throughout the day and also in the "Good for Me" game. It is better, however, to focus reinforcement on a specific area with the child as increasing desired behaviors takes a lot of effort on the part of the child. For example, in Tamar and Arnon's case the focus of the reinforcement in the "Good for Me" game with Shelly will be on her ability to say, in explicit words, her own wants, feelings, and thoughts.

In the treatment work with Tamar and Arnon, they decided that mother will play the game with Shelly weekdays from Sunday to Wednesday and the remaining days of the week into the weekend, father will play the game with her. Sometimes couples decide that only one of the parents will play the game with their child. In this case, it is very important that the parent with the high-tension relationship with the child be the one to play the game, because that parent is the child's critical assessor.

In the parent's game with Shelly, emphasis was put on reinforcing her ability to express clearly what she thinks, wants, suggests, and feels. The expressions in the "Good for Me/You" game were found in phrases like these, "Good for you that you said you want to go visit Grandmother. I really like it when you say what you want." "Good for you that you said in words that you were angry. That way it's easier for me to help you." "Good for you that you told your brother you do not want to play Monopoly. It's very important to say 'no' when we don't feel like doing something." The secret slogan chosen by Shelly and her mother was, "We're strong and not afraid." Shelley's secret slogan with her father was, "We'll talk out loud and stand proud."

COMPLIMENT
Why compliment? Because a compliment lets us feel we exist.
A compliment is a positive message sent without any connection to a behavior. That said, similar to reinforcement, when it's given too much, it isn't effective. Such compliments become compliments without content. Therefore, we should pay close attention to complimenting at reasonable and effective intervals. For children (and adults) with low self-esteem, there is a tendency to fend off compliments. This is why it is important to combine the sending of positive messages along with how a trait or behavior of the child affects me, for instance, "I love the way you look," instead of "You are so beautiful." When a message is passed in this manner, the tendency is to accept it more easily.

Parent's Homework Assignment: Complimenting their child at least once a day. Sometimes it's important to compliment the very fact that this child is a part of our world. For example, "It's so great that I have a child like you," "How wonderful that I have you," and other similar phrases. It is important to genuinely mean what you say and not hand out empty compliments. Turn the child's face towards the parent's face, look into their eyes and smile when sending your message. Through the knowledge accumulated in the use of this model, we have found that this type of compliment, about the child's basic existence in my world, is best done once a week. I call it a "Sabbath Compliment." There is substance and intimacy in the way parents learn to give compliments of this kind. As with the entire model, practice in the therapy room is required before any tool is practically applied at home.

It is worth paying special attention to a crucial point in the application of The "Warm" Model. It is advisable not to exaggerate implementing the model in such a way that is not suited emotionally or behaviorally, so as not to create a sense of saturation. Compliments, or reinforcement, without limits or compatibility, are liable to have the opposite effect of what we intended. The goal is for parents to become the "critical assessors" for their children, with the use of coordinated and effective messages. For this reason, the model is designed in harmony with the family's character, the parent's and the children's needs, while constantly monitoring the manner in which the model is applied. For example, with teens we won't apply the "Good for Me" game as it appears here, but rather in a unilateral fashion where only the parent reinforces his child: "I wanted to tell you good night and good for you for helping your sister do her homework. It's great to have someone to count on."

Game Activities for Young Children that Implement Self Love

Young children respond well to messages from the adult world. They absorb these messages with all of their senses, and therefore, there is a great advantage in passing along these messages from a very early age. The same is true about a child's self-love. When the message is sent via a repetitious game, it touches deep in the mind of the child and becomes one of the child's inner voices, molding his self-perception.

Game suggestion: "I Love Myself Just the Way I Am"

The game "I Love Myself Just the Way I Am," is generally taught to the parents of children around four years of age.

We play the game with the child using consistent wording combined with hand movements. To begin, we play the hand game, and afterwards, we add the words. The game starts with simultaneous hand clapping and then patting hands in mid-air, and this is repeated. Then, to the hand-clapping, we add a sentence: "I love myself just the way I am and it's fun. My name is Naomi." I begin with my sentence, then teach them their own sentence: "I love myself just the way I am and how fun my name is…" We continue in this manner while alternating and increasing the tempo.

Parents, as we mentioned, try out the game while in the therapy room, and only afterwards, play the game with their child at home. In addition to the pleasant and relaxed atmosphere that is created in the session with the parents, it turns out that this little game is a favorite with children and they ask to play it again and again. The rewards children receive from playing these types of games is multi-leveled, from the actual experience of playfulness with the parent and the contribution to the feeling of belonging and resilience. The intent of the sentence about self-love denotes a desired way for a child to think of himself. As the child watches the parent liking themselves (modeling), he finds legitimacy for a similar feeling in his own sense of self-love. Moreover, the child experiments with verbalizing, which imbues a positive connection within himself. Some parents choose to play this game directly following the "Good for Me" game, and they play it near their child's bedtime.

Self-Esteem and Rehearsing For Failure

Coping with failure is one of the most important tasks in this modern era of achievement and competitiveness. For people with low self-esteem, it is more difficult to deal with failure than for people with a higher self-esteem. This is due to their tendency to over-generalize the negative implications of failure and due to their habit of emotionally over-reacting, more so than those with a higher self-esteem (Brown & Dutton, 1995).

Yochai and Hila are parents in their thirties who arrived for treatment in light of their twelve-year-old son Eitai and his distress in social situations. During the intake session, it became clear that Eitai was an energetic child, a perfectionist who reacted to every failure, even the smallest setback, as if it were a catastrophe and the end of the world. "I'm that way too," said Hila. "I can't cope with failure. You have no idea what I do to avoid mistakes."

T:	And what happens when you do make a mistake?
Hila:	To me, it's the end of the world.
T:	Because…
Hila:	Because I can't stand myself.
T:	Do you think there's a connection between what you experience, the "end of the world" after failure, and Eitai's experience, which you described earlier?
Hila:	I'm sure there's a connection, but I don't know how it started and I don't know what to do about it.
T:	Let's start with understanding things and after that

we'll suggest solutions, and how to handle them. Is that okay with you?

After obtaining the couple's agreement, I turned to the psychoeducational explanation of the link between perfectionism, self-esteem, and emotional distress.

Psychoeducational Explanation:
Research (Speirs Neumeister & Finch, 2006) shows that the more a child is exposed to perfectionism in his parents, the more he develops an inflexible way of thinking, higher expectations, anxiety over disappointing others, and thus his self-esteem is increasingly more reliant upon the high-intensity power of achievements and the response of others to those achievements.

In reference to the self-esteem kettle, we can say that levels in the kettle shift according to the individual's accomplishments. When there's success, the kettle fills for the time being and there is a sense of euphoria, but any failure, even the slightest one, destabilizes the kettle and drops it back down to a lower level ("If I failed – then I don't count"). On account of the labile movement in the kettle coinciding with achievements and the influence of external surroundings, the mood of a person with low self-esteem, who single-mindedly strives "to be perfect," is more intense and more extreme, especially when he is required to cope with failure. We can graphically illustrate this with the following:

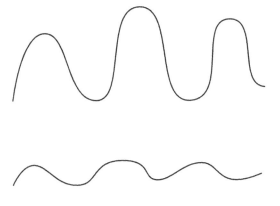

The intensity of influence by achievements and failures of a person with low self-esteem

The intensity of influence by achievements and failures on a person with high self-esteem

We all have a picture in our mind of what the ideal situation would be or of the perfect "Me." From the earliest of times, people have realized that suffering is linked to the gap between the ideal and the real. The question is what happens to us when this gap appears. For the perfectionist, there is a picture of perfection in their mind that must not be altered. They are busy, obsessively so, with an endless striving for perfection, without having the capacity to accept a given situation that is not flawless. Generally, I use the metaphor of a picture to clarify this point.

Let's take for example, a "Picture of Perfection" like the one drawn by Mirel Goldenberg (Epel, 2013):

What would happen if we draw some black spots on the face of the sun? The picture will not be perfect anymore; it will change and not be a description of an ideal situation as it was earlier illustrated.

There are people who aren't bothered by the dark spots in the picture, and then there are those who experience the changes as damage to what they saw as an ideal picture, which is now unbearable and insufferable to look at. This inflexible way of thinking of reality as black and white, along with a demanding and absolute inner dialog – "It has to be perfect/I have to be perfect" – leads to a situation where every failure is seen as a disaster and as catastrophic. This perception often leads to the inclusion of failure into ourselves, "If I failed – I am worthless," and to an insufferable experience, "I can't stand it," and is even liable to cause unbearably intense negative emotions, which can lead to an emotional and psychological crisis (Ellis & Dryden, 1987).

The ability to live in harmony with the black dots in the metaphoric picture in a given situation, and in life in general, therefore, produces a mental resilience and to more effective coping with failure. The messages we pass on our children concerning success and failure will determine their view and ability to cope with undesirable situations. The higher our self-esteem, the more accepting we are of the black spots on the whole picture. Perfection comes in small pieces. The trick is to "catch those perfect moments." For example, when I am sitting by the sea and watching the sunset, listening to the whisper of the waves, feeling the wind on my face – I mark that as a perfect moment. When my child runs to hug me or when my daughter makes me laugh until I cry, I regard those moments as sublime. I would like you to snatch moments like these during the day, magical minutes, and not latch onto a constantly perfect picture.

T: Hila, what goes through your head when you hear what I've said?

Hila: What does it mean? That's the story of my life. I feel just like what you said. I have the same feelings all my life, including the emotional distress you mentioned. But when I hear the explanation, it helps me make sense of it all. I don't really know how to grab hold of the perfect parts; I'm always criticizing myself, and maybe the people around me, too. Now it's clear to me what's going on with me and what happens with Eitai. The question is what can we do? Not make any demands of him?

T: It is interesting that you bring up the matter of demands on Eitai, because I recently read a research article that found that one of the principle reasons for anxiety among children was the exaggerated pressure from their parents to achieve (Luthar, Barkin & Crossman, 2013). We will deal with the issue of demands on Eitai and if they are compatible with his stage of development. For now, I would like you to focus on your perception of the concept of failure, because it's connected, in the end, to your demands on Eitai. The demands on Eitai are the behavioral expressions of our concepts of success and failure. Your messages, verbal and nonverbal, contribute, it seems, to the inflexible perception Eitai has about possible failure and his attempt to avoid failure, by pleasing everyone around him. Every disappointment you have, or disappointments that happen in the environment, push him towards anxiety and lowers his self-esteem.

In order to better understand the connections between the variables, we will illustrate them on the following diagram:

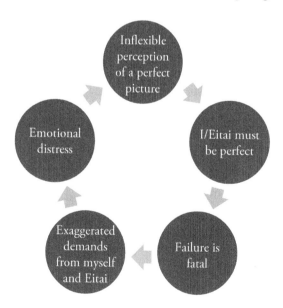

Many paths can lead to a change in this cycle of behavior, and you, as parents, play a vital role in that change.

Practice For Failure Situations

The main goal when working with perfectionist children, children who cannot accept undesirable situations at all and failure, in particular, is to change their perception of failure. For this to happen, we must first help the parents to change their own attitude and concept of failure. Later on in the chapter, under the sub-topic, self-efficacy, I will cover the matter in detail, but the basic message is to look at failure as an opportunity and not as a misfortune. Indeed, failure is very unpleasant and it turns out that when we aren't afraid of it, failure can be a great impetus for personal growth and the attaining of personal goals. Research done on people who are incredibly successful in a certain field (sports, politics, music, etc.), has revealed that they succeeded by right of their capacity to learn from failure and continue to progress forward. I often give the well-known example of Michael Jordan – one of the most successful basketball players of all times – it goes like this: "I have missed more than 9,000 baskets during my career, and I have lost almost 300 games. I failed again and again in life and that is why I succeed."

It is possible from an early age to send out messages that enhance the skills for coping with failure. The following are a few examples and tools that may be of assistance:

How to Tell a Story?

Already, in the early years of a child's life, before language and words, our messages have significant influence on a child; at this point, they simply observe our behavior. When a toddler builds a tower from blocks, for instance, parents who could not accept an imperfect tower of blocks, fixed the arrangement of blocks. The message to their child is – lack of belief in the toddler's ability to cope on his own. The child will learn to wait each time for the parent's correct arrangement, something which may lead him to develop low self-efficacy. The child may well develop a reliance on the parent's feedback and will be wary not to make mistakes. At a later time, we may see the child angrily ripping apart his drawings when they aren't "perfect," and suffer when things don't go well.

At the stage when words begin to arrive, we have a dramatic opportunity to impart messages, values, and attitudes to our children. Take, for example, when we tell our children a story. The stories may be personal or perhaps classic tales, from a book or made up spontaneously. When we have before us the classic stories of Cinderella or the Ugly Duckling, this is an opportunity where we can do a lot of groundwork. Many of the classic children's tales relate to coping with problems such as rejection or abuse in the family or in society. We have a golden opportunity to make a connection between self-love and coping with difficulty or failure. For instance, in the familiar story of Cinderella, we should highlight the point that in spite of the difficult situation Cinderella found herself in, she believed in herself. When we come across undesirable situations in our own lives, it is important to remember who we are, how wonderful we are, and that we can overcome difficulties and unpleasant situations. The same is true for the Ugly Duckling; a parent, together with a child, can guess about how the duckling turned into a beautiful swan; he was always beautiful on the inside, but when he was able to love who he was, then others could also see how truly beautiful he was. How important it is to believe in who we are, accept ourselves, and love what we are. This gives us the power to prevail and feel strengthened from the inside.

Modeling for Failure with a Margin of Error

Stories are not enough. Children need to see things in actual practice, see how their parents deal with difficulties and failures. Our message as parents to our children is: no one is perfect (not even us), we make quite a few mistakes and we'll make mistakes in the future, but the smart thing to do is to learn from mistakes and try again. Failure, in this sense, is a blessing, because we learn from it no less than from success.

Children learn from us and imitate us in the smallest things. We should be prepared to experience the challenge of possible errors and become a model for coping with failure for our children in everything we do, even the small stuff. We need to allow our children and ourselves plenty of margins for possible errors – a place where a mistake is accepted as part of the learning process and not perceived as a catastrophe. Therefore, we bless our errors as parents and also bless our children's mistakes as well, while we send the message: "Nothing is perfect," "Every error is educational," and "Failure isn't a disaster." In order to make it easier for parents to send these kinds of messages, we will practice "The Possible Error" game in the therapy room.

Oops! The Game of Possible Mistakes

This wonderful game is one I learned from a trainee of mine and it works well in child-direct therapy, in parent training, and as a game for parents to play with their child. For the perfectionists among us, we strive to maintain control in order to avoid possible error. This game, in contrast, gives us the option of aiming for the target but without having full control; being in a situation where there is the possibility for errors while still being able to accept the mistake and its imperfections. Let's go back to Hila and Yochai:

T: So that we can connect with the experience of imperfection without being frightened of it, I will ask you to cover your eyes and draw a picture of a man or woman with as many details as possible. Can you take a guess how this trial exercise will be for you?

Yochai: (smiling) I imagine it will be harder for Hila than for me.

Hila: I can't even cover my eyes.

T: Because...?

Hila: I don't like being in situations where I don't have full control of what's happening.

T: Great. That is exactly the point of the game, to let you experience a trial run of some lack of control and prove to you that it's not the end of the world. It's important to me that you play the game even though you may feel uncomfortable. Our aim is that you succeed, and eventually, play the game with Eitai.

Hila and Yochai drew a figure of a man while their eyes were covered. As expected, the figures were far from being "perfect."

T: How was it for you?

Yochai: It was nice enough. I was curious what would come out in the end. It's making me laugh.

Hila: To tell you the truth, it wasn't as bad as I imagined. I even enjoyed it a little because I was curious how it would turn out.

T: Like the children say, "Whatever happens, I'll be happy."

Hila: Okay, let's not exaggerate. I'm not happy about how everything came out.

T: You're right. When we make a mistake or fail at something, we aren't exactly thrilled about it. The point isn't that we should be happy about failure, but rather know how to accept it, learn from it, not be afraid of it, and not incorporate it into our personalities. The person you drew is not perfect. Does that mean your value is lessened?

Yochai: The truth is when she makes a mistake, she's even more attractive to me, because then I feel I'm allowed to be imperfect and make mistakes, too.

T: That reminds me of the time I went to visit a friend I knew from the army. I walked up to a beautiful house, very neat, very shiny, everything in its place, like a museum. I was amazed at how beautiful it was and at the same time I began to feel how I was taking smaller steps, so as not to get anything dirty or accidentally move or break something. In order to feel comfortable, to feel secure, we need room for possible errors. You as well as Eitai, need room for possible errors – it's part of life and part of what builds our resilience. I really liked what you said just now, Yochai. Because by the way you said it, Hila can understand that when she's not perfect, you feel closer to her. This is true for all of us. It's hard to be close to "perfect" people who expect us to be perfect, too. When Eitai comes home with a grade of 62, instead of saying, "You could have done better," it's better to say, "Not so terrible, next time it will be better. Let's understand what happened so that you can improve your grade for the next time." We don't stop aspiring to progress, to improve, and to succeed; we allow margins for error, for possible failure as something we can learn from and continue to progress.

Family Friday Activity

As part of the parental model for coping with mistakes and failure, I ask the parents to introduce a regular weekly activity every Friday at dinnertime, which includes addressing the week's successes along with the less successful parts of the week.

While having your family dinner, each member of the family, including parents, tells about something good that happened to them that week, something they succeeded in and felt proud of themselves for, and then reveal something else that didn't go as planned, something they wished they could change. The parents say, "Good for you" for the successes and another "Good for you" for sharing about the failure. Afterwards, the parents ask, "What did you learn?" and the parents and children tell what they learned and get reinforcement for doing so, for learning from the mistake. When parents tell about a failure they had that week, it's best to add a phrase such as, "I'm only human; I can make mistakes," "Maybe I made a mistake but I still think I'm a great person," or "I'm not perfect. Making mistakes is part of life." I recall a family who introduced this activity, "Personal Family Friday," and turned it into a real celebration. One by one, each family member told their story about what they were proud of that week and was rewarded with applause; the failures won a round of applause, too. The applause stood for the courage to admit an error and for taking responsibility for that error. Whoever succeeded in saying what they learned from the mistake received not only applause, but also a piece of chocolate. This is a wonderful example of how we can create a new dialog in the family, a positive and accepting atmosphere with margins for possible error, for owning responsibility, for cooperation and learning. As we will see in the next chapter, learning from mistakes has a decisive importance on a person's ability to guide himself towards achieving his goals.

Fostering Self-Efficacy

Self-efficacy refers to the belief of the individual in his competence to function in tasks or take on challenges and cope with them. According to socio-cognitive theory, the belief of an individual in his capabilities is the basis for human motivation, well-being, and personal accomplishments (Bandura, 1997). Every motivation is rooted in a person's core belief that they have the capability and the power to affect their performance – to control their life. This belief is the basis of effective thinking or non-effective thinking, of negativity or positivity, of fortitude in the face of distressing situations, of selection processes, decision making and problem solving (Bandura et al., 2001). Tied to this belief are the expectations for results: whether a performance will be successful or whether it will fail. The higher the self-efficacy is perceived to be, so are the efforts the individual invests in attaining the goal or challenge he has set for himself.

At this point, it is worth differentiating between two contiguous concepts: the perception of self-efficacy and the skill of self-control.

Bandura (1997) maintains that self-efficacy relates to a person's belief in their own competence to direct their lives towards their aims and goals. Bandura places emphasis on one's belief of competence. He sees this belief as the driving force, the determining factor of whether a person is capable of acting for the sake of attaining his goals. Rosenbaum (1990), in contrast, refers to the person's mastery of his competence to function for the sake of achieving his goals. We are speaking of a collection of cognitive skills that enable an individual to overcome and affect behavioral changes without external coercion (Ronen, 1992). According to this approach, a person is able to achieve his goals only if he activates his mastery of self-control. That is to say, one is capable of overcoming cognitive, emotional, and behavioral obstacles in order to reach one's goals. Therefore, the behavioral function of self-control takes place when an individual surmounts conflict, waives immediate gratification, and chooses the behavior that will be most economic for himself (Rosenbaum, 1980). According to Ronen and Rosenbaum (2001), the skill of self-control is activated only when an individual comes up against an obstacle that hinders them from reaching their target. Specifically, one's goals and the obstacles that stand in one's way of obtaining those goals, are what determine whether or not he will exert self-control.

A person's ability to direct himself towards his goals requires a belief in his capability along with his mastery of the skills, which enable that person to realize their belief.

We dealt earlier with the skill of self-awareness, for example, automatic thoughts and chain responses, enacting self-instruction, and the assertive communication model. We will continue to discuss these in the chapter that covers child-direct therapy. For now, we will focus our attention on fostering self-efficacy in a child. How can parents assist their children in developing their belief in their own capabilities to obtain their objectives?

The higher the self-efficacy, so too rise the personal accomplishments and the sense of personal happiness (Bandura, 1994). Individuals with high self-efficacy approach difficult tasks as challenges they need to cope with and not as threats they need to avoid. This attitude of reality stimulates internal interest, curiosity, enlists full attention to the task and imbues a strong commitment to achieving their goal. Individuals with healthy self-efficacy succeed in maintaining their efforts and their personal self-belief when faced with failures. They relate to failure as part of an ineffective effort or lack of knowledge and mastery that remains to be acquired. They will continue in their attempts to reach their objective with the faith and security that they have the ability to influence and control inhibitory processes on the way to reaching their goal. Another result of high self-efficacy, aside from producing personal achievement, is a decrease of possible emotional anguish (such as: anxiety and depression) in the face of failure (Bandura, 1977, 1994, 1997).

In comparison, individuals with low self-efficacy avoid difficult undertakings (which they may perceive to be threatening), have low ambitions, and have a feeble commitment to goals. When up against demanding tasks, they may focus on their own personal frailties, the obstacles that stand in their path, and their own expectations for negative results. They tend towards giving up on reaching their goals when they run into obstacles. In contrast to those with high self-efficacy, they relate failure to their own lack of ability to cope with the situation. Therefore, chances are they won't try to change those negative results, and as a consequence, lose faith in their competence and often experience states of panic, anxiety, and depression.

Self-efficacy, similar to self-esteem, has the property of providing resilience when coping with life's challenges. Parents who succeeded in taking actions to foster these two variables – self-efficacy and self-esteem – enable their children to enjoy a better quality of life.

Rona and Yaron are the parents of an eleven-year-old daughter, Shir, diagnosed with an attention disorder and significant learning disabilities. In addition, Shir is described by the parents as a child who can't seem to read the social map; she shies away from social situations, clings to her parents, and is overly dependent on them, has trouble falling asleep at night, is afraid of the dark, and afraid of heights. Following the intake process, we tried to define the problems that led them to seek treatment and we rated the problems according to their degree of difficulty as perceived by the parents:

1. Very low grades at school.
2. Inept in social skills – doesn't know how to make contact, is socially rejected, and seems to suffer from social anxiety.
3. Afraid of the dark, afraid of heights.
4. Clings to parents, especially at night, dependent on parents for schoolwork assignments and other various tasks.

T: Does it seem to you that there is a connection between all of these problems?

Rona: It seems to me she simply doesn't believe in herself. She doesn't even try to cope.

Yaron: I think it's connected to how we sort of feel sorry for her. We try to make things as smooth as possible for her. It's very difficult for her. We are worried because she is such a poor darling. In every area of life, it's hard for her – socially, schoolwork, even at home she's always clinging to us. On one hand, it exhausts us and we're angry at her. On the other hand, we feel sorry for her.

T: It would seem that both of you are right. In light of what you have described, I have a theory that I'd like to check with you. When I listen to what you say about Shir, I see in my mind a girl who doesn't believe in her ability to get along in many areas. Does that seem reasonable to you?

Parents: Very.

T: Shir does have some personal issues that burden her. She has an attention disorder and learning disabilities, so it's not easy for her to learn new material. And it seems these traits are also a detriment in social circles, especially the trouble with verbal dexterity that we saw in the diagnosis you brought, which can be a real social stumbling block. She has developed a fear of the dark and of heights, which is quite common at her age, and so it reasons that she clings to you more. But what looms over all these problems is, it seems, that Shir has a low perception of self-efficacy. She doesn't believe in her competence to progress towards her aspirations. When self-efficacy is low, the world looks more threatening and the feeling of helplessness is greater. Let's try to understand this by our own personal experiences. Rona, you said earlier that you work in a travel agency. Imagine, if you will, yourself in a situation where you'd taken care of a client's request for a vacation for two in Greece and they were late for their flight. The plane took off and they are extremely upset, so they call you on the phone. What goes on through your head?

Rona: (smiling) That they aren't the first ones to ever miss a flight.

T: Do you believe you will be able to solve the problem?

Rona: Of course, I will solve it. It's what I do every day.

T: How do you know you will succeed?

Rona: What do you mean? That's exactly what my job is. I'll call the airlines and arrange a new ticket for them. At the very most, they'll have to wait a bit, but they'll get to Greece soon enough.

T: For that to happen, you were aided by a movie in your head, where you put together the solution; you know who to call, what to do, and you have the belief that you will resolve the problem. When we have that sort of faith, our motivation to solve the problem is higher and we invest the necessary effort in finding the solution. We call this belief: self-efficacy. This is to say, we believe that we are capable of achieving our goal. I suppose that with Shir, this belief has been severely damaged. Let's try to see what makes up self-efficacy and how it is expressed with Shir. First, we will use your example, Rona, and try to illustrate it graphically on the board.

Cycles of Self-Efficacy:
Example of a Positive Cycle of Self-Efficacy

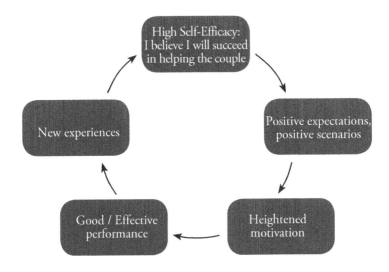

T: We can see a positive feeling about the solution, expectations for success, investing energy in a desired direction, a successful result, and a new experience with those sorts of problems. But what would have happened to you, Rona, if a couple of times in a row you weren't able to help the couples that got stuck at the airport? Or what would happen to you, Yaron, if, as a mechanic, you couldn't fix the cars that came in for repair?

Yaron: I would be very exasperated and frustrated. That is exactly the same thing that happened to me in school. I can understand Shir, since for me the school part was the same. I simply could not understand anything in the classroom, and in the end, I quit school in the eleventh grade.

T: I see that you clearly made the connection with Shir. That's quite correct, according to Bandura, who developed the concept of self-efficacy; people who judge their efficacy as being low have a tendency to imagine themselves in scenes of failure. Those thoughts weaken motivation and bring about a low performance level. One's failure to perform often pushes a person to despair or to fear additional failure, which in turn causes them to avoid another attempt.

Self-efficacy influences a wide variety of behaviors. It can halt or encourage people to make attempts and also determine how much they will commit to the effort of attaining a particular goal. Let's imagine what happens to Shir, for instance, in her school work:

Example of a Negative Cycle of Self-Efficacy

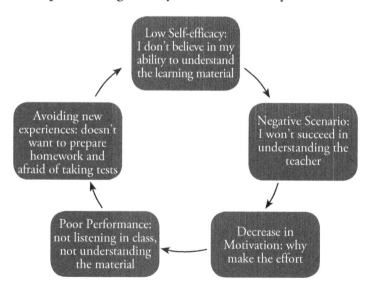

Yaron: You can understand why we said she's a poor thing?

T: At the moment, it is apparent she is having some anxieties. Apart from the low self-efficacy, there is a good chance this has influenced her self-esteem as well. I imagine that in a situation like this it would be hard for her to feel worthy. It may be difficult for her to love herself, and therefore, we should help her, by nurturing her self-esteem and also try to change the cycle of low self-efficacy. This is where you come into the picture. We're about to be students for the moment, in order to get a better understanding of what is known from the research done on self-efficacy and what we can do about it on a practical level. Is this all right with you?

After receiving the couple's consent, we turned to the psychoeducational explanation of how we attain self-efficacy.

Psychoeducational Explanation:
How Do We Acquire Our Perception Of Self-Efficacy?
Bandura (1994), whom we mentioned earlier, explains in a very clear manner how we obtain self-efficacy. This explanation will help you to understand what needs to change in order to help Shir. Bandura claims there are four significant factors that influence the development of self-efficacy.

1. Successful experiences in performing tasks – Success in a task and receiving positive reinforcement generates higher expectations for similar tasks in the future and a higher sense of self-efficacy. The emphasis here is on the experience of control over events. The success of completing a task strengthens self-efficacy; failures diminish that belief, in particular if the failures occur before a sense of self-efficacy is well established. If people experience episodes of easily achieved success – without exerting effort – they become accustomed to expecting quick results, so when they do experience failure, it's hard for them to tolerate it. A high sense of self-efficacy requires experience in overcoming obstacles by persistent and determined efforts. The perception of reality as something where I can achieve my goals if I make the effort, enables us to recover quickly in situations of defeat and allows us to renew our attempts and proceed onward towards the goals we set for ourselves.

2. Modeling – Observing the successful endeavors of others, who are similar or significant to us, strengthens one's sense of self-efficacy; "If he can do it, then so can I." The more alike the model is to ourselves, so too will their influence ensure a stronger impact on our self-efficacy. Here, too, the emphasis is put on the effort one invests. If I see someone who is accomplished, without also being aware of the effort they have invested, I might relate their success to luck, extraordinary personal traits, or suchlike. For my self-efficacy to rise, I must see the efforts that were invested by the person I perceive to be a model for attaining his goals. Similarly, the failing of someone comparable to myself is liable to lessen my self-efficacy and lower the effort I am willing to exert to reach my goal.

3. External persuasion – Persuasion or verbal encouragement from significant others cause one to believe one has the capability or inability to complete a given task. Positive persuasion raises the sense of self-efficacy and must be based on realistic estimates of aptitude and talent. Verbal persuasion concerning our aptitude to do something ("You can do it"), significantly contributes to one's ability to muster the necessary energy and effort exerted to execute actions directed towards a goal. Conversely, when the external environment casts doubts on these abilities ("I don't think you can do it"), it causes one to develop self-doubts and direct inner-attention to weaknesses and frailties when dealing with diversity. This, in turn, causes one to lose motivation and even abstain from contending with obstacles and forfeiting the accomplishment of one's chief goals.

4. Psychological/Emotional Arousal – The higher the level of arousal in stressful/threatening situations, the more self-efficacy decreases. When we are calm and experience a sense of control, at the psychological level, the perception of our self-efficacy increases. In this case, the emphasis is on the conditioning that has been formed between our internal experience and the performance of the task. If, for example, I must study for a test, and while studying I feel I am not concentrating, I may very well interpret the physical signs of a lack of concentration as an inability to perform the job. I may very well slide into a bad mood, lose my motivation to learn, and give up on making an effort to study for the exam. The struggle to increase self-efficacy arises due to my negative interpretation of emotional and psychological events I have encountered. Individuals with high self-efficacy view the state of arousal as positive energy and a performance enhancer, while those with low self-efficacy view the state of arousal as a performance hinderer.

After this rather long explanation, we'll try to see how we can help Shir modify her cycle of efficacy.

T: In light of what I just explained, do you have any possible ideas what can be done?

Yaron: The thing that rings loudest for me from your

explanation is in the effort invested. Not to give up. We're doing the exact opposite. We're always conceding to her because we feel sorry for her. I also identify with her, because I went through the same thing with my schoolwork, and now, I think, what if my parents had come to you and heard that explanation, maybe my whole life would have been different.

T: What should they have done differently?

Yaron: In our house, I was the "black sheep," the one who didn't succeed. I felt my parent's disappointment and it was very important for me to please them. There were so many arguments about homework assignments and about school in general. I hated school. I would sit in class and not be able to concentrate and not understand anything. I thought I was stupid, that I'd never amount to anything.

T: Do you still think that way?

Yaron: No. Thank goodness, we've grown up…

T: What led you to realize you weren't stupid?

Yaron: In the eleventh grade, I started working at a garage and the garage manager took me under his wing. He was always saying to me, "You're number one," at first I didn't think he really meant it, but when I could find the mechanical problems that others didn't notice and I fixed complicated things, I understood that I did amount to something.

T: Now we can understand what your manager did, in contrast to your school setting where you didn't have any experiences of success. At the garage you succeeded even more than the others, this is what we meant when we said we are experiencing jobs successfully performed. Your manager encouraged and reinforced you for those successes and caused you to believe in your own professional proficiency.

Rona: That's not the only thing. Everything you explained before, happened to Yaron. Do you remember when you told me if Ya'akov (one of the employees at the garage) can repair something – I don't remember exactly what it was – then you could fix it, too?

T: Just as you could, so can Shir. What the garage manager did for you, Yaron, you can do the same for Shir. He didn't pity you. He gave you tasks as part of the job and encouraged you. He persuaded you that you were capable.

Yaron: (with tears in his eyes) I truly owe him so much. He really saved me.

T: He was a significant figure in your life, just as you are in Shir's life today.

Yaron: Yes, but about the school work. I swore to myself that I wouldn't do to my kids what my parents did to me. It will be hard for me to make demands on her.

T: One of the things we will try to do here is modify the conditioning that exists with you and with Shir, which interprets school and learning as a negative experience. With both of you, a connection developed according to which school studies are an unpleasant experience and it's best to avoid them. It's also linked to the attention disorder and the difficulty to concentrate and take in the learning material, and there is an additional reaction to the environment. The criticism and arguments you had with your parents intensified your sense of low self-efficacy. I would like to suggest to you to try at home with Shir, an exercise I call 20/10. This exercise will let you break the negative preconditioning towards homework assignments.

How We Can Assist Our Child with Homework – The 20/10 Exercise

For children with an attention deficit, there is difficulty with goal directed behavior due to problems in the executive functions located in the brain's pre-frontal cortex. These executive functions are responsible for a person's upper cognitive control processes: the ability to plan, to make decisions, to learn from mistakes, to initiate, to persevere, to adapt to new situations, and regulate emotions. This has a dramatic influence on their personal, social, and academic functioning (Barkley, 2001). Children with ADHD have a basic problem developing the self-control necessary for maintaining goal oriented behaviors. They require external mediation in order to cope with life's adversities. It is no coincidence that many people with attention disorders often marry spouses with superior managerial skills.

Rona: Yes, it's the same with us. Even if Yaron was never diagnosed, I'm sure he has an attention disorder. He's like another child at home. I have to remind him about things all the time. That drives me crazy, because a lot of times I can't rely on him. I will ask him to do something and later on he apologizes for not doing it. I have to do everything.

T: That's a familiar situation. What you're describing characterizes the lives of couples where one member has an attention disorder. It can exhaust the "caretaker" partner and also provoke hostilities and anger. On the other hand, there are quite a few advantages to having an attention deficit. It's no coincidence that in the eleventh grade Yaron already succeeded in locating mechanical malfunctions in cars even when the other mechanics couldn't. In fact, because their attention is blocked, they manage to organize information differently; they think outside of the box and they have remarkably creative thinking. I suppose we'll be able to see this with Shir, if she can believe in her own abilities.

Rona: As a matter of fact, Shir is an amazing artist.

T: So, it seems she has a wonderfully creative side. We will think of how to nurture her creativity. At the same time, we will try to strengthen her efficacy in school work through the homework assignments. In particular, in those areas where you have control over the messages you send and the ability to change the conditioned behavior responses that have been reinforced over time.

Rona: The truth is, I do a lot of her homework assignments for her. What I mean is, I sit with her and when she starts to cry, it's hard for me to see her like that so I tell her the answers and sometimes even write the entire assignment for her. Sometimes she wears me down so much and I get angry with her. I really want to help her, but it exhausts me. Of all things, her homework is the hardest for me. I have a million things to take care of and I find myself spending many hours helping her succeed. It's too much, I don't have the strength anymore.

T: I imagine this happens to many parents who want

very much to help their children succeed. Some of us express anxiety over our child's poor performance and you do what many parents do – you try to protect her from the possible consequences of failure, and you are angry with her because she doesn't stand up to your expectations. We can see this in the cycle that has been created and which keeps repeating itself.

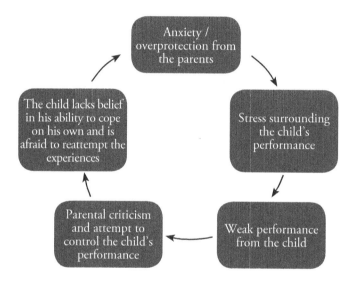

Rona: So, what can we do?

T: In order to change this cycle, we will aim at returning the responsibility for preparing homework assignments back to Shir. We want to make her rely on herself in order to strengthen her experience of self-efficacy by sending a new message about homework, and in doing so, alter her learning experience. The way to do this is by sending a new message about homework and the conditions regarding homework =

threatening experience combined with criticism, lack of success, and lack of efficacy. We will change the conditioned response to: homework = challenging, but perhaps pleasant, combined with positive reinforcement and a sense of competence. In order to promote a change in the conditioned responses, we will begin practicing the 20/10 exercise with her for preparing homework assignments. I'll demonstrate for you how I'd like it to be done in a role playing exercise. Which one of you wants to be Shir?

(Rona volunteers herself)

T: Shir sweetheart, I noticed that it's really hard for you to do your homework. I can see how much you're struggling and I really understand your difficulty. Sometimes we do the assignments together for more than two hours and that seems to me like too much time. I would like us to change that. I thought it would be good if we use the "20/10 method" I recently learned. It will help us turn doing homework into a more pleasant experience. There are children who can only concentrate for short periods of time, and afterwards, they lose focus. I think this happens with you too, and so, we will work with your mind instead of against it. Every day you'll spend twenty minutes preparing your homework. Only what you know and only what you understand. After twenty minutes, the timer will buzz and signal you've finished your homework. After the timer buzzes, the two of us will play Ping-Pong, your favorite game, for ten minutes. If you want, you can continue with another round. That means, if you decide to do another twenty minutes of homework, you will earn another ten minutes of Ping-Pong. How does that sound?

Shir
(Rona):   It sounds fine, but what if I don't get all the homework done?

T: I'll talk with your teacher before we start to use the new system. I will explain to your teacher how important it is to me (and you) that homework assignments be a better experience for you than they are now.

Shir:
(Rona):   What if my teacher doesn't agree?

T: If the teacher doesn't agree, we will find a solution. It will be my responsibility to take care of that.

Before implementing the exercise at home, it was agreed that Rona would call Shir's teacher and speak to her about the therapy program, about our aim to strengthen Shir's self-efficacy, even if the price was not finishing all of the homework assigned to her. In addition, it was agreed that Rona would try to set up a meeting at the school, with my participation, in order to build a comprehensive program suited to Shir's needs.

In the next session with Rona and Yaron, they told me about the conversation they had with Shir's teacher, who was understanding and supportive and willing to cooperate in the application of the exercise at home. They reported that Shir was happy about the idea, which surprised both parents. Shir managed to do a great deal in the twenty minutes allotted, much more than she had done in a whole hour prior to the new arrangement. Shir's motivation to prepare homework assignments was higher and she eagerly sat down to do them. Rona sat with her while she did the homework, made sure to reinforce her after the twenty minutes ("I'm really proud of you") and then held up her end of the bargain by playing ten minutes of Ping-Pong. We began to see the changes we had hoped for. The next step was to foster Shir's efficacy in the area of independent functioning with the homework, and the aim was to lessen her reliance on Rona when doing homework assignments. Rona learned another technique that would help them in this direction.

When faced with boring and unrewarding tasks that seem exhausting to them, children with attention disorders will find it difficult to perform those tasks and will be tempted to do something else they deem more rewarding. Therefore, immediate and consistent, positive encouragement is important, and will turn a task into more of a challenge (Barkley, 1995). In practice, we will want to combine challenges with immediate positive encouragement. I demonstrated for Rona how to present this to Shir by role playing. I gave Rona (who played Shir), a simple arithmetic exercise: $256 + 342 = ?$ and then asked her how much time it would take her to solve the equation?

Shir   Half a minute.
(Rona):
T: And I'll bet it will take you one minute. Let's see who's
            right? Whoever guesses closest to the time it actually
            takes you – is the winner.

We set the second hand on the clock in front of us and Rona solved the exercise in ten seconds.

T: Rona, how did you feel when competing against the clock?

Rona: Even though it's only a role playing game, I felt a kind of positive tension and wanted to win, I mean, to solve the equation as fast as I could. I think this will be great to do with Shir.

T: In the beginning, we will let the child win and say a longer amount of time than the child says. After about six rounds of playing this game, it's best to give a genuine estimate of time; how long it would take to solve the equation or exercise. Since during the twenty minutes allotted there will usually be more than one exercise to do, the child will find the motivation to do another exercise in order to win against the clock or the parent. If the child wins, they receive verbal reinforcement such as, "Good for you," and nonverbal reinforcement, perhaps applause, a hug, or a kiss. If the parent wins, the message is, "That was a complicated equation. Good for you for doing it. Let's move on to the next exercise and you'll have another chance to beat me."

In our following session, Rona arrived feeling quite pleased, but surprisingly, it was Yaron who opened the session.

Yaron: I have to tell you something. There has been a 180-degree change. Rona used what you taught her, to the letter. Shir was very cooperative and I don't even recognize her now! They set the agreed hour for homework at six o'clock. Yesterday at five-thirty, I heard Shir remind Rona they had school work to do at six o'clock. Shir looks happier and the most important thing – no more arguments over homework assignments. The entire atmosphere at home has changed and the tension Rona was feeling has eased up.

T: I'm glad to hear it. Rona, do you feel the same way?

Rona: It really works. It's clear to me what I have to do and how I should do it. I feel we are on the right track.

T: I'm very proud of you, Rona. Quite often we teach parents to use effective tools, yet due to any number of reasons, they find it difficult to apply them and to be consistent. Your success comes as the result of your steady and consistent work. It's important you continue with this. There may be additional setbacks along the way. For instance, when you might be busy with other things, or if Shir comes home from school and doesn't feel like doing her homework. Don't be upset when these situations occur and don't give up. It's all right not to do homework for one night or to shorten the time allotted for doing them. Our goal is to create a positive conditioned response between homework and a challenging, non-threatening experience. Consistency is necessary for establishing the conditioned response. We will continue to follow your progress during our sessions and monitor how the process is moving along. Our goal is for Shir to be able to do her homework for twenty minutes without your immediate presence. At a later stage, we will increase the time limit to twenty-five minutes and perhaps even more.

The next two follow-up sessions were dedicated to learning The "Warm" Model for use with Shir, in an attempt to increase her sense of efficacy and better experience her self-worth. In light of the positive results with the homework assignments and the generally pleasant atmosphere at home, we could now proceed onward to our second goal – treating Shir's fear of the dark and fear of heights.

Self-Efficacy and Anxiety in Children

T: In the exact same manner that efficacy is linked to tasks like homework, it is also connected to the ability to cope in stressful situations. You both share a vital role in modifying the preconditions that have been created. I'd be happy if you would share with me the chain of response that is linked to Shir's anxiety. Do you have an example from this past week?

Situation	Automatic Thought	Emotion	Behavior
At eight-thirty it's time to go to bed. Shir won't fall asleep without our being in the room.	Rona: I am exhausted. All day long I am with her. I need some time to myself. Yaron: I feel sorry for her. It's important to me that she sleep well and for the right amount of time. Otherwise, she'll have a hard time at school tomorrow.	Rona: angry Yaron: pity, helplessness	Rona sits next to Shir until she falls asleep. Yaron sits next to Shir until she falls asleep. Sometimes he falls asleep next to her until the early morning hours.
The incident for Shir: my parents sit next to me until I fall asleep.	I can't deal with the fear on my own. Only when my parents are next to me, I can relax.	Calmness	Sleep Result: Increase in dependency on the parents

Psychoeducational Explanation:

From what we have seen here, we can understand how Shir developed the sense that she can't fall asleep without you. I imagine this attitude exists with her other fears as well. That is to say, your experience of protecting her and/or your anger at her is liable to perpetuate her fears and even heighten them. When you pity her you are complying with her inner voice that says, here is something she can't cope with on her own but only with your help. Her dependence on you increases and she avoids having to deal with her fear. If Shir is afraid of the dark and you stay next to her until she falls asleep, it's as if you were

saying. "Yes, the situation is dangerous and we should remain by your side because you can't be on your own."
Let's examine this via the cycle that has formed and which perpetuates her fear.

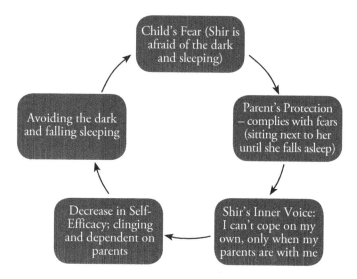

In order to break this cycle, we'll learn how to guide Shir towards her self-efficacy. This can only happen if you, as parents, make a change in your compliance with Shir's fears.

From the treatment aspect, there are two options: one option is to work together with Shir, on the process of decreasing her fears, which is the preferred option in my opinion, and the second option is that Shir come in for direct therapy sessions for treating anxiety/fear. This should be done simultaneously with your training of the methods for making change in the cycle of which we have just spoken about.

Rona and Yaron, having experienced success with the homework exercise, decided to try by themselves to deal with

Shir's fears. We agreed between us on continuing the parent training in order to aid Shir in lessening her fears and only if it would become necessary, we would combine this with direct therapy for Shir. Rona and Yaron did a wonderful job and implemented step-by-step, everything we practiced in session. As a result, it was not necessary to introduce direct therapy with Shir. All the changes were done with the hands-on involvement of the parents.

In the following chapters, we will delve more deeply into the ways parents can aid their children in contending with fear.

Part B:

Child-Direct Therapy

The treatment of children and the choosing of intervention methods are complex matters. Ronen (1994), in her outstanding book, endeavors to detail the artistry and skill of child-direct therapy and the integral questions that accompany the treatment of children: Whether to treat the initially specified problem or take up the issues that become apparent during interviews (intake)? Should the therapist deal with each problem separately or construct a comprehensive program of treatment? What to treat first? Who to treat? The child? The parents? The family? Is treatment even required? These critical decisions will be the result of in-depth systematic assessment including, first, the child's parents.

In my professional opinion, it is not possible to treat a child without having parent training. Parents are the primary and most significant agents of change for a child, and it turns out that parents are also far more effective in modifying their children's behavior than any unfamiliar therapist (Kazdin, 1984). Parent training before and during child-direct therapy substantially increases the positive results of treatment (Bernstein et al., 2005). At the institute where I administrate, I have established an iron-clad rule: every treatment of a child begins by meeting with the parents. Furthermore, we will not rush to admit a child for therapy before the parents themselves have begun a process of change. Cohen (2006), clearly states that it is necessary to implement genuine parent therapy and not only parent training, whose purpose it is to provide the specific tools required to address the child's problem. Cohen refers to the pursuit for better understanding of parenthood and the constructing of a plan of intervention not only focused on the child's needs, but also on the needs of the parents, at two key levels: (1) the systemic-ecologic level, which pertains to the environment's power to assist or hinder the parents efforts to contend and cope; (2) the intrapersonal level, delving into the internal processes of development and change in parenting methods. These internal processes touch upon the realms of expectations, needs, beliefs, cognitions, attitudes, interpretive and reflective capabilities, and the ability to regulate emotions and behaviors.

In the treatment of every child, we view the parents as a therapy resource, as active participants in the treatment and invaluable to its success. In some cases, we even view them as line-therapists, according to Briesmeister & Schaefer's definition (1998).

Since we recognize the great importance of working with parents and we understand they are the most significant facilitators of change for a child, especially younger children, this book initially focused on parent training for various children's issues. At this point, we will address child-direct therapy, the existing complexities inherent in this type of therapy, and the unique treatment process that develops between the therapist and the child.

When we work directly with a child, it is imperative we take into account a number of factors. In most cases, the individual requesting treatment is not the child himself, but rather someone from his immediate surroundings, his parents or from his educational framework. In these cases, the child steps into an unknown realm, one not of his own choosing. Even if the child clearly states that he would like to receive help, a child doesn't always fully understand the significance of that assistance. Next, the individual requesting treatment generally has a definite opinion about the desired direction of change and quite often disparities arise between the requesting factor's goals and the child's goals. For example, a child is referred by his parents for treatment of social issues and while in therapy he asks to be treated for the relationship with his parents. In the event of a conflict of interest between the needs and goals of the child and the parents, it will be necessary to intervene on these exact questions and then determine clear treatment targets. The matter becomes even more complicated when parents request that the therapist see their child, even though the child's problems are entirely normal and linked to the proper functioning of the developmental process. Parents, whether young and inexperienced or highly apprehensive, may be convinced that their child suffers from a severe problem that requires treatment. This, by the way, is another reason that stresses the importance of beginning with parent training in the treatment of a child. The child's age and stage of development will determine the correct methods for intervention. It is impracticable to employ a similar form of intervention for a child of six as for a child of twelve. We should also take into account language development, the ability to articulate (naming and retrieval), particularly if the child has learning disorders and attention deficits, which will greatly hinder long-term talk therapy. We ought to consider the cognitive developmental processes, the ability to conceptualize, make judgments, and comprehend internal processes. Accordingly, a cognitive-behavioral therapist for children requires not only knowledge of childhood development and possible protocols for treatment of problems, but must also retain a great measure of flexibility and creativity in order to tailor tools, ideas, dialog, and progress according to the child's specific needs and development.

A common metaphor among therapists is, "Tailoring a suit," according to the child's exact measurements, which is quite apt in this case. As therapists, our ability to align ourselves with the child's needs calls for open-mindedness, creativity, and the courage to breakthrough our own limitations. Therapists who occupy themselves with the question of how to apply what they have learned on their young clients, without constantly being attentive to their client's needs, are liable to thwart the treatment process. I see this process as "sailing on the sea." Before me I always see a lighthouse; where do I want to take the child? What are the goals we want to reach? All the while, I must consider the ship I am sailing in – what are its dimensions, its capabilities, and what are the conditions of the sea. Is the climate (of the child) stormy or calm, sunny or overcast?

In the first chapter of this section of the book, we will demonstrate the manner in which I set sail, how I will detect a child's strengths and weaknesses, how I will build a bond of trust with him and begin the work of our joint journey. Following this, in the next chapters, I will try to describe that journey, the tales of the sea, via three examples of therapeutic intervention: therapeutic intervention for anxiety with a description of treatment for childhood fears, therapeutic intervention for behavior issues through an example of the treatment of anger and aggression. Last I will focus on therapeutic intervention in the sphere of social proficiencies, through an example of treatment for social rejection.

4

The First Session with the Child

On the kibbutz where I grew up, it was decided to send me to speech therapy in the second grade. "She doesn't know how to speak correctly. She is straining her voice too much. She yells too much and her speech has to be improved." I recall when the woman in charge of the children (the "replacement" mother on a kibbutz who takes care of many children in the children's house – where they live and sleep) came to me and said, "On Tuesday at six you have a speech lesson, because you don't speak correctly and this has to be taken care of." The message was clear; I spoke poorly. They had noticed the problem. This was an issue to be addressed, and they had taken steps to give me the necessary treatment. I understood this. There was no question as to whether this was appropriate or not, or what sort of treatment was required in my case, or what I thought about it, if I wanted to go at all. The following Tuesday. I went to a small room next to the member's clubhouse where the lessons were to be given. A little woman greeted me at the door, her hair was long and unkempt, and I immediately noticed that something was strange about her. Right away, I saw that her eyes were shut and that her eyelids fluttered continually, and

I wasn't sure at all what this meant. The petite lady greeted me with a smile, introduced herself and added, "I have been blind since birth." If she hadn't stated this, it's more than likely I wouldn't have been able to concentrate during the speech therapy session, and maybe even refused to go.

When we are working with children, we must explain to them what they are seeing. A child who arrives for treatment and immediately begins to play games with the therapist, before understanding the purpose of the visit, is liable to remain confused and not understand what is taking place. Why is the "lady" or the "man" talking to me/playing games with me? Who are they? What are they doing here? A child who cannot provide himself with the answers to these questions will not be able to make the most of what therapy can offer. Therefore, in the first session with a child, I recommend that matters be handled in such a way that the child feels he knows where he is and why he is there.

After several sessions with the parents of Edo (a ten-year-old boy), he came into therapy accompanied by his parents. When the three of them arrived, I came out of the therapy room to greet them, I smiled at Edo, shook his hand, and said to him, "How nice that you've come. Soon we'll get to know one another." As I mentioned earlier, a greeting of this sort allows the child to feel he is both expected and that we are happy he has come.

Meanwhile, I said goodbye to the client who had been in my therapy room and called Edo and his parents to come inside. In the first session with young children, I let them choose whether they want to come in alone or with their parents in order to heighten the child's sense of "a safe haven." Edo chose to enter together with his parents.

T: I'm so glad to meet you, Edo. At the meeting I had with your parents, I heard many good things about you and I was looking forward to meeting you. Have you heard about me, too?

Edo: I only heard that you help children.

T: That is correct. For many years, I studied how to help children. Do you feel you need help?

Edo: Don't know. My parents say I don't behave very well.

T: And what do you think about that?

Edo: That they don't treat me very well.

T: What do you mean?

Edo: Don't know. They should tell you.

T: Dear parents, do you understand what Edo meant?

Mother: We have a lot of arguments over the way he treats his sister. Edo is ten years of age and she's six years old, and he is teasing her all the time, insulting her and hitting her. We also know he hits children at school, too.

Edo: That's right. She annoys me, and at school they irritate me.

T: Then it's a good thing you came to me. Together with you, I will try to find some solutions. The first step is trying to understand what irritates you, Edo, and what happens to you when someone annoys you. After that, we will try to understand what can be done so that you won't become so annoyed, and how your parents can change things so it can be nicer for all of you. Do you agree with my plan?

Edo: Yeah, I guess so.

T: Okay then. It's very important to me that you tell me what you understood just now. What is our plan?

(It's very important to get feedback from the child about the things that were said, if and how they understood them).

Edo: That we should understand what makes me angry and find a solution.

T: It's a very basic plan. This is what we'll do in the beginning, but it might change if we decide together to change it. Okay?

Creating an initial goal right away in the first session with the child is very important. Adults understand processes; they understand that getting to know someone takes time and that it's necessary to examine the problem closely before beginning a treatment. Children do not yet comprehend this concept, and the younger the child the more difficult it is for him to understand. Moreover, children who clearly grasp the purpose of the sessions make a greater effort to begin change at an earlier stage as part of their willingness to please an authority figure, which enables the therapist to reinforce positive change, generate motivation for the therapy alliance, and augment change in the desired direction. It is not surprising then, that when Edo returned with his parents for their second session, they reported that over the past week there had not been any behavior problems. In this case, it is important to reinforce and also get a deeper understanding of how this came about. What helped their child to change his behavior? Did he say to himself something different than he usually does? Has he noticed new things? How does he explain the change? If there is no emphasis on the inner and external dynamics that led to change, it will be difficult for him to repeat that behavior change later on.

The Diagnostic Process for Children

Comprehensive CBT diagnosis includes, among other things, intake and the replies to questionnaires, which provide an even more precise picture of the client's problems. While it is easy enough to use questionnaires with adults, more specifically with parents (we can quite easily use structured or semi-structured questionnaires), when the diagnosis is done directly with a child, we will need to use more creative methods that are appropriate to the child's age and stage of development. An examination based solely on an oral/frontal interview is suitable for only a small portion of children. Young children five to nine years of age are not always able to identify, comprehend, and give a name to feelings, emotions, and thoughts. It is not always easy for them to be exact when rating the degree of difficulty they are faced with. Therefore, it is best to use creative means for producing, as much as possible, a broad picture of the child's world in a short space of time. One of the techniques I have found effective for this purpose is drawing the child's, "Rays of Sunshine."

Rays of Sunshine Drawing for the Initial Assessment of a Child

Noa, an eleven-year-old girl, came in for treatment of what her parents defined as "social troubles at school." Noa did not want her parents to come in with her for our first session. We respected Noa's request and I sat with her on her own. Noa is an introverted girl who has difficulty opening up. When I sensed this was the situation, I decided to use the "Sunshine of Niceness."

Explaining the activity to a child:

So that I can get to know you better, I would like us to draw your sun. Every person has their very own sun: mother, father, teacher, and friends. We all have a sun. Our sun has rays of sunshine and sometimes those rays are very nice and warm, while at other times they can be scorching hot and not very pleasant. I want us to try and get to know the rays of niceness in your sun. Is that all right with you?

In order for me to know about your sunshine, I'll ask you to draw your sun, with all the rays of sunshine shining out of it, and on the inside of the sun we'll write your name. This way each ray of sunshine will be connected to your life, for instance: father, mother, your brother, friends, school, sports and hobbies, and so forth. On each ray of sunshine, we'll write how nice it is for you. The nicest ray of sunshine is a ten and the least pleasant ray of sunshine is a one.

Nice Ray of Sunshine = 10 ----------------- Not Nice Ray of Sunshine = 1

(clockwise) 10 – Dance Lessons, 5 – Dad, 9 – Mom, 6- School, 8 - Classes, 2- Friends, 8- Gili, 10- Debbie (bottom), 1 – Yoav, 6 – Stav, 10 – Nana and Papa (mom's parents). In the middle center: Noa

Noa's drawing clearly represented a different picture than the one described by her parents. Noa came for treatment of what her parents referred to as a "social issue" in her class. In their view, she is rejected, lonely, and in emotional distress due to social troubles with her friends at school. While working with the sun drawing, it became apparent that Noa was feeling uncomfortable with her friends at school, but she is also close friends with two girls in her grade that are not in her classroom (Gili and Debbie). She spends time with them at recess time, and essentially, going to school isn't such a problem for Noa (rated a six). As a result of the work on Noa's rays of sunshine, it became clear that Noa had developed a strong hostility towards her brother, Yoav (he was rated a one), who, according to Noa, taunts her all the time. He insults her and laughs at her while she doesn't say anything back to him. Sometimes she cries. Noa says that her father loves Yoav, plays soccer with him all the time, and never gets angry with him. The parents had mentioned the strain in relations between Noa and her brother, but had not given it much importance. They linked her sadness, withdrawal, and quietness to her experiences in the classroom. As was mentioned earlier, in this case, we, as therapists, are placed in a conflict of loyalties. Should we stick to the parent's aim for treatment of social dysfunction or should we treat the child's objective? Who is our client? Who are we committed to?

In a similar fashion, we often find children who express a desire to treat social difficulties at school while the parents' intention is to deal with their child's conduct and behavior at home. Sometimes there may be a conflict of interests between parents and children, or a difference of priorities on what should be dealt with. My professional opinion is that we should work with the problems the child indicates in session. In this case, the child's motivation for affecting a process of change will rise, he will feel the therapist is attuned to his needs and cooperation will increase. At a later stage, it may be possible to integrate the parent's aims, whether in direct treatment with the child or in joint sessions with the parents and the child.

Using " Rays of Sunshine" for Examining Strengths and Solving Problems

When I go through the details on the rays of sunshine, I don't make due with an explanation about the rays and their degree of niceness, instead I ask, "What needs to happen so the sun's rays will be nicer?" For example, when we got to her father's ray of sunshine, I asked Noa what needs to happen to make her father's ray of sunshine reach a grade of seven or eight. Noa answered, "He should spend some time with me. He should show me that he loves me like he loves Yoav." In fact, Noa had just designated one of the goals of therapy – strengthening the bond with her father. In order to pinpoint further therapy goals, we will move on to the second stage of examination, according to the "Niceness Sunshine," where we aim for a shared treatment target with the child. This stage is called, identifying the sun's energy. This stage is intended for children with good cognitive abilities and is recommended for age ten and above.

Identifying the Sun's Energy Explaining the activity to a child:
Just like the sun, we too have a limited amount of energy. Do you know what energy is? Energy is power. With people, it means how much effort they put into thoughts, feelings, and their imagination. For instance, did you have an unpleasant thought today? Or perhaps you felt an unpleasant feeling? Whenever there is something that distracts me, or annoys me, maybe frightens me, sometimes even excites me or makes me curious, I spend energy

on it. I think about it. I think about how to solve the problem. What I have to do. Who I have to talk to and what to say. We all distribute our energy between different things. For example, today my cat is sick, so I spend a lot of energy on questions like: How is he feeling? Should I take him to the veterinarian again? Maybe I should do something else that I haven't done before? Do you have something that is on your mind, too? Something that you spend a lot of energy thinking about? Do you think about it constantly? Do you imagine it all the time?

Quite often children will readily cooperate at this stage and tell about the things that bother them, about their feelings, and even about their thoughts linked to these topics. Often, it is difficult to internally gauge the order for addressing each of the child's problems, and therefore, we should move on to another phase and employ graphics. I asked Noa to divide the circle of her sun into sections in such a way that would show and express the amount of energy she allocated to each of the different problems. On her drawing of the "Niceness Sun" there were four areas that received low scores for levels of niceness: Yoav, friends, her father, and the paternal grandparents. In the distribution of energy that she invested in each of these areas of difficulty, she noted only three, and in the following manner:

According to the drawing, most of Noa's energy is invested in the connection with her brother, Yoav. From this, we can derive, together with Noa, the first goal of treatment – the relationship with Yoav – to understand the essence of the relationship, identify its elements, and try to offer possible solutions for the resulting feelings, thoughts, and behaviors attached to the relationship.

Since Noa is a verbal child, cognitively developed for her age, we could easily move into the phase of closely examining the connections within her relations with her brother, Yoav, in a more focused manner. In this instance, I chose to work with Noa's "cycle of emotions" concerning her brother.

Goal Centered Cycle of Emotions

T:　Noa, what do you understand from your drawing of the Sun's Energies? What demands most of your energy?

Noa:　My stupid brother…

T:　If you are so angry at him, then you must have a reason (validation). Let's understand together a little bit more about that anger.

Explanation to a child:

Anger doesn't just happen; anger is a feeling that has a reason. It tells us that something is wrong. Many times we can feel all sorts of emotions about people in our family, about friends, and about people in general. There are reasons for all of our emotions. Let's try to understand the feelings you have towards Yoav.

The Intervention Process:

T: What emotions do you recognize?

Noa: Anger and happiness.

T: Any others?

Noa: Maybe fear. Sadness, too.

T: Lovely, you have already told me about four emotions: anger, happiness, fear, and sadness. Are there any more emotions?

Noa: Yes, but I don't remember them now.

T: It's natural that you don't remember more emotions. We'll recall them little by little. Every emotion has a purpose. If my son tells me that he loves me, then I feel happy. When do you feel happy?

Noa: When Mommy hugs me.

T: And when are you sad?

Noa: When Daddy plays with Yoav.

T: When your father plays with Yoav, are you more sad or jealous?

Noa: Both of them.

T: That means there are times when we feel more than one feeling. When your father plays with Yoav, you feel both sad and jealous. These are very natural feelings and it's a good thing they exist, because they tell us something about ourselves and about others around us.

Let's look and see what your feelings are telling us about Yoav.

I would like you to write down everything that comes to your mind when I say the name, Yoav. Let's draw it on the paper like so, that way it will be clearer for us. Let's draw it like the rays of the sun, okay?

Handwritten

Diagram: (From top clockwise) Aggravating – Anger 10: He does it on purpose – Anger 9: Sometimes he wants to play with me – Nice 8: I hate him – Hate 10: Dad loves him the most – Jealous 8: He Hits Me – Afraid 8: He takes things from me – Anger 10: Makes fun of me – Ashamed 10. Yoav (in the center).

After you've written down everything that pops into your mind about Yoav, let's check the feelings you have about him. You wrote, for example, that he hits. When someone hits us, what do we feel?

Noa: Fear.

T: That is right, fear. When Yoav hits you, how much fear do you feel, from zero to ten?

Noa: *Ten…* no, actually… eight.

T: You lowered it to eight because…?

Noa: Because Mommy comes over and separates us.

T: Let's write the name of the feeling with another color next to "hits me." The name of the feeling is f-e-a-r.

Next to the name of the feeling, we can list how strong that feeling is; your fear of Yoav when he's hitting you is eight, correct? Now let's see which feelings you have for all the other things that came to mind in connection to Yoav.

After sketching the central emotional cycle, it is possible to introduce the process of intervention in correspondence with the goals of therapy, which arise from the emotional cycle. The goal will be to enable Noa to see the connection between the feeling, the thought, and her chosen behavior with Yoav.

In the event that the child has difficulty in processing the emotional information, and more specifically – a problem with identifying and naming emotions – it is advisable to work with the following therapy cards: verbal emotions (for instance, the Inner Voice cards) or nonverbal (for example, Feel Me cards) or both of them at once (example, Feel Like [margishon] cards), in order to broaden the recognition of different emotions.

Additional uses for emotion cycles

We can also utilize the emotion cycle for examinations where there is no specific focal problem. In this case, we will want to identify the principle emotional focus in the child's life, with whom they appear and when they appear. An explanation to the child in these cases will go something like this, "From what you've described, there's a bit of a mess in your life, and I would like us to try to tidy things up together. What might be of help is for us to understand what is troubling you during the day. What thoughts are running through your head from the moment you wake up until you go to sleep at night?" For children who have difficulty in identifying thoughts that perturb them, we can ask them which feelings they experience during the day, with which people, and at what time those feelings are expressed. The purpose of this is to help the child, and ourselves, create an emotional and/or cognitive map, where we can identify the heart of the matter.

1. Begin with the emotions and check which emotions the child recognizes within himself, how he divides them inside the circle, with whom they appear, when, and at what intensity: with mother – I feel angry in the force of ten, especially when she tells me to do my homework.

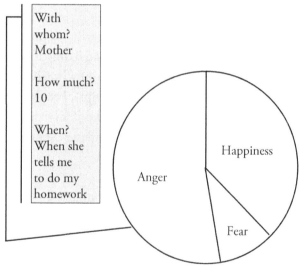

2. Begin with the thoughts that run through your head during the day, or the thoughts related to an issue or a problem and examine which emotions are connected to those thoughts along with their intensity. We can identify the thoughts crossing our mind during the day and check how much space each of those thoughts takes up in our brain. With older children, we can use percentages. What

percentage of the day do you spend thinking about failing a test? About thinking you are weird? That other children can't stand you?

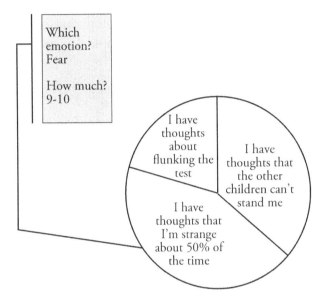

This diagnostic device centers attention on the feelings, emotions, and thoughts of the child, as an integral part of constructing therapy goals. Through the use of these tools, we can comprehend where problems are located and what positive strengths the child exercises. During the treatment, we will aspire to gradually teach the child to understand that his behavior is related to the thoughts and feelings that preceded their chosen behavior. It is possible to add tables and charts for self-monitoring thoughts, feelings, and behaviors, as is acceptable practice in the cognitive-behavioral approach.

In this section of the book, I will introduce examples of

direct intervention with children in three of the most common problematic areas among children:

Anxiety, behavior, and social skills. In each area, I chose an example case and through them we can see how the therapy process with a child develops, how therapy goals are determined, and how various tools are applied in order to bring about change.

5

Examples for Child-Direct Therapy Intervention

As was noted in earlier chapters, the decision to apply child-direct therapy is not an automatic option. Even when parents come for treatment with the clear pronouncement that their child needs immediate therapy, the decision for treatment will be made only after a thorough and comprehensive assessment of the problem via the parents. Every treatment of a child should begin with parent training and instructions in the application of tools, which will aid their child with his problems. Moreover, every child-direct therapy should be closely accompanied by parent training for the duration of treatment, including joint sessions with the parents and the child in order to firmly anchor the process of change.

The many books written on the subject of child-direct therapy with the cognitive-behavioral therapy approach place emphasis on a didactic intervention process for monitoring through the use of tables and personal observation. This is an extremely important intervention unlike any other, but still it is not enough.

Many of the therapists, whom I have trained over the years, have understood what they must do when treating a child, but they did not always understand how to do the treatment. They did not apprehend the therapy process. They did not perceive the path or know how to speak with children about their problems. In what manner should the psychoeducational explanation be presented to children at different ages? What are the kinds of tasks and missions that we can impose on a child? How can we work in close collaboration with the child's parents?

The three examples I will cite in this section of the book attempt to provide answers to these specific questions. I have chosen to present examples of treatment in three of the most common areas of therapy work with children: fear, behavioral conduct, and social skills. Each analogy will represent a specific frame of context from which contents can be gleaned for other types of therapy, whether by the manner in which the therapy process is generated or whether in the choice of tools that aid in realizing therapy goals.

Now is the time for us to set out on a journey into the children's world and meet Shai, Aviv, Yaniv, Na'ama, and Gali. We will meet each one of them and discover their personal circumstances and the processes of change that each one faced, in the framework of the following three stories:

1. "The Wonders of Gargamella" – for treating childhood fears.
2. "Storm in a Barrel" – for treating anger and aggressiveness.
3. "If Only I was…" – for treating social rejection.

1. "The Wonders of Gargamella" – Treating Childhood Fears

We are all afraid at times and we all have fears of something and/or someone. What differentiates us are the intensity and the frequency of those fears. The intensity and the frequency of anxiety are linked to the **panic level** we feel in a given situation or from our senses. Not long ago, I was instructing a group of therapists whom I have been advising for several years and who know me quite well. I usually smile, am pleasant and calm (as much as I can be calm…). While I was getting them some ice cubes out of the new fridge-freezer I had recently purchased, I heard an odd and very loud noise from inside the refrigerator, and it crossed my mind that it might be something dangerous. Perhaps it was about to explode or maybe cause an electrical short circuit in the house. Due to my complete ignorance of these occurrences, I became very upset. My calmness changed into helplessness, fright, and confusion. I hurried to wake up my son who was asleep at the time. He couldn't understand what all the fuss was about, and in a few seconds, released the ice cubes and solved the problem. I saw what he had done and received a sensible explanation from him about the problem and soon I became an expert at fixing the ice-cube problem. Now, whenever I hear that noise, it becomes clear to me what it is, what I have to do, and how to handle the situation. A lack of understanding of internal and external processes, of emotional and physical experiences, is liable to lead to panic. Panic is one of the principle elements in most anxiety disorders. Children (and adults, too) who experience anxiety and do not comprehend its significance, the manner in which it is generated, what it is composed of, or its modes and effects, may very well experience emotional distress, helplessness, and confusion that, when left untreated, can become severe, even critically damaging one's ability to function.

In his highly important and comprehensive book on the subject of anxiety among children, Peter Muris (2007) notes that epidemiological research shows how anxiety disorders are among the most widely found psychopathological disorders in young children. Without the proper treatment, they are at risk of being chronically characterized well into adulthood. In addition, Muris points out that anxiety disorders in childhood are predicators of psychological disorders in later years. Other anxiety disorders, sleeping disorders, behavioral disorders, attention deficit disorders, depression, damage to social functioning, low academic achievement, abdominal pain, headaches – impair overall functioning. According to Muris (2007), the course of anxieties in children is directly correlated to neurological and cognitive development. With infants, fears are primarily centered on immediate and concrete threats, like loud noises and loss of physical support. At around nine months of age, when their cognitive skills reach a level of maturation, which allows them to differentiate between recognized faces and strange faces, the fear of separation and the fear of strangers begins to appear. At a later stage, around kindergarten age, fears of imaginary creatures (monsters, witches) begin to develop and the supposition is that this occurrence is linked to the imaginative thought process of preschoolers. With the transition to school, at approximately six to seven years of age, children are able to arrive at conclusions based on cause and result and foresee possible negative results. For this reason, more realistic fears sprout up and the matter of worrying creeps into questions such as, What will happen? Am I and/or my family safe? And more... (Muris, 2007).

Cognitive-behavioral therapy has been found to be very effective in individual, group, and family therapy, for treating children's anxieties (Victor and Bernstein, 2008) and incorporates six basic principles:

1. Psychoeducational Explanation of Fear – for children and their parents.
2. Somatic Therapy – relaxation, breathing.
3. Cognitive Construction – identifying and monitoring negative or irrational thoughts and replacing them with rational/functional thinking.
4. Problem Solving – self-found solutions, increasing self-efficacy.
5. Exposure – gradual exposure and desensitization to the source of the anxiety.
6. Preventing Recurrence – decreasing the number of sessions, lessening the dependency of the client with a clear program for future incidents.

Cognitive-behavioral therapy abounds with protocols for intervention in the realm of childhood anxieties (Hudson, Lyneham & Rapee, 2008; Kendall & Hedtke, 2006a; Kendall & Hedtke, 2006b; Lyneham & Rapee, 2005). Therapy protocols are very structured and contain worksheets, tasks, psychoeducational explanations, and tailored systems of exposure.

The example I have presented here is found in dialog with a theoretical basis and current existing protocols. However, the emphasis will be on the therapy process, on creating a therapy alliance with the child and with the parents, and on the process of weaving a therapist-client (child) relationship. Step-by-step, we will strive to create the desired change while fully considering the methods for determining goals, the explanation given to the child, and the choosing of intervention techniques. There will also be emphasis placed on situations where the parent is a participant in sessions along with their child and how we can better utilize the parent as a resource for therapy and a stimulus for growth for the child and for the parents.

The anxieties that characterize childhood are many and various. Here, I chose to present an example of childhood fears, a very common intervention. Most children go through the experience of childhood fears without requiring intervention, while for a small percentage of children, these fears develop into chronic anxiety, which can damage their quality of life.

Research indicates that more than 70% of children between the ages of four to twelve are afraid of the dark, nighttime, monsters, and other creatures (Muris et al., 2001). By kindergarten age and during the early years of elementary school, there is confusion between reality and fantasy, so fears seem quite real to a child, even if those frightful threats do not exist in reality. The older the child, the more those fears become realistic (robbers, for example).

Childhood fears are a normal part of a sound development. For only a small percentage of children, anxiety may intensify, and in extreme cases significantly impair the child's ability to function. In cases like these, we can see physical and emotional symptoms similar to those that appear in adults. However, we may distinguish symptoms characteristic to children, such as, stomach pains, headaches, difficulty sleeping (trouble falling asleep and/or falling asleep alone, waking up in the middle of the night), reverting to bed-wetting, clinging to the parents and fearing to remain at home alone, a sense of helplessness, tantrums, and difficulty concentrating.

Environmental factors contribute considerably to the development of anxieties in children. Not only traumatic events and/or life events and negative experiences augment the occurrence of anxiety with children, but there are also subtle learning processes linked to verbal and nonverbal messages that children receive, which can dramatically influence the progression of anxiety (Field, 2006). Over the last few decades, some researchers (Twenge, 2000) claim there has been an increase in the levels of childhood anxieties, apparently due to mixed messages, stressful and threatening, from immediate and distant surroundings, which cause the child to feel a lack of security. This increase in anxieties occurs simultaneously as the family's position as the provider of safety and security is on the decline.

Our reactions to our children's fears, as parents, can fluctuate between identifying with them to pitying them, which is expressed in the parent's attempts to lessen the child's response to anxiety by anger, scorn, and ridiculing the fear, or their child's reactions when faced with his fears. In all of these cases, not only is the parent's reaction not beneficial, it may even perpetuate the child's anxiety or intensify their fears. Therefore, in every treatment of anxiety disorders with children, even with child-direct therapy, it is necessary to counsel the parents and train their reactions and attitudes to the fears and anxieties of their child. Otherwise, therapy will simply be just "spinning the wheels."

The Process of Working with Parents
First Session:

Rinat and Yoram, the parents of eight-year-old Shai, arrived for their session, and right from the start stated that they didn't believe in "interrogations." They came to me because they had heard that my method was quick and very effective and more importantly, was not invasive. Rinat and Yoram did not believe in psychological therapy, but since their son had simply ceased to function, they understood they had no other choice.

T: There's always a choice, but it's possible that you too will gain from the therapy, especially if we are able to help Shai. What you have described reminds me of what happened to me when I went for acupuncture. I didn't believe it could help me and I even joked about the whole matter, but my back pain was so severe, I gave it a chance, and then, after two treatments I felt much better. I learned not to argue with success. Here, too, we will continuously check if the things we are doing have worked or not worked. In the Cognitive-Behavior Therapy approach, we are constantly monitoring the results of intervention. We're doing actual research about what works and that's why this type of therapy is so effective.

Let's agree that even though you don't believe in psycho-therapy, you will try to commit yourselves to this first session, and then, together, we will consider how we'll proceed from there.

On the telephone you said that Shai was deathly afraid. Can you expand on this?

Rinat: Yes, he has behaviors that we've never seen before. He simply stopped functioning: doesn't want to go to school, won't agree to fall asleep unless one of us stays with him, won't shower alone, even when he goes to the toilet, he leaves the door open.

T: How long has this been going on?

Rinat: About six months, it worsened and now it's impossible.

T: Do you have any ideas as to what this fear is connected to?

Yoram: It seems to me it started over the Passover holidays. Although he has always been the timid type, during the Passover holidays it turned into a really bad situation.

T: Do you have any idea what happened during Passover that caused him to be frightened?

Rinat: (turns to Yoram) It seems to me that it started after you two went on that fun-day, right?

Yoram: Yes, we went to the amusement park and afterwards to a movie, and that same night he wouldn't stay in his room alone, so he came into our bed.

T: What was the movie about?

Yoram: *The Smurfs*, not anything to be afraid of in that…

T: Really? What may seem harmless to us might frighten children to "death." We have quite a few children who come to us for treatment of anxieties and fears, which developed after watching a movie. We even have children who are afraid of clowns and dolls. What we, as adults, perceive as harmless and even funny, is liable to be grasped by children as something very scary and threatening.

Yoram: It doesn't seem reasonable to me that it's connected to the movie. What difference does it make? Why is he so afraid? We need to give him the tools to overcome his fear and that's all.

T: First of all, you will receive the tools for coping and afterwards we will decide if Shai should come in to get his own set of tools. You should understand the crucial role you have in dealing with Shai's fears. I would like to explain to you the meaning of the anxiety we see happening with Shai and where you come into the picture.

Psychoeducational Explanation:

Anxiety is an exaggerated fear, panic, or extreme concern without a rational basis or any genuine immediate threat.

A fear of things that threaten us exists to help us survive, to flee or fight when faced with a dangerous situation. Anxiety appears as a result of negative and frightening thoughts, without any connection to any real danger that might threaten us. In this case, the brain is liable to mark an event or thought as a dangerous thing, and a chain of responses is then created. The purpose of this chain of response is to prepare us for contending with the danger.

This preparation of the body is linked to the release of hormones that enhance the body's alertness and also produce physical manifestations such as a faster heartbeat, quicker breathing, perspiration, and more. Therefore, even when there is no real danger, a person's inner alarm system is activated as if there was a genuine hazard. The individual may experience physiological sensations, which may well frighten him, and this causes him to avoid the perceived element of peril. This situation is liable to lead to a complete evasion, injuring one's mental well-being and one's ability to function day-to-day (Beck, Emery & Greenberg, 1985). As with adults, children too experience the accompanying physiological reactions (shaking, quickening of the heartbeat, stomachaches, etc.). These symptoms are unpleasant and are liable to frighten any child. Most children will experience a sense of anxiety from the appearance of these symptoms and they will attempt to avoid them (Muris, 2007). As a result, expectations and tensions rise in the face of any hint of a threat in the vicinity. Paradoxically, evading the menacing elements (darkness, creatures, witches, monsters, and so forth), over time intensifies the level and frequency of anxiety. The child feels a lack of control and helplessness. Let's try to see this in a graphic manner and then we can better imagine the process Shai goes through:

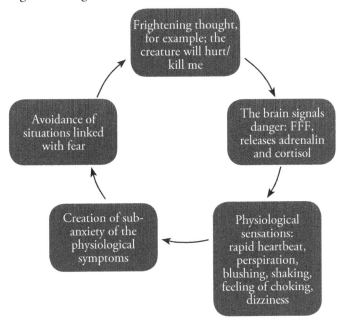

There is a strong probability of a connection between something that happened on your day of fun (amusement park rides, movies, etc.), and an experience of fright and danger. Quite a few children come into treatment with a fear that a creature, witch, monster, movie character and/or other images, might hurt them.

This a life-threatening thought for the child, and this thought activates the amygdala, which is a part of the limbic system of the brain responsible for recognizing dangerous situations and preparing for them. The moment the amygdala identifies a possible danger nearby, it activates an entire survival mechanism, including the release of hormones, in particular, adrenalin and cortisol, which assist in implementing one of the three basic forms of survival existing within us and animals in nature: to **fight**, **flight** or **freeze** (referred to as the **FFF system**). This survival mechanism causes a high level of alertness in all our body's systems so that we can survive when faced with a threatening situation (Beck, Emery & Greenberg, 1985). If we were to encounter a snake, this alertness would enable us to run away from it or attempt to kill the snake.

In my youth, I worked in the kibbutz's dairy farm. I had four years of great times until I reached eighteen years old and began my army service. Once, when I was loading hay with a pitchfork, a very long, very black snake slithered across my boot. It looked about two meters long. Even though I had a pitchfork in my hand and I could have smashed the snake, my automatic reflex was to freeze in place. My breathing halted while I held the pitchfork high above my head. It seemed to me as if I stood like that for many long minutes, not moving, even after the snake had passed on by. When we are in a peril situation – the upper brain – the cortex, responsible for cold and rational thought processes, hardly operates at all. We function automatically according to the survival directions sent from the amygdala.

When I counsel parents about their children's anxieties, I give this example in order to explain the fear mechanism. I check if and when they were frightened, how the three F's functioned with them, and what the physical symptoms they had experienced were.

T: Now that you've heard the explanation for anxiety,

how it develops and intensifies – can you recognize similar processes within yourselves?

Rinat: Without having to dig too deeply, I've known that I have very strong feelings ever since our children were born. When they were first born, every time I had to leave them, I had stomach pains. I had difficulty breathing and I would do anything so that I didn't have to part from them.

T: Without digging to deep, what were you afraid would happen?

Rinat: That something horrible might happen to them. That I wouldn't be there to help them.

T: So let's look at the cycle you developed and then we'll go back to talking about Shai.

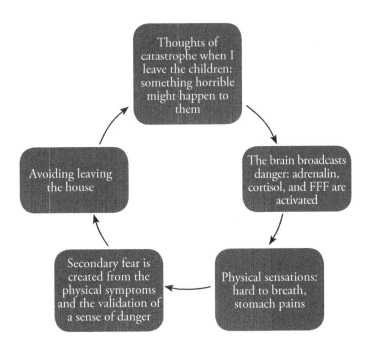

Yoram: For me, ever since I was young I've had anxieties about having head colds. I know it's not very rational, but when I have a cold, I'm afraid I won't be able to breath and I'll choke.

T: You probably do many things to ensure this will not happen.

Yoram: Yes, I regularly take vitamins to strengthen my immune system. If there's someone sick nearby me, I find ways to avoid contact with them. I also try to sterilize all sorts of things. I always carry some sterilizing hand lotion.

T: So, you've developed a whole strategy to prevent yourself from catching a cold, including preventative habits. The difference between you and Shai is that you understand it's not very rational. Yet it's difficult for you to get over the anxiety you've developed. With children of Shai's age, the reality and the imagination are liable to become mixed up. In Shai's experience, he's standing next to a snake; he is facing a real and very frightening threat.

Many children, like Shai, will scream, run away, seek protection with their parents, avoid going to the bathroom, the shower or anywhere else that seems threatening to them. They may be afraid of the dark and afraid to fall asleep. All of these reactions are natural and normal in a situation of anxiety. Our goal in therapy, first with parent training and perhaps later on in direct therapy, is to restore your child's sense of security and control. By using the cycle of anxiety, which we sketched earlier, we can better understand how we intend to do this. We will try to replace the frightening thought with a more practical thought. The body is in constant alertness mode and triggered for approaching danger at every moment, thus we will teach to self-regulate and relax by learning breathing and relaxation methods. We can lessen the avoidance response through exposing the child to the element that frightens him and thus teach the brain that while this may be scary, it is not dangerous. We will teach the child techniques to help him acquire more experiences of control, which also contain elements of fear, without being frightened by them.

These goals cannot be attained without the parents' assistance. The parents will be the most important agents of change for their child. Additionally, without modification, the parents are liable to perpetuate the child's anxiety and possibly even intensify their fears. In general, family processes create, worsen, and maintain dysfunctional patterns of thinking, feeling, and acting (Friedberg, McClure & Garcia, 2009). More specifically, concerning anxiety disorders among children, certain parents are liable to view the child's anxiety as some sort of catastrophe, measuring their own value and capabilities as parents, according to their ability to protect their children, and hence, inadvertently undermine their child's self-efficacy (Ginsberg et al., 2004).

When parents are ready and willing to attempt applying the process for change with their child themselves, it is recommended to use children's books as aids that allow for the creation of a program that is clearly understood by the child. Parent training, with the use of children's literature, fills numerous functions for passing along the message to parents in regards to their parental efficacy and their ability to become primary participants and take an active role in the cognitive change, emotional and behavioral, of their children (Friedberg,

McClure & Garcia, 2009). Many wonderful books have been written for the purpose of enabling children to better cope with fears. I have chosen to bring a working example of mine, *Grandfather Jamiko's Light Switch* (Epel, 2011), and show how this type of work can assist children to overcome situations of fear anxiety.

Grandfather Jamiko's Light Switch (Epel, 2011)

The children's book, *Grandfather Jamiko's Light Switch*, was written as straightforward children's literature of its own right, and as the unfolding tale of a child contending with his fear of an imaginary creature. However, it does represent a form of therapy protocol that enables therapists and parents to work with children who are afraid of all different sorts of things, in particular, imaginary creatures. Even though the book was written as an aid for coping with childhood fears, it is suitable for many types of anxieties on account of the cognitive behavioral process that corresponds with the storyline: normalization, psychoeducational explanation, relaxation techniques, breathing exercises, cognitive structuring, and problem solving.

The book tells the story of Edo, who is frightened by a creature, but reluctant to tell his mother about it. With much sensitivity, his mother encourages him to speak about the creature and Edo's grandfather teaches him how to deal with the scary beast.

The book offers several principles for parents to learn, whether or not they are using the book itself. In the event they are using the book, the parent reads the story to their child, pausing at each page to process the information in an interactive fashion with the child.

The Principles Appearing In the Book and the Manner in Which to Utilize Them When Working With Parents

1. When a child tells us about a fear that he experiences, we should relate to it seriously, expressing understanding and empathy for his fear.

This principle is expressed in the book when the mother shows interest in what Edo is telling her about his fear.

Edo stares down at the ground, as if he's looking for something there.
"I'm scared…," says Edo.
Mother sat on a big rock underneath the pine tree and asked Edo, "Why are you scared?"
"I can't tell you."
"It's not good to keep things inside. If we hold on to things on the inside, it can hurt," said Mother.

Edo's mother encourages him to speak about his fear, but without applying pressure. When Edo tells her about the creature, his mother asks questions and tries to understand his fear.

2. We should help the child to recognize and define his fear, picture it, and give it a name.

In the book, mother helps Edo recognize up-close, the source of his fear. She helps him to conceptualize the fear, give it a name, and draw a picture of it.

"Creature is something small and scary that hides in all sorts of places."
"What kinds of places?" Mother inquires.

"Everywhere, even right here," whispers Edo.
"And what does it look like?" asks Mother.
"It has big eyes, a long bent nose, pointed ears, and sharp teeth, and it changes colors – sometimes it's blue, sometimes red and even yellow."
"Perhaps he's only in your thoughts? Sometimes we all have frightening thoughts," said Mother.
"But the creature is real… he's not only in my thoughts," insisted Edo.
"Maybe you can draw a picture of him for me…that way, if I should ever meet him, I'll know it's him."

At a later stage in the book, Edo gives a name to his frightening creature with the help and instruction of Grandfather Jamiko. Grandfather tells Edo the story of how he found a name for the scary witch that once terrified him:

"I was afraid of a creature that looked like a scary witch. In my house there was a large picture hanging in the living room. The picture was a painting of a boat sailing in the ocean and all around it there were trees dancing in the wind. I thought the boat was the mouth of a witch and the trees were her hair."
"What was she called, Grandpa?" queried Edo.
"I called her Agoonina," replied Grandpa. "What's your creature's name?" inquired Grandpa.
"Don't know. It doesn't have a name. It's just a creature," said Edo.
"So, let's give him a name…" suggested Grandpa.
"Maybe he's the son of Agoonina, so we can call him Agooziggy – Ziggy, for short," Edo proposed.
"Good idea," said Grandpa.

The ability to define the fear and give it a name assists in regulating the feelings of fright when faced with that fear, and enables the experience of sensing a control over them and later on, aids with the process of cognitive restructuring.

3. We can help the child to increase his sense of control over the fear through alterations of the drawing .

Altering the child's drawing promotes cognitive structuring, in that a new focus of attention is set within the picture, one that is associated with the fright stimulus. Changing the picture can be done through humor, metaphors, or any other creative mode, which aids in altering the negative interpretation of the situation in the direction of a more functional perception.

Edo took the drawing out of his pocket and gave it to Grandpa. Taking a pen, Grandpa made all sorts of scribbles on the drawing. But when Grandpa gave the picture back to Edo, all of a sudden Ziggy had round eye-glasses, a clown's hat, and wore a pair of zebra-striped coveralls.

Edo laughed.

"What did you do to Ziggy?" asked Edo.

"When you meet up with Ziggy, you'll see him just like this, or you can change him any way you want to."

In this instance, our aim is to disassociate the link between the scary image and the experience of danger. That is to say, whenever Edo thinks about Ziggy, his image will be less frightening and certainly won't be menacing.

4. We can share a frightening experience from our childhood with the child.

Grandfather Jamiko, who helps Edo with the process of

overcoming his fear, shares with him his own childhood experiences:

Grandpa went on and added: "I was mostly afraid of being left alone, without my mother or father. Every time they went out to the theatre or a movie, I cried and begged them not to go."
"That's exactly what I do," says Edo. "When they are about to leave, I'm convinced the creature will come. My body starts to shake, my heart begins to pound really fast and I'm afraid."

This kind of sharing generates a normalization of the fearful experience, while at the same time it provides a model for the ability to overcome that fear. When the child understands that his significant figures (role models), had similar experiences, he feels that what he himself is experiencing is normal. In the process of acquiring self-efficacy, he learns from his significant figures (role models) that these fears can be conquered. Grandfather Jamiko shares with Edo his own experience with fear as a child, including the solutions he found for getting along with scary creatures. Grandpa became an accessible role model for Edo, and thus, increased Edo's personal experience of self-efficacy (If Grandpa can do it, then so can I).

5. We shall explain to the child about his experience with fear by giving a psychoeducational explanation, which is suited to his age, language skills, and current stage of development. This sort of psychoeducational explanation appears a number of times throughout the book. For instance, when Grandpa explains to Edo about his childhood experience with fear, Grandpa presents the explanation in the form of a metaphor:

Grandpa patted Edo's head and smiled, "When we're afraid, our
brain releases materials that make us feel uneasy.
Our heart beats faster, like a horse galloping through a field.
Our stomach shrinks up like an accordion,
and it's hard for us to breath."
"Yes, Grandpa – that's exactly what happens to me when I think
about the creature…I mean, Ziggy.
Even just talking about it makes my stomach start to hurt…"

Explaining to the child about his experience of fear enables
him to get a sense of control through the knowledge he has
gained, understand the processes he goes through, and lessens
his apprehension of these fears.

Another example of the psychoeducational explanation is when
Grandfather Jamiko explains to Edo about the connection between
thoughts and feelings via the metaphor of "The Gnomes' Home":

"Sometimes the Gnomes sleep a long time. Then the Gnomads wake
up, and when they're awake, we are in a bad mood because they only
think about mean things," says Grandpa. "And another thing…"
Grandpa whispers, "The Gnomes and the Gnomads can't be awake
at the same time. That's why we have to wake up the Gnomes and
put those Gnomads to sleep. That way it'll be nicer for us."

Grandfather Jamiko's explanation of our thought process, in the
form of gnomes, lets Edo understand that he has control over
the thought process and the emotions that adjoin them. We
are the ones who decide which gnomes will be awake. Whether
they be the calming thoughts about the friendly gnomes, or
perhaps, they will be the anxious and scary thoughts about the
worrisome gnomes.

6. We can teach the child to manage his own anxiety without being frightened.

There are two main approaches in cognitive-behavioral therapy directed at an individuals' ability to cope with stressful or fearful situations. One approach adopts the method of distancing the threatening stimulus or declaring cognitive combat against them (Clarke, DeBar & Lewinsohn, 2003), while the other approach accepts the threatening stimulus and accommodates it without judging (Linehan, 1993). In actuality, we are talking about two systems of self-control that will be addressed in depth later on in this book. One system opens up to the experience, whereas the second system shuts down the experiences (Rosenbaum 1998, 2000). *Grandfather Jamiko's Light Switch* contains references to both of these mechanisms. On one hand, Grandfather Jamiko teaches Edo techniques that distance the threatening experience, as in the use of the humorous drawings of the creature or as in the application of self-instruction (details to follow). On the other hand, Grandfather Jamiko teaches Edo techniques for enabling the inclusion of fear without being frightened, such as breathing and smiling. Even the matter of speaking to oneself when facing the creature is not specific to victory or warfare, but rather acceptance and observation, and afterwards, a distancing from a place of control.

"When Ziggy comes, don't be frightened. Just the opposite, smile at him. A smile helps us overcome the fear.
Smile and say to him the magic motto that keeps away the creatures: 'Ziggy... you're here? How are you doing? I don't have time for you right now.
Sorry, see you some other time.'"

7. We'll use metaphors like, "the Gnomes' Home."

Working with young children on the direct cognitive process is quite intricate, since the development of their cognitive processes has not yet matured. Young children are better able to derive benefit from an amusing metaphor (Friedberg, McClure & Garcia, 2009). In the book, there is a wide use of metaphors linked to the psychoeducational explanation and with the tools that aid Edo in coping with his fear. The home of the gnomes is a metaphor, one which helps a child recognize and comprehend the difference between negative thoughts (Gnomads) that cause him to feel uncomfortable, and friendly thoughts (Gnomes), allowing him control when coping with unpleasant situations. Grandfather Jamiko explains to Edo:

"Inside this house, (which everyone has, me and you, too), there live two big families: The Gnoble Family, with their Gnome children and the Gnood Family with their children the Gnomads.
For the Gnoble Family, life is always pleasant and nice because all the Gnomes think only agreeable thoughts.
There's a happy gnome and another gnome who's always gleeful about everything.
In the Gnood family, things aren't so agreeable because the Gnomads think about unpleasant things. There's a nervous Gnomad and a grumpy Gnomad and a worry-wart Gnomad."

When working directly with a child, it is advisable to utilize creative ways to identify their Gnomes and their Gnomads. The child can sketch them, sculpt them, perhaps glue a paper drawing on a popsicle stick, and even hold conversations between the two gnome families as a game played with a parent or therapist.

8. We'll help the child find their own personal light switch.

In the book, *Grandfather Jamiko's Light Switch*, the light switch becomes a constant phrase the child says to himself each time a fear arises, and which helps him to wake up the nice gnomes. This is essentially a self-coping statement, one that helps create a sense of control by way of a cognitive manipulation (Rosenbaum, 1990). A self-coping statement (self-instruction) constitutes the first line of intervention for contending with thoughts that arouse anxiety for the purpose of generating a new cognitive structuring (Friedberg, McClure & Garcia, 2009; Kendall & Suveg, 2006). Self-instruction functions at the speed of thought within the brain. According to Bandura and his colleagues (Bandura et al., 2001), a large part of our upper brain's thinking process is done with the igniting and extinguishing of thoughts and ideas. For instance, behaving according to moral standards or an action, which is opposed to our moral norms, necessitates a rapid ignition or a quick extinguishing, similar to pressing on an electric light switch. The idea of the "light switch" was formed with the intention to change the inner dialog that arouses anxiety and create a new strategy for coping. One of the techniques for finding the light switch is by brain-storming with the child. Sometimes the parent (or the therapist) can suggest a self-instruction phrase, but it's important to remember that self-instruction will be effective only if the child connects cognitively and emotionally to the phrase, which he is meant to repeat to himself. It is important to examine the effectiveness of any self-instruction phrase. The child will need to practice using the self-instruction phrase against threatening stimulus. If the self-instruction phrase does not work, this is a sign the self-instruction is not tailored precisely enough to the child, and we must search for a new self-instructing phrase.

Now that Edo understands the advantages of activating the nice gnomes, Grandfather Jamiko guides him towards finding a self-instruction phrase.

"But how do we wake up the gnomes?" Edo asked.
"We'll turn on the light switch for them," says Grandpa
"And how will I turn on the light switch?" wonders Edo.
"Everyone finds his own light switch," replies Grandpa.
"What's your light switch?" Edo asks Grandpa.
"I take a deep breath, hold the air inside for a moment, then let the air out very, very slowly and whisper to myself:
'I'm strong. I'm not afraid; they're only bad thoughts and that's that. Gnomes, wake up. It's time to work!'"

"I have a light switch," declares Edo:
"Ziggy, Ziggy, diggy, diggy,
He's the gnomad's friend.
Ziggy, Ziggy, diggy, diggy,
Wake up the gnomes."

9. We'll teach the child how to regulate states of arousal with relaxation.

Physiological relaxation, through breathing or muscle relaxation, is a simple and effective way to create a sense of calm, increase the experience of self-control, and regulate negative states of arousal (Kendall et al., 2002).

In the book, *Grandfather Jamiko's Light Switch*, emphasis is placed on two relaxation techniques as regulators of arousal processes. One technique includes slow breathing (Grandpa taught Edo to breathe deeply and release the air very slowly), and the other technique involves relaxation of the body with assistance from the parent ("magic dust").

The magic dust technique was designed to assist the child in regulating emotional stimulation and the tension that accompanies his anxiety. For children who suffer from anxiety, it is difficult to fall asleep. Coping with the dark, separation from the parents, the stipulation of being alone, and their negative connection with the source of a fear (creatures, monsters, ghosts), creates a state of "loss of control" and contributes to the development of night fears (Kushnir & Sadeh, 2012). In order to provide the child with a greater experience of control and a new correlation between going to sleep and relaxation, we can implement the idea of "magic dust," which appears in the book. The idea of sprinkling some "magic dust" before going to sleep helps the child relax as a precondition for sleep and is suitable for children from three years of age and above. The parent tells the child to imagine they have a magic wand in their hand and the wand has the power to relax everything it touches. The parent gradually and thoroughly sprinkles "magic powder" all over the child's body while the magic powder relaxes each area of the body. The parent softly strokes the child from the top of his head down to the tips of his toes, all the while noting each part of the body and tying it into the relaxation experience. For example, "Now the magic powder floats over your eyes and soothes them. Good night eyes." Upon reaching the soles of the feet, the parent will gently rock the child's body while holding the legs and saying, "Now the magic dust is sprinkled all over your body. Your body is relaxed and ready for sleep."

It's a good suggestion to also teach the child about gradual muscle relaxation. This technique teaches a child how to tighten a group of muscles (hands, stomach, legs) for up to eight seconds, and then to quickly relax them all at once. For instance, in the process of tightening the hands, we'll ask the child to imagine he is juicing a lemon and trying to get out all of the juice. In addition, for the process of relaxing the arms and shoulders, we ask the child to imagine he is a drowsy furry kitten who wants to stretch (Koeppen, 1974). A detailed description of Koeppen's (1974) muscle relaxation exercises written in Hebrew can be found on the Shitot Institute's website: http://www.shitot.net.

There are many techniques for teaching children breathing awareness, for instance, by blowing on a candle or blowing soap bubbles. I've found that "breathing through a straw," is a very effective technique for children and adults alike. I learned this technique a few years ago at a yoga workshop somewhere in southern Israel, and I have tailored it for working with children.

Breathing Through a Straw
Every training exercise begins with a psychoeducational explanation for the child. The child must understand what he is doing and why he's doing what's been asked of him. When we are teaching the parents how to instruct their child, we must equip them with the same explanation the child will receive. Meanwhile, the parents can practice in the session room, using role playing games, the explanation they will deliver to the child. Rehearsing the breathing awareness exercises provides an excellent opportunity for initiating collaboration between parents and children in the form of one of the most important techniques for enabling an individual to regulate themselves.

Psychoeducational explanation:
At times of tension, without our being aware of it, we are inclined to have short and shallow breathing or rapid breathing.

Controlling the rate and quality of our breathing causes a decrease in the emergency hormones in the blood and an over-all sense of calm. Slow breathing and the focusing of our attention on breathing is one of the simplest ways to induce relaxation.

For this exercise, we will need a straw, a device which will help us realize the difference between unconscious automatic breathing and slow conscious breathing. For children, we can introduce this exercise as the "Breathing Game" or the "Straw Game."

I ask the parents (or child) to count how many breaths they take during one full minute. A single breath is counted as an inhale and an exhale. Then we record the results. Following this, I request they hold a straw in their mouth, inhaling through the nose, and slowly exhaling through the straw for one minute. The following results will show a decrease of approximately fifty percent or more in the number of breaths after breathing through the straw. In this way, it is easy to demonstrate how we can quickly gain control over our rate of breathing. Continue to practice the straw exercise a number of times during the session and monitor both the parent's and the child's experience. In the majority of cases, relaxation is reported. They are requested to continue practicing the straw breathing exercise at home and even place straws in different places around the home (next to the bed, under the pillow, in a handbag), in order to remind them of the slow breathing and to practice breathing like this during the day.

10. We will give the child reinforcement when he displays behavior of overcoming his fear.
All through the book, Edo receives reinforcement for his

progress. In the work process with the parents, I suggest to them the use of the "Good for Me" game, which we learned earlier, in order to encourage their child while he is overcoming the fear during the day. For example, "Good for you that you took a shower all by yourself, which means you're making an effort to get over the fear and I'm very proud of you."

Dweck (2006), points out the importance of reinforcing the efforts made that contribute to the child's success and not to the child's attributes. Phrases such as, "You've succeeded because you're smart/brave/best," cause the child to develop concerns over disappointing those around him when overcoming challenges he may face. Children who receive reinforcement for the effort invested and their attempt to cope ("How wonderful that you tried and you succeeded"), will more easily endeavor to cope with the next challenge they meet. This in no way contradicts simply complimenting the child without any connection to their behavior (see "Warm" model).

The Process of Working with a Child

Despite the definite importance of focusing on parent training, sometimes pressure is placed on the therapist to meet the child before completing the change process with the parents. As I stated, I do not hurry to meet with the child, in light of all the reasons I mentioned earlier in the book, and also so as not to objectify the child. As a therapist, I must be thoroughly convinced that there is a significant advantage in meeting with the child, as relative to the training sessions with the parents.

After two counseling sessions with Rinat and Yoram, they again requested I meet with Shai. "He's in a terrible state. Now we understand his situation better, but it will take a long time to implement all the things that you've taught us and we prefer you meet with him and work with him." In a case like this, I act according to the parent's wishes and utilize this as a motivation for continuing the treatment. My message to Rinat and Yoram was – I agree to meet him, but on the condition that I continue to meet with you for further instruction. When the parents are active participants in direct therapy with their child, as we will see later on, the treatment process can be brief and highly effective.

In the first session with the child, it is the child's choice whether or not to invite the parents into the therapy room with him or for them to wait outside in the reception room. The parents' presence is an important resource for therapy. Their attendance in sessions enables me to pass along the same messages to the parents and the child simultaneously. It allows the child to be better understood by the parents and lets the parents – via the therapist's modeling – learn how they ought to respond to the child, on a verbal and nonverbal level. Many parents, who accompany their child during therapy sessions, absorb the verbal and nonverbal information and use it with the child outside of therapy sessions. Some parents will go through a therapy process of their own concurrently with the child, on account of the anxiety, which they themselves also experience. The parents learn about the anxiety, comprehend it, identify it, and ascertain how to manage the anxiety. In the case where a child enters the session alone, it is recommended to allow ten to fifteen minutes at the end of the session for sharing with the parents what took place in therapy. Before asking the parents in, it is advisable to coordinate with the child, which items are to be shared with the parent. Involving the parent at the conclusion of a session accords the child the opportunity to summarize for himself, and afterwards, by speaking aloud, to tell about the process he went through in session. The child's problems become more comprehendible to the parent and they become witnesses of the process their child is going through. Many parents reinforce their child at this stage and this strengthens the child's sense of self-efficacy and self-esteem. In addition, often at the conclusion of a session, we will update the parent, or parents, on the homework assignments the child was given. Sometimes we require the assistance of the parent in order to complete those tasks (this is especially critical during the processes of exposures where the child has to carry out exercises: driving the child to various places when the child suffers from agoraphobia, giving the child money to buy something at the store when a child has social anxieties, and so on…).

Shai asked to enter the therapy room with his father. It is apparent that Shai is somewhat introverted, clings to his father, and displays sporadic eye contact. He seems to me to be embarrassed and bashful. After about ten minutes of "defrosting," where we spoke of school, what he likes to do, and my role (helping children solve problems), I began to guide the session towards its intended purpose.

T: I understand from your mother and father that sometimes you are afraid and that's why you came here. It's important to me to tell you that most children your age are afraid of something (normalization). This is completely natural, but it's possible to help you get over the fear. So that we can help you, we'll try to get to know your fear. Is that okay? So, tell me a bit about this fear.

Shai: I don't know how to describe it.

T: Can you tell me when it began?

Shai: I don't know exactly.

T: I have a game that can help us. Let's play "Hot/Cold." I'll tell you all sorts of things that children are afraid of, and if it's close to your fear, then say it's "getting hot," and if it's really far from your fear then you say, "cold." Agreed?

Shai: Yes.

T: Clown?

Shai: Cold.

T: Animal?

Shai: Cold.

T: Witch?

Shai: Hmmm…not exactly.

T: Monster?

Shai: Stop, don't say that.

T: Does that mean it's "hot"?

Shai: Sort of.

T: Can you draw me a picture of it?

At this point, Shai drew a picture, which looks to me like a "monster."

T:	What would you call what you've drawn?
Shai:	It doesn't have a name.
T:	So, let's find it a name.
Shai:	But I don't have one.
T:	Dad, do you have an idea for a name?
Dad:	Hmmm… (Smiles)
T:	Dad, were you afraid of monsters or creatures when you were Shai's age? (Normalization)
Dad:	Yes, I was afraid of a neighbor who looked like a witch to me. I would imagine she was a witch, with a witch's laugh, and I was really scared of her. I was even afraid to leave the house because I thought she might come out.
T:	Was she really a witch?
Dad:	No, she never talked and only looked at us when we went by, but I imagined all kinds of things…
T:	Did she have a name?
Dad:	She was called Birdy, but my brothers and I called her Birdzilla, because besides that, she looked scary. She had crossed-eyes.
T:	Seems to me that there's no one who wasn't afraid of something as a child. Dad, how did you handle the fear?
Dad:	My parents explained to me that she was a poor woman who had been through many hardships in life. They tried to help her with all sorts of things and they told me she was a nice lady and never hurt anyone.
T:	Shai, what do you think when you hear that story?
Shai:	Dad, why didn't you ever tell me? Is that lady already dead?
Dad:	Yes, she died a long time ago.

Shai: Do you have a picture of her?

T: What Dad has told us is very interesting to you, correct? You'll probably ask a lot of questions about that lady; it's quite intriguing. Dad, are you curious to know about Shai's fear?

Dad: Very. He only told me that he's afraid. But until today, I didn't know what he was afraid of.

T: We don't really know Shai's fear yet. But when you see Shai's drawing and understand that something is frightening him, what goes through your mind? Do you think he can get over the fear like you did?

Dad: Of course. Probably even better than me.

T: I think so, too. But for that to happen, we'll need to get to know and understand the fear. That way it will be much easier for us to get along with the fear.

The purpose of the session was to identify, understand, and express the fear in order to strengthen the child's experience of control. However, it is not always so simple, and therefore, flexibility is necessary for smooth working, while at the same time, attempting to return to the treatment's goal. Our aim during the first stage is to recognize the fear. Shai gave a name to the monster he drew: "Gargamella." Then we realized the monster was related to "Gargamel," the evil character who chases after the Smurfs (which was the movie he saw with his father at the amusement park). Not surprisingly, there were clues in Shai's drawing. Many times children develop an anxiety after watching a movie. Due to the thought processes that characterize young children, they are convinced the image they saw in the movie presents an actual threat in reality. In the assessment process we ask when the fear began, but it is important to also ask the child if they have any idea why the fear appeared. Did they hear a scary story? Had they seen or heard something frightening? Did they watch a movie that scared them? Many times childhood fears are linked to triggers in the child's environment and it is important to locate them in order to initiate a change in the conditioning that has formed within the child.

At a preventive level, it is immensely important that the parents check with their child what kinds of content he has been exposed to in order to mediate reality for them. Quite a few children are embarrassed to talk about their fear because it makes them seem weak. For this reason, when parents are present in session with a child, we normalize through them, the child's situation and validate his feelings (as was done with Shai) and a great importance is placed on the explanation the child will receive concerning his situation. A psychoeducational explanation immediately lessens many worries with the adults and the children. An understanding of cognitive, emotional, and behavioral processes is formulated and then linked to the distressing experience, which the child is contending with. This understanding creates a sense of control, power, and the motivation for change. At this point, Shai and his father receive a psychoeducational explanation of fear.

Psychoeducational Explanation for the Child:

T: Shai, do you have an idea why it is important to be afraid?

Shai: So we can run away.

T: Exactly so. Nature is very smart. With us and with the animals, fear helps us survive and better cope in dangerous situations. Let's try to understand how fear works. When you are afraid, do you have many kinds of sensations in your body?

Shai: Yes, my heart pounds. It's scary (clings to father).

T: Let's understand why our heart pounds so hard when we're afraid. Imagine you run into a snake. Is a snake dangerous?

Shai: Very.

T: That's right. Many snakes are dangerous. So what should you do if you see a snake?

Shai: Run away.

T: Correct. What should the body do so that we have the strength to run away?

Shai: Don't know.

T: We need to breathe in a lot of oxygen so that the body will have plenty of strength to run away. When we feel danger, the body has a mechanism that works like an electrical switch, and this turns on a whole system so that we can run away quickly. The heart beats harder to pump blood throughout the body, the muscles tighten up in preparation for action, and our whole body readies for survival. But when there's not really any snake – and the brain only thinks there's a danger – all those sensations remain and since they feel unpleasant and strange to us, we're afraid to feel them. Are you afraid to feel all those sensations in your body when you're scared?

Shai: Yes.

T: That is natural. None of us likes to feel uncomfortable sensations. For instance, if I pinch your hand very hard, it will be uncomfortable, right? Want to try it?

Shai: Okay, but I want Dad to pinch me.

T: Gladly. Dad, will you pinch really hard on the skin between the thumb and the index finger of Shai's hand? I want to ask you, Shai, to tell me how uncomfortable it felt from one to ten. Ten is the most uncomfortable.

(Dad pinches as instructed.)

Shai: Eight.
T: How many seconds do you think you can stand the painful feeling?
Shai: Ten seconds.
T: Dad, please pinch the same spot on Shai's hand again, and this time we will time how long he can stand the unpleasant feeling.

Shai managed to put up with the pain for more than a minute.

T: What can we understand from this exercise, Shai?
Shai: That Dad is strong (we all laugh…).
T: Dad, what do you understand from the exercise, besides being strong?
Dad: I actually learned that Shai is really strong. He managed to put up with the pain for more than a minute.
T: Dad, I think the same thing as you. When we are able to cope with something unpleasant, it means we are strong. When we are afraid, we have an unpleasant feeling in our body – the problem is we are very frightened by those sensations. This is interesting since sometimes we have the exact same sensations when, in contrast, we are doing things that are actually fun for us. For example, think for a moment of a singer you

Shai: really like. Imagine you are going to meet them. What sorts of feelings are going on in your body now?

Shai: When I met Yuval Hamebulbal, my heart was beating so hard.

T: That's it exactly. When we are happily excited, those sensations are also present: a pounding heart, butterflies in your belly. When is another time you were happily excited?

Shai: On my birthday, when my cousins came. I hadn't seen them for a while. And when my Grandpa brought me the game that I wanted most of all.

T: Do you remember what you felt in your body?

Shai: Not really.

T: Dad, do you remember what you feel in your body when you have a happy excitement?

Dad: Of course. A pounding heart and butterflies in my stomach.

T: Those are sensations similar to feelings of fear, aren't they? Only that when we get excited, we aren't frightened by the feelings and with fear, we are frightened. Because we are frightened by these feelings, we stop doing all sorts of things. There are children who don't want to bathe alone and are afraid to sleep in their own beds. What's it like for you Shai?

Shai: (Lowers his head, grins, and clings to his father).

T: Maybe your father can help us, since he's seen your behavior...

Dad: (Hugs Shai) For a long time now, Shai is afraid to go to sleep, scared when it gets dark, frightened to shower or go to the bathroom alone, and clings to us all the time.

T: Everything that Dad has described is very natural when we are afraid. When it gets dark, what goes through your mind?

Shai: That soon it will be nighttime and I hate nighttime.

T: Because...

Shai: Then the monster comes.

T: Do you mean Gargamella? What happens when she comes?

Shai: Stop, I can't talk about it...

T: Are you afraid to talk about it?

Shai: Yes.

T: This is a good time to check what's going on in your body right now. Notice how the sensations in the body change when we're scared. What might really help us is to breathe the fear out. Take a deep breath, you can close your eyes, too. Dad, you're invited to breathe as well. We are breathing slowly in order to tell the brain that everything is all right and there's no reason to be afraid. Then, just like the mechanism that confuses our body is turned on, slowly, slowly, the mechanism for making us calm and quiet is switched on instead. If you want, you can raise your arms every time you take a breath and when you let the air out, slowly, slowly, lower your arms. Because it's difficult for you to talk about Gargamella, we'll go back to the picture you drew. Let's look at the picture together. Does it remind us of anything that's not scary at all, maybe even funny? To me, Gargamella looks like she's afraid herself, she has frightened eyes. I wonder what she's afraid of.

Dad: It's not nice for me to say, but to me it looks like she is making doo-doo...

All of us: (Laughing to tears…)

T: Shai, what do you think? Maybe you can imagine she's trying really hard to make poo? Can you add that to the drawing?

Shai drew Gargamella making poo and added an annoying fly sitting on her nose.

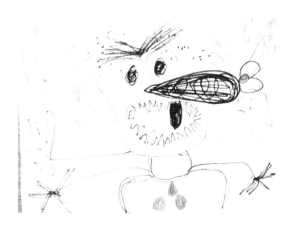

Integrating humor is marvelous for clients and especially for children. In spite of Shai's high level of anxiety, the session was characterized by a positive atmosphere, which inspired Shai's motivation for further work. Shai received a homework assignment to do at home: every time he thinks, or imagines, Gargamella, he has to picture her making "number two" and fighting off the fly on her nose.

In the next session, it will be easier to do cognitive-emotional work on the fear. Generally, we will aspire to pinpoint those thoughts that stand as the basis for the fear. We will want to teach the child about the connection between those thoughts and his sense of fear. However, it's not always possible because of the age of the child or his level of development and ability to cooperate. In the event that it is difficult to create a linear process, where the child learns that each behavior is linked to a preceding thought, it's better in the first stage, for the therapist to be the initiator of the problem solving process. The therapist will designate the goal of the first session and implement the process of intervention. The second session with Shai included coming up with a self-instructing phrase.

Turning on the Light Switch: Discovering Self-Instruction

In the book, *Grandfather Jamiko's Light Switch* (Epel, 2011), the guiding self-coping statement (self-instruction) appears in the form of a "light switch," which Edo turns on to wake up the gnomes. It is possible to find self-instructional phrases with the aid of the book and ask the child what his light switch would be. However, it is also possible to do an additional process in order to ensure the self-talk statement is exactly suited for the child.

Self-instruction is an inner dictum whose purpose is to replace negative automatic thoughts. From the vantage point of the thinking process, this acts as a sort of light switch. When we are held back by negative thinking (as in this case, frightening thoughts), the mind focuses its attention on every negative thing, internal or external, which actually intensifies the fear. As a result, a cycle of negative and fearful thinking is created. An effective self-coping statement immediately enables the client to guide his attention towards more positive and practical thinking. When working with teenagers and adults, it's best to come up with a self-instructing phrase after a thorough and comprehensive process of clarifying automatic thoughts, conditioned thoughts, and core beliefs. The more precise and exact the self-talk phrase is to one's core beliefs, so too will be its efficacy. The self-guiding statement is based on compelling corrective thoughts, which are specific to an individual. There isn't one self-instruction phrase suitable for all clients. A meticulous process is required for finding the most efficacious self-statement for each individual.

With younger children, it is harder to develop a linear progression, which begins with clarifying automatic thoughts and concludes with discovering a precise self-instruction. In cases like these, we can "flood" with numerous alternative phrases. In Shai's case, we brain-stormed together with his father and wrote down all the sentences that might "give us power" over Gargamella. Here are some samples of those phrases:

I'm strong. I'm safe – Gargamella, stop making a mess.
Gargamella – go take a poo.
Oh my, you have a fly on your nose.
It's a little scary, but not dangerous.

When searching for a self-instructing phrase, we can use a process of elimination. With adults, we are aided by guided imagery along with grading the phrases from one (not so good) to ten (excellent phrase). With children, we work more with grading the self-instruction, combining rhythm or even melody, hand movements, hand-clapping, and so forth. The marks that Shai gave for the self-coping statements were as follows:

I'm strong. I'm safe – Gargamella, stop making a mess. – 8
Gargamella – go take a poo. – 10
Oh my, you have a fly on your nose. – 8
It's a little scary, but not dangerous. – 9

Eventually, we played around with the phrases and arrived at a self-instruction, "It's scary, but not dangerous; I'm strong and safe." A self-guiding statement like this is capable of being more effective than the phrase that was rated ten (Gargamella – go take a poo), since it is broader and responds to a wider variety of situations. Nonetheless, we won't waive the self-instruction that received the highest mark, so we chose to make a combination of two phrases. This is the assignment Shai was given to do at home:

1. Hang the funny drawing on the wall. In the morning, when Shai wakes up, he has to look at the picture, say, "Good morning" to Gargamella, with a smile, and ask, What? You haven't made doo-doo yet? Go take a poo! This assignment made Shai laugh. We rehearsed it several times. Shai received reinforcement from his father and myself for each time he successfully completed the exercise.

2. During the day, and especially after dark, Shai has been asked to say the self-instruction he chose ("It's scary, but not dangerous; I'm strong and safe"), particularly when the fear becomes more intense.

In the next session, Shai and his father reported an improvement in moods and on clinging less to his parents over the past week. Before reaching the next stage of exposures, it's important to me that Shai understand the pathways of anxiety and what is worthwhile doing in order to make a change.

T: Shai, good for you. You've succeeded in completing the homework assignments. Thanks to your efforts to overcome your fear of Gargamella, especially due to your completing the assignments, there's been an improvement. The assignments were meant to send a message to your brain that Gargamella isn't dangerous at all.

Shai: This week I wasn't afraid of her.

Dad: But you still won't go to the bathroom or shower alone, and you're still afraid to fall asleep alone.

T: This means we have more work to do but we're moving in the right direction. In order for your brain to understand there isn't any danger in the shower, bathroom, or bedroom, we need to prove it. This is the reason we will be moving into a really important stage of treatment, where we do scary things on purpose. In this phase we'll do things that you specifically avoid doing because of the fear. Let's try to understand why it's so important to actually fool the fear. I'd like for us to write down together the process of fear and what we can tell ourselves about it.

We traced out different diagrams, which Shai wrote himself. It took him quite a while to write them since he hasn't yet completely mastered writing skills, but he very much enjoyed writing them himself and getting our help from time to time. Below is an example of one of the diagrams, containing the relating psychoeducational explanations and self-talk:

I'm afraid of Gargamella. Gargamella is a scary monster and she can hurt me.

It's natural to be afraid at my age. Can she really hurt me? It's only scary but not dangerous.

The brain activates a system that helps me when I'm afraid. I breathe faster to take in more oxygen. The muscles tighten and the heart beats faster and harder.

That's how the body behaves when it's afraid. It's not comfortable but it's not dangerous.

I'm afraid to feel like that and I won't go into the shower. The dark scares me because maybe the monster will be there.

I'll get into the shower anyway. I'll smile at Gargamella and tell her to go make a doody.

In the next step, we drew up a list of things that Shai doesn't do on account of his being afraid of Gargamella, and we graded the intensity of the fear from zero to ten (the peak of fear). For example, getting into the shower alone (9), going to the bathroom alone (8), going to sleep alone (10), going into the bedroom at night (5), staying in the bedroom alone with the door closed (10), and so on...The list was long and we decided to begin the exposure process right then and there, in the situations with the lowest grades of anxiety, going into the bedroom at night with the door open.

While exposures with adults are done symmetrically, with children it's preferable that the exposures be accompanied by a pleasurable and playful experience in order to more easily create new conditioning. It's possible to devise graduated exposures that include positive reinforcement according to the progress of the exposure process. At this stage of the process, it is suitable to integrate games that encourage and motivate further exposure, and the desired change upon the negative conditioning that had been formed. With Shai, there was a lessening of his fear of Gargamella, but regrettably the conditioning for fear of the dark and being alone were already well established (in the bedroom, in the shower, and the toilet). For this reason, we moved along to the stage of "Fight the Fright" games.

Fight the Fright Games
Darkness Games

The purpose of this game is to desensitize the fear of the dark, by means of exposure combined with a game. To begin, the exposure takes place in the therapy room together with the parents, while we gradually dim the lights until the room is in total darkness. The exposure exercise should only be implemented at home after practicing it in the session room. While remaining in the dark, it's possible, for instance, to play guessing games such as, which letters are drawn on the back of a hand, or the thumb game, where hands are held cross-wise while the thumbs of the parent and the child are trying to "catch" one another. For the next stage, the parent will sit at a distance from their child on the other side of the room, while singing a song. After this step, the parent will exit the therapy room while continuing to sing the song from the other side of the door. Following this step, playing the game will be timed. Can you remain alone in the room for five seconds? The time is measured with a stopwatch and in each round the time lapse is increased. The length of time the child manages to remain alone in the therapy room determines the exposure time used for playing the game at home. Which is to say, if we succeeded in reaching an exposure time of twenty seconds alone in the darkened therapy room, then the assignment at home will be to remain alone in the darkened room every day for twenty seconds. In every exposure process, there is continuous monitoring of anxiety levels (How afraid were you from one to ten?), along with a review of techniques that will aid the child when coping with challenges. For example, saying the self-instruction phrase, regulated breathing, physical relaxation, singing a song, guided imagery, hand-clapping, and so forth. Reinforcing Shai's success at each stage of the process is done with symbolic reinforcement alone (Good for you. You've succeeded; that means you can go on to the next stage) and not practical or social reinforcement. It's also possible to use these types of reinforcement according to the child's needs.

Beyond the consistent process of desensitizing, it is advisable to integrate games, which aren't necessarily included in systematic exposure, since they aid in building a child's fortitude when facing fear and anxiety by simply participating in the experience of the game. One of these games is called, "Witch-Watch." This is a game played in the dark, which my children particularly enjoyed. This game produces positive excitement, pleasure, and cooperation between all members of the family, and combines some direct exposure for the fears of darkness and scary creatures.

The Witch-Watch Game

The Witch-Watch game is one I played with my children when they were small. They loved the game so much that we kept on playing it for many years, even after they had grown older...

As we have already mentioned, games that parents and children play together strengthen the sense of belonging for both the parents and their children while providing a strong foundation for building a child's psychological resilience. This particular game causes a high level of excitement, but one that is positive and enjoyable. In addition, the game lets the parents practice playfulness, since in order for the game to succeed, the parents must step outside their usual boundaries of familiar behavior patterns and truly play a game.

How to play the game;
The mother or father (or the therapist, at the learning stage) plays the witch. The children remain in a room that is completely dark. The instructions for the children are as follows:

Soon a witch who wants to eat you will enter the room; you can melt her, but only under these three conditions:

1. If you smile and she sees your white teeth in the dark,
2. If you say magic words that chase away fears (such as, "We're not afraid; we're brave," "Hey witch, you're not scary," "We're not afraid of you – fly far, far away").
3. If you clap your hands three times.

In the first stage, one of the parents is in the room with the children. Everyone gets under a blanket, covering even the head, so that the whole body is covered. The other parent is on the outside of the room's closed door and begins to drum on the door with their hands, at first quietly and then louder. For the courageous among us, at this point, we might want to add a loud scary laugh, like witches' laughter. When the parent/witch enters the room, they say things such as, "I'm a witch, big and strong, and I like to eat big children and little children, yellow children and green children…" While saying these things in the tone of a witch, the parent/witch tickles the children and the other parent who is in the room with them. From the clinical experience that we have gathered in the use of this game, we found that in the beginning, the children melt the witch right away, but after a few times, they prefer to keep up the state of heightened excitement. The next step is for one of the children to play the role of the witch. In homes where all the members of the family play the game together, often times they each take turns and most of the time the children choose to be the witch "bait" and not the witch herself.

Shai and his parents implemented the exposures extraordinarily well, including the witch game, played with the whole family. The willingness of the parents and Shai's cooperation brought about much change; within eight sessions, there was a dramatic decrease in Shai's feelings of fear and the resulting avoidance. Towards the conclusion of treatment, we dedicated an entire session to summarizing and to relapse prevention.

T: Shai, as agreed, we are about to move on to the next stage of treatment, and we will meet again in one month for a follow-up session. A month from now we'll check together how you have applied everything you've learned here. How Gargamella is doing and how you are getting along with "fooling the fear." It's important to me to prepare you for the coming month and the following months after that, because there will be times when the fear mounts. The fear may come due to Gargamella or because of other things, and so we will make a plan of what needs to be done in case that happens. Let's begin with you choosing two cards

from the deck (from Bikovsky's "Feel Me" cards), one
that reflects how you were feeling when you first came
here and the other to describe how you feel now.

Shai chose two cards.

T: Excellent. Now we'll tape them to the page, in their
proper place, and check what helped you get from the
first card, which shows you when you arrived here, to
the second card, which illustrates how you are today.

We had a fruitful discussion about the tools that had helped
Shai: turning on the light switch (the self-instruction), smiling
at Gargamella, breathing through a straw, muscle relaxation,
and fooling the fear (exposures). Shai's father and I helped
remind him of the tools that had been forgotten. Shai and his
father then wrote them down on the page. Following that, we
searched for a self-instruction phrase, one that would be useful
for any fears that might come along later. Shai came up with
this one: "Fear, fly away like a witch. I'm turning on the light
switch."

I photo-copied the page that Shai and his father made, and
gave it to Shai. We agreed that if the fear comes back, this page
will remind him what he needs to do about it. Father suggested
they laminate the page and Shai decided to hang it above his
bed.

Shai started by asking himself how he felt when he arrived
– then he chose a card showing how he feels after the session.

In Handwriting

How was I when I got here? (top)

How am I now? (bottom)

What helped me? (left side)

Telling the fear to buzz off, Gargamella poops and waves a fly from her nose.

Breathe through a straw and smile at the fear (left bottom)

What do I tell myself when fear appears? (right side)

Run away fear. I am pushing the courage button. (right bottom)

Shai continued with regular monthly follow-up sessions for three more months, and afterwards, we said our goodbyes.

2. "Storm in a Barrel" – Treating Anger and Aggression

Behavior problems among children and adolescents constitutes one of the greatest challenges facing parents, teachers, and professional people, due to the possibility of injury to others entailed in behavior issues. Accepted practice is to relate to behavioral disorders chronologically, at a developmental level, beginning with Oppositional Defiant Disorder (ODD), characterized by patterns of hostility and rebelliousness towards childhood figures of authority, continuing on to conduct disorders expressed as patterns of injury to others and the violation of social norms during adolescence, and then dealing with anti-social personality disorders from adolescence onward, typified by disregarding the rights of others and displaying a lack of morality and empathy.

The common denominator between all behavior disorders, with no relation to age, is aggressive behavior. Aggression is defined as behavior intended to cause harm to another individual who wants to avoid injury (Anderson & Bushman, 2002; Joireman, Anderson & Strathman, 2003). Children who already display chronic physical aggression at pre-school age are found to have the highest risk for physical aggression and criminality during adolescence (Broidy et al., 2003).

Aggression constitutes one of the principle and most concerning social problems in the western world due to the grave consequences it imposes upon individuals and groups (Bandura, 1973), and is found at the center of psychological research (Anderson & Bushman, 2002). In the last few decades, there has been a marked rise in the frequency and intensity of aggressive behavior (Kazdin, 2003), all over the world, and in Israeli society in particular, especially among children and adolescents (Ronen, Rahav & Moldawsky, 2007). Research findings indicate that the phenomenon exists among children and adolescents of different ages, populations, and geographic areas. We are witnessing aggression in schools, at clubs, on the sports field, in shopping centers, and at entertainment and amusement sites. Beyond the injuring of others, aggression demands a high personal cost. Aggressive children, who do not learn to adopt pro-social behavior, pay a high price for aggression throughout their lives. Their aggression has far-reaching consequences upon their maturation, their relations with family members, their children, their place of work, and friends (Tremblay, 1999).

Broidy et al. (2003), in their long running research spanning over a decade, in different countries, found that with most children there is a decrease in physical aggression as they grow older, while only a small percentage of children demonstrating severe chronic physical aggression in childhood, continue to express physical aggression at a later age. These young children are found to be at significant risk of developing severe behavior problems as adolescents, including criminal behavior. A second advocacy of these findings is provided in the research done by Campbell and her colleagues (2006), where it is shown that when children demonstrate a higher level of physical aggression, so the aggression is more constant over the years and linked to higher levels of behavior issues and lack of adaptation.

Aggression is the product of an individual's internal processes while interacting with external-environmental factors, combined with cognitive, emotional, and behavioral development (Bandura & Walters, 2010; Bandura et al., 2001). In these processes, a person's self-regulation mechanisms play a central role, allowing one to take control of aggressive behavior.

Physical aggression, expressed by intentionally causing

physical harm to another, includes cognitive and emotional elements. The cognitive component is linked to an individual's hostile thoughts and is related to fixed negative thinking concerning his surroundings (Anderson & Bushman, 2002). The source of this type of thinking stems from the manner in which an individual encodes social situations, interprets them as threatening or unjust, and therefore, not worthy of their trust. During the processing of social information, there exists among children with hostile thoughts, a tendency to interpret situations in a negative and erroneous fashion and to connect hostile intentions to others, an interpretation that leads to aggressive behavior (Crick & Dodge, 1994; Dodge et al., 2002).

The emotional element associated with aggression is anger (Buss, 1961). Usually anger is short-lived, yet among those with characteristic hostile thinking, the anger is liable to continue for a longer period of time (Bushman et al., 2005; Denson, Pederson & Miller, 2006). This type of anger enables an individual to preserve their aggressive intentions over time by means of deepening their memory of the event and increasing his intent to harm others (Berkowitz, 1990). Control over anger is achieved when one is capable of identifying emotional stimulation and interpret it as anger; comprehend, interpret, and evaluate the angry feeling that is being experienced; and express that anger in a manner that will benefit the individual (Southam-Gerow & Kendall, 2002).

There is a direct positive relation between the three elements of aggression: anger, hostility, and physical aggression. The higher the levels of hostility and anger, so the level of aggression is higher (Epel, 2007; Buss & Perry, 1992; Crick & Dodge, 1994; Dodge et al., 2002).

We can exhibit this graphically in the following manner:

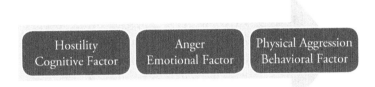

There are children who are capable of controlling their aggressive behavior in spite of hostile thoughts and feelings of anger (Epel, 2007). Who are these children?

The Art of Self-Control and Pro-Social Values

Children, who are able to control their behavior in spite of hostile thoughts and feelings of anger, are endowed with high skill levels of self-control and well developed pro-social values (Epel, 2007). These children adhere to the attitude that it is important to them not to hurt another person, even when this value is confronted by other doctrines, such as hedonism, ambitiousness, and so on (Chadha & Misra, 2004).

In contrast, children who have not adopted pro-social principles and acceptable social norms have difficulty relating to the needs, feelings, and rights of others (Hastings et al., 2000; Ludwig & Pittman, 1999). These children are more offensive, more hostile, less social, less emphatic, and less cooperative with those around them (Dodge et al., 2002; Eisenberg, 2006).

Therefore, children with high pro-social orientation, which is expressed by giving assistance, co-operation, and empathy, will have significantly less negative thoughts, hostility, and vindictiveness, and they will be less aggressive towards others. Although, pro-social attitudes alone are not enough to prevent hurtful behavior. In order for a child to be able to control his aggressive behavior and not injure others, he must be equipped with the art of self-control (Epel, 2007). Self-control is comprised of a collection of cognitive skills enabling a person to overcome and change behavior without external coercion (Ronen, 1992), when coping with emotions, thoughts, pain, and other obstacles, which interfere with the proper implementation of purposeful intended behavior (Rosenbaum, 1990).

Children can be differentiated from one another according to their skills of self-control and their social goals and principles. A child with positive social aims (not to hurt others, to get along with the other children, etc…), will endeavor to utilize the art of self-control in order to achieve his social goals. In this type of situation, in spite of any heightened hostility and anger the child experiences, he won't express his feelings with aggressive behavior. We find that in circumstances where a child retains high pro-social values and self-control skills, he won't express physical or verbal aggressive behaviors, even when he is feeling hostile and angry (Epel, 2007).

The therapist's ability to understand the aggressive behavior of children and adolescents based on these two variables, the art of self-control and pro-social principles, is most significant for diagnosis and treatment (Epel, 2007, 2012).

In fact, we find that theoretically there are two pivotal points around which we should examine the aggressive behavior of children: the axis of pro-social values and the axis of self-control skills.

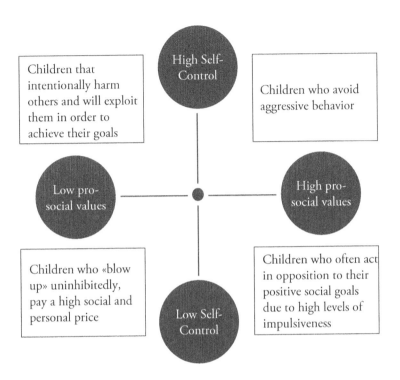

When pro-social values and self-control skills are high, a child will tend to avoid aggressive behavior. When the pro-social values are low, but the child has high self-control, there is liable to be intentional injury to others in order to attain their desires. In these cases, it is important to work with the child on acquiring pro-social values in order to lessen the aggression. When the pro-social values are high and self-control skills are low, the child will not be able to achieve his aims and may harm others due to his impulsive reactions. If this is the case, it is important to equip the child with the art of self-control. In this way, he can realize his social goals. When pro-social values and self-control are low, the environment and the child himself are at risk, and this may take a high toll on all concerned. These children have the highest levels of aggression (Epel, 2007) and treatment with them requires the instilling of pro-social principles in addition to self-control skills.

The implication of these findings is that when we prepare to construct an intervention plan for lessening aggression with these children, it's highly advantageous to take into account their value system in addition to self-control proficiency. Contrastingly, in practice, personal and group therapy with children suffering from behavior disorders is mainly focused on acquiring self-control skills, which will enable the children to better cope in different situations (Ronen, 2005). The main difficulty in existing therapy approaches is that there is no differentiation made between children who need to obtain self-control skills and those that are in need of encouragement for the development of their pro-social values.

In this chapter, I will bring two examples of therapy intervention: treatment of a child with low pro-social standards who harms his surroundings, and treatment of a child with high social standards and low self-control, which do not allow him to effectively express his social values.

Skateboards and Pro-Social Values

Aviv is twelve years old. He has come for treatment as one of the conditions the school has set for continuing his attendance there. By the second grade, Aviv was already diagnosed with Oppositional Defiant Disorder (ODD), which was characterized by his not entering the classroom, not recognizing authority, loitering, offensive and abusive speech towards the school's staff, along with exploiting and extorting children younger than himself.

The dialog with Aviv was complicated. He would hide his face under his cap. His cooperation was meager in spite of my many attempts to reach him. The first breakthrough in therapy happened when I explained to him what causes us to hurt others.

T: I want to talk to you about the reasons we might injure someone else. I treated someone your age a few years ago and he told me that when he insults a teacher or threatens someone, he feels strong. He feels in control. Do you know anyone like that?

Aviv: Yes.

T: There's no one in the world who doesn't like to feel strong and wants things to go the way they want them to. Don't you agree?

Aviv: Yes.

T: The question is, how do we get what we want? How much do we take into account the existence of others and that maybe they want different things than we do?

Aviv: I don't care about other people.

T: You don't care about all the people in the world or is there maybe one person you do care about?

Aviv: I don't care about anyone.

T: Yourself, maybe?

Aviv: Not really.

T: It's not easy to live like that. In fact, you can't really enjoy what life has to offer you. I'd like to give you a gift. A big present for living life, and that gift is the ability to develop concern for yourself and for others.

Aviv: Not a chance.

T: I don't give up so easily. I think it's a waste if you can't enjoy what the world has to offer, and I think it's even more of a waste if the world can't enjoy what you have to offer.

Aviv: I've got nothing to offer.

T: There's no such thing. You weren't born for no reason. There's no person that doesn't have a gift to give the world. There are people who don't know what their gift is and there are people who know but choose not to give. Sometimes they choose to cause hurt, and there are those that give their gift to the world and the world gives them all sorts of gifts in return. Those are the people that benefit the most. Which are you?

Aviv: Me? I don't have any gifts for the world. I don't even understand what gifts you're talking about.

T: I'll give you an example from my life. I help people feel better. When I succeed it fills me with joy. I feel I have a purpose in life. Helping others makes me feel that I have given a gift to others. Not a tangible gift, but an emotional gift, a favor for the heart. But I also receive heartfelt presents from them, such as gratitude, appreciation, love, and a bond. Have you ever felt that when you do something it gives you a feeling of joy?

Aviv: Only when I'm skateboarding.

T: Describe to me the feeling you get when you're skateboarding.

Aviv: It's fun like, I don't know how to describe it.

T: From what I understand, you have to know how to control the skateboard, then you can succeed to do whatever you want to, right?

Aviv: Yes.

T: Life is like that, too. We want to do something
       and in order to achieve it, we have to control our
       movements. Exactly like on a skateboard, you have
       to direct yourself along the course. It is the same in
       life. We have to direct ourselves. We are the ones who
       decide what we will be. Can you control a skateboard?

Aviv: Of course.

T: What kinds of tricks do you know how to do on the
       skateboard?

Aviv: Ollie (jumping with the skateboard by kicking the
       back end) and Slide (sliding down an object with the
       board).

T: I'd really like it if you'd bring the skateboard next time
       and show me. That's a great example of a gift that you
       have to offer the world.

During the next few sessions I learned a lot about skateboarding
and even more about Aviv. What kinds of tricks he knows how
to do and which trick he likes the best. What trick does he
really want to learn? How does he intend to learn it? Who can
teach him? What do you have to do in order to control the
skateboard better (concentration, control, inner quiet)? Thanks
to the skateboard, we learned relaxation techniques, breathing,
and guided imagery, all for the purpose of improving his
skateboard performance. Home assignments included watching
skateboarder videos on You-Tube, where he had to pick the
best clip and show it to me. Watching the video clips led us
to talking about the other people around him. How does he
prefer to be taught? If he had to teach someone, how would he
do it? What does it take to be a good skateboard teacher? The
ability to see what someone else's needs are and how he needs

to receive them? When a bond of trust was formed between us, and cooperation had grown, I felt comfortable enough to display for him the matrix of pro-social values and self-control.

T: We spoke about what a good skateboard teacher is, and I want to tell you that in my view, there have to be two really important traits that will turn them from an ordinary teacher into an excellent teacher. Do you have an idea what those two traits are?

Aviv: That they should be nice.

T: Yes, that's in the right direction, since one quality of a teacher is that he will be in favor of the student – that they want to help students and not hurt them. You might call that "values for the good of society." How would you call that trait?

Aviv: Good values.

T: A second characteristic, which is truly important for a great teacher, is that he have the ability to control himself. Imagine that you are learning with a really good teacher, one who knows all about skateboarding – at the highest levels – but he doesn't know how to control himself. Suppose you really irritate him because he's teaching you a trick and you didn't do it exactly the way he explained, what would happen?

Aviv: He'd yell at me and maybe slap me on the back of the head.

T: Then what would happen?

Aviv: I'd kick him.

T: Then you wouldn't be able to study with him anymore, would you? What's it called, the part where he doesn't control himself and hurts others?

Aviv: Out of control.

T: Excellent. Now, let's look at something interesting. I want to show you a table that explains to us what makes a great teacher. A teacher who'll be fun for us to learn with and who we'll think is great, and someone else who is a really awful teacher.

Teachers with good values care very much about their students. They will do everything not to harm them. Teachers with weak principles can hurt their students, insult them, and are not interested in how their pupils feel. There are teachers who care very much about their pupils, and even so, they cause them harm, because they don't have control over their own behavior. Time after time they will be sorry and apologize. The worst types of teachers are those who both don't care about their students and don't make an effort to control their own behavior. I sincerely hope they don't employ teachers like those at your school.

Aviv: Is that what you think? All the teachers are like that. They all yell, act crazy, and they don't even care about the kids.

T: Let's check what you said. Try to fill in the table with the teachers you know and maybe some of the kids you know, too.

Good Values	Not Good Values	
		No Self-Control
		Self-Control

We filled in the table while we tried to understand what the characteristics of the teachers and the children in the class were. By the end, we came back to Aviv.

T: Where would you place yourself, Aviv?
Aviv: I don't have such good values. (Long silent pause)
T: How do you know that?
Aviv: If I want something, I just grab it from one of the other kids. I talk back to the teachers. I force kids to give me their snacks.
T: So, we do have a problem with the values. You only see what you need and want and don't see the needs of others. (Silence)

Now it's much clearer to me what gift I would like to give you. I would like to give you the possibility to see others and not only yourself. This will make you a better friend, a better skateboarder, and maybe in the future, a better teacher, if you want to teach skateboarding. What do you say?

Aviv: Okay.

Aviv's treatment bore good results. A significant improvement began in his ability to be empathetic and also with his behavioral issues. The road was bumpy and complicated. I not only had to talk about things, I had to do them, to leave the session room and go with him to see the skateboarders doing their stunts. As matters progressed, I had hoped to be a role model for him of someone who sees the needs of others. I endeavored to give him the feeling that I saw him and his needs; that I was attentive to his world and would guide him towards being able to recognize me and also see the needs of others.

On Self-Control, Secret Jars and Shields

Yaniv, an eleven-year-old boy, came to treatment because of behavioral problems at the explicit request of his school. In the session with his parents, it became clear that Yaniv reacted with physical and verbal violence when faced with various social situations at school. Parents and the school system have a decisive role in everything connected with the development of aggressive behavior. This is due in part to the complex difficulty of sending clear, unified messages and complications in the application of authority and their impact on children (Omer, 2002). Accordingly, therapy work with children's behavior problems must involve the systems that surround the child, at home and at school.

In parent training with Yaniv's parents, which took place over several weeks, much emphasis was put on the parental messages, the parent's ability to communicate assertively and clearly with Yaniv, on conveying messages that contribute to Yaniv's sense of self-efficacy and self-esteem, as was earlier addressed in the section concerning parent training.

Although there was a slight improvement in Yaniv's behavior, particularly at home, I thought it appropriate to meet with him on account of his behavior in school, where the parents have less control over what has taken place.

Blue-eyed Yaniv, with his robust build and facial expressions of curiosity and embarrassment, entered the therapy room.

T:	(Smiling and shaking his hand) Nice to meet you, I'm Naomi. You must be Yaniv, right?
Yaniv:	(Nods, puts out his hand, smiles, and says nothing)
T:	Do you know why your parents made an appointment for us to meet?
Yaniv:	Because of school.
T:	And they told you who I am...or would you like to hear a little?
Yaniv:	They said you help children solve problems.
T:	That is correct. They are right. That's exactly my role. We all have problems. That's part of living. In order to cope with our problems, we need to recognize them and understand them and find solutions. I help children, and adults, too, to better deal with their problems.
Yaniv:	I don't think my problem has a solution.
T:	What's your problem?
Yaniv:	Everyone at school hates me.
T:	If you think that then you certainly must have a reason. Give me an example of the hate you feel at school. What is it they do that makes you feel they hate you?
Yaniv:	They're always blaming me and punishing me.
T:	Who is blaming and punishing?
Yaniv:	The teachers.
T:	All of the teachers?
Yaniv:	Mostly the home-room teacher, the math teacher, and the Bible Studies teacher.
T:	And the other teachers?

Yaniv: They don't like me either but it's not as bad.

T: How do you know they don't like you?

Yaniv: I feel it.

T: Is there a teacher who is nice to you or perhaps you feel they care about you?

Yaniv: The art teacher is mostly okay. She's actually all right.

T: Does she hate you?

Yaniv: I don't think so.

T: So, we can make an important assumption: Not all the teachers hate you. There's at least one teacher who's okay with you. What about the kids in your class? Do they hate you, too?

Yaniv: Except for Michael, all the other kids hate me and I hate them.

T: What is it they do that causes you to hate them?

Yaniv: They tease me.

T: Give me an example.

Yaniv: Don't want to.

T: You know, when I was about your age, there was someone in my class that couldn't stand me. She would laugh at me, talk about me behind my back, and even tried to organize a ban against me.

Yaniv: What did you do?

T: It was really hard for me, because before then, we were best friends. I remember I was very sad and didn't know what to do. I think I told myself that it wasn't worth me being so sad just because of her. What do you say to yourself when they tease you?

Yaniv: I don't say anything to myself. If somebody starts teasing me, I beat him up.

T: So are they afraid of you?

Yaniv: They'll be sorry if they mess with me.

T: Does that mean you'll hit someone if they mess with you?

Yaniv: Yes. I won't hit without a reason.

T: That's amazing. Everything you're saying reminds me of a book I wrote a few years ago, about a boy who is a lot like you.

Yaniv: What book?

T: The book is called *Grandfather Jamiko's Secret Jar*, and it talks about the exact same subject we're talking about now. I'd be very happy if we could read the book together. What do you think?

Yaniv agreed and we read the book together.

Therapy Treatment with the Book:
Grandfather Jamiko's Secret Jar (Epel, 2003)

The hero of the story is a reactive boy who responds aggressively and impulsively to any threat or provocation (Dodge & Coie, 1987; Hubbard et al., 2001; Poulin & Boivin, 2000). The boy tends to put the blame on those in proximity and doesn't know any other way to prevent them from "messing with him." For reactive children, characterized by impulsiveness and a difficulty with self-regulation, it is of primary importance to provide them with self-control skills, which will aid them to better cope in a variety of social circumstances.

The book deals with self-control proficiencies for children who display aggressive behavior. The purpose of the book is to teach these children two types of self-control by employing metaphors. Closed self-control, in the form of a "magic shield," and open self-control, illustrated with a "secret jar."

Michael Rosenbaum (1990, 1998, 2000), an eminent researcher on the subject of self-control, distinguishes between two response systems that operate when we interact with our environment. The **open system** allows us to approach an experience as it is, without judgement or evaluation are based on rules of logic and analytical thinking. Most of our attention is directed towards the current stimulus with acceptance and containment. The third wave of CBT treatment deals almost entirely with this type of openness to experience.

In contrast, the **closed system** helps us to distance ourselves from an immediate experience by way of avoidance or via cognitive transformation of the same experience, a cognitive interpretation and organization on the basis of an existing concept (Rosenbaum, 1998, 2000).

The jar that appears in the story is a metaphor of our capacity for containment. In the story, a child comes across a variety of different containers, meant for collecting unpleasant incidents: small sacks with little capacity for contents, or translucent balls that bounce about unrestricted, delicate and fragile vessels like glass jars, bigger containers the size and strength of an oak barrel, and even flexible containers that change their shape with each aversive stimulation.

The story's hero recognizes his own vessel, similar to a balloon, which stretches and expands until it explodes. The advantage of working with metaphors is that it is not necessary to precisely identify an emotion in order to illustrate an episode. For young children (and older ones, too), it is not always easy to identify, understand, and accurately put a name to emotions (Southam-Gerow & Kendall, 2002). The opportunity to use the "vessel's language" facilitates emotional communication. Take for instance, in kindergartens where they use the book, a conversation evolves around the feelings of the children and of the teaching staff: "My box is about to explode; I'm going away to calm down," "Talk to me in a few minutes; my sack is really full right now." Parents who have been aided by the book have reported that their children are better able to clearly communicate their experiences when they speak the "language of the jar." In one of the family sessions where we worked on the ability to accommodate through reading the story, a child in the first grade said, "I noticed that at home my tank is much smaller than when I am at school." By utilizing the book, we can then promote dialog about unpleasant experiences at a systemic, familial, and personal level. At the therapy level, we will want to identify, along with the child, what kind of vessel they have, what it's made of, what size it is, how unpleasant things get inside the vessel, what happens to them once inside, and how we can "empty the tank," so there won't be a flood.

While working with Yaniv, after reading the book together, we began by identifying his vessel and understand how it operates.

T: What sort of vessel do you think you have?

Yaniv: I don't know exactly how to describe it, but it's awfully full.

T: Do you think you can try to draw a picture of it?

Yaniv drew this picture:

T: It looks like your vessel is not only full but that there's a storm inside. Am I seeing correctly?

Yaniv: Yes, it's a very messy vessel. Everything's a mess.

T: How wonderful that you could draw a picture of the vessel. What are those lines?

Yaniv: That's me blowing up.

T: What does it look like when you blow up?

Yaniv: It's not very nice. I'm really angry.

T: If I was a camera that photographed each moment, what was happening to you, what would the camera capture on film?

Yaniv: Me hitting.

T: And what else?

Yaniv: Me yelling.

T: And then…?

Yaniv: Cussing.

T: So, when your vessel blows up, you hit, yell, and curse. Can you tell me for how long this goes on?

Yaniv: Don't know. At the same moment I explode, nothing matters to me.

T: If you could think of what material your vessel was made of, what would it be?

Yaniv: Don't know.

T: Is it more like plastic or metal, or maybe rubber?

Yaniv: It's sort of like the balloon the kid in the book had, the one that blew up so big it burst, but inside there's no air, there's pieces of glass and metal.

T: Ahh…like a bomb that explodes and scatters all the pieces?

Yaniv: Yes, exactly. Like a bomb.

T: What happens when a bomb explodes?

Yaniv: Nothing is left of it.

T: What else?

Yaniv: There are dead and wounded people, like in a war.

T: That's right. When we blow up the way a bomb explodes, there are injuries. Can you tell me what happens to the wounded when your bomb explodes?

Yaniv: I don't mean to hurt, but when a kid tells me, "Shut up fatty," I automatically hit him.

T: Does that help?

Yaniv: Sometimes.

T: What do you mean?

Yaniv: There are kids who don't dare mess with me, and then there are the kids who mess with me on purpose. They tease me even more and it makes me mad.

T: Children your age can sometimes enjoy making other children angry. I discovered that it doesn't matter who they tease, or about who and what they insult. It makes no difference if I'm fat or skinny, blue or red, have a big nose or small nose, if I have glasses or have red hair. What matters is how we react when they tease us. When children your age become angry, hit back, yell, and swear, they become the "best show in town." Then instead of the punches helping you, they actually hurt you more, since it means they succeeded in making you mad. What would you like the other children in your class to think about you?

Yaniv: That I'm strong and not to mess with me.

T: And if you had another way to send the same message without hitting, would you be willing to try it?

Yaniv: Yes, but I don't think it will help. I'm already really irritated when they start up, so I don't think I have a choice.

T: You're talking about something very important called "self-control" – how much we can control our reactions. For instance, if I really have to urinate, I can hold it in until I get to the lavatory, right? It's the same for you and your mother and father. Why don't we urinate in the street whenever we like?

Yaniv: Because it's not nice.

T: Let's say I really have to go and I can hardly restrain it.

Yaniv: But peeing is something private that you don't do in front of everyone.

T: That's correct. You're right, and it's great that you know what's private and what isn't. But if I need to urinate in the lavatory, I have to control my bladder, to hold it in and not urinate in the street. This is really interesting because the bladder is a sort of vessel. It fills up more and more until we feel a pressure and then we go to relieve ourselves. We learn to recognize the pressure in our lower belly and know that we have to go to the toilet. The same

thing happens with our vessels. We have to find a way to
know when our tank is full and find a way to empty it
so that it doesn't explode. What do you say about that?
Would you like to learn some methods to do that?

Yaniv: Yes, very much.

T: Let's go back to your vessel. We saw how your vessel
was a confusing mess, much like a bomb about to
burst when it's filled up. What can we do to prevent it
from exploding? What can be changed in your vessel
so it won't blow up?

Yaniv: You can make holes in it.

T: If we make holes in it, what will change?

Yaniv: Then things can get out of it and not fill it all the way
up, and it will not explode.

T: I really like that idea. Essentially, you're suggesting a
way to empty the vessel. Can you draw a picture of it?

T: Can you explain the change?

Yaniv: The vessel has holes and the unpleasant things are spilling out of them.

T: Where are they spilling out to?

Yaniv: I don't know. Maybe into the air.

T: Out into the air is a good idea. It's linked to one of the methods that helps us empty our vessel. One of the ways to empty our container is by breathing. We're always breathing, otherwise we wouldn't be alive, but I mean being aware of our breathing. Close your eyes and focus on your breathing. The air coming in and going out. Now, try to take a deep breath and hold it for a moment in your tummy, and then slowly, slowly, let the air out. When you don't have any more air in your chest, hold onto the "no air" feeling for just a moment before taking in another breath of air.

We practiced the breathing for a few minutes with Yaniv's full cooperation.

T: How do you feel now?

Yaniv: Relaxed.

T: More relaxed than ten minutes ago?

Yaniv: Yes.

T: What happens to our body when we breathe deeply?

Yaniv: I don't know. It simply relaxes me.

T: A good deep breath is relaxing. This happens because slow, deep breathing slows down the body processes, and when that happens, we feel more relaxed. A deep breath tells the body to relax. When we are angry, our body becomes turbulent, like in the vessel you drew.

Breathing is like one of the holes in the vessel that you drew, since it helps to empty the vessel. Can we think of any more things that might empty the vessel?

Yaniv: I don't understand. If I breathe then I won't be irritated?

T: It will help your "nerves," more specifically, your anger, and that is why I'd like you to practice the breathing we learned, at home. Especially when you feel your vessel is somewhat full. Remember that every breath empties it a little bit and lets out the unpleasant items into the air. In our next session, we will learn how to control our behavior. We will learn how to tell ourselves things that help us feel differently and behave differently.

The Bouncing Game

In the next session, we learned about our thoughts, our feelings, and our behavior, by playing the "Bouncing Game" (Zetler-Rom & Epel, 2014), which helps us to identify thoughts that pop into our heads.

The purpose of the game is to allow children to identify automatic thoughts, and after that, to understand the connection between occurrences, thoughts, emotions, and behavioral reactions. From clinical data compiled at the institute that I direct, we found that children love to play the game and ask to play it over and over again. Even thirteen and fourteen-year-old children can easily relate to the game if the explanation of the game is suited to their age level.

In this game, the child learns to bounce automatic thoughts, similar to bouncing a ball. The rationale for the game is that, for children, cognitive conceptualization is very difficult. Children have a hard time sorting out automatic thoughts and struggle to identify those thoughts. The process of conceptualization is critical, since it assists in the self-monitoring of thoughts and the ability to cope with them (Zetler-Rom & Epel, 2014). Hence, the use of special techniques for children is necessary, in order to aid them in understanding the concept of "automatic thoughts."

The "Bouncing Game" enables us to provide an explanation of automatic thoughts, while conceptualizing them from within the child's world. I explained to Yaniv that all of our behavior is connected to "automatic thoughts" that "bounce around" inside our heads. Our goal is to try and "catch" those rapidly passing automatic thoughts.

The game includes four phases:

Phase One
A Simple Association Game

T: Let's see how our mind bounces thoughts inside our brain. Suppose I say the word "sun." What's the first thing that pops into your head?

Yaniv: Moon.

T: Excellent, that's a thought that pops up without having to think much at all about the word "sun." We call this kind of thought an "automatic thought." Now we'll take a ball and play catch. I'll say a word, throw you the ball, then you say the word that pops into your mind and toss the ball back to me.

Phase Two

T: It's fun playing catch with you, Yaniv, you're a great thought bouncer. Now we'll move on to the second phase of the game. I'll say words that are connected to places or people, for example, "school," "mother," and such. Then you tell me the thought that pops into your head, using more than one word. Let's begin with the word "school."

Yaniv: I hate school.

T: Hate is a feeling. Love, happy, angry, embarrassed, sad, glad – all these are emotions. Emotions arise because of a thought that pops up in our head. What might help us to catch a thought is when I say a word, like "school," and a feeling like hate appears. I'll ask you the reason for the feeling. All right? Let's try it again, "school"

Yaniv: I hate school.

T: Because…

Yaniv: Because at school everyone is disgusting.

T: Terrific, now you've bounced a thought. So that we can remember all of your thoughts, we'll write them down.

We wrote down the thoughts that arose along with the words: father, mother, brother, sister, sea, pool, bible class, math class, etc. In this case, only I toss the ball. Yaniv catches the ball and "bounces" a thought according to the word I "tossed" to him.

Phase Three
We are playing catch with the help of Yaniv's thoughts, which

we wrote down earlier. We each choose a phrase and toss the ball. The catcher has to guess which feeling comes up for the ball thrower in relation to the phrase, and we check if it's correct and if there are any other feelings that might be added. If there is difficulty in saying a specific feeling, we say whether the feeling is pleasant or unpleasant.

For example, Yaniv chose the phrase, "Mom annoys me because she doesn't listen to me." He throws the ball to me, then I guess, Anger. Yaniv accepts my answer as the emotion he experiences and says that there are no other feelings attached. Next, I chose the phrase, "The sea is freedom." Then I tossed the ball to Yaniv and he said, "Fun, happy." I affirmed those feelings and I also added the feeling of "calm." While playing the game I try to understand, along with the child, what exactly are the thoughts and what are the emotions accompanying them. In this manner, we are exposed to a variety of feelings and can observe how a certain thought is connected to a particular feeling.

Phase Four
The "bouncing" is linked to a situation, for example, "A kid says to you that you're stupid," "The teacher yells at you to open to page fourteen," "Mom looks at you and says she loves you." In each situation the child says the first thought that "jumps" to mind and what the accompanying emotion was for that thought. After the child has gained some mastery over identifying emotions, we can move along to the phase of understanding chain responses.

In order to chart the chain of response, we look for an incident that occurred that week where I had an unpleasant sensation.

Here is an example of a chain response chart that was drawn during therapy with Yaniv:

Situation	Automatic Thought	Emotion	Behavior
When playing football (soccer), I stole the ball and a guy swore at me, "You maniac!"	"I'm a maniac?" He's a maniac! I'll show him! No body cusses me out!	Anger	Punch him in the stomach, yell at him. His friends grab me. The teacher comes.
Punched him in the stomach, yelled at him. His friends grab me. The teacher comes.	What does the teacher think? "He's always causing trouble; he should be punished." What do my friends think? "He's crazy." What was the kid I punched thinking? "I'll get him for that."	Angry at Yaniv Fear Anger	The teacher takes me to the office. I get punished. They don't want to be friends with me. They stay away. He'll try to get back at me later on.

T: When you look at the chart, does it seem to you when you lose control, hit and curse, that it helps you or hurts others?

Yaniv: Of course it hurts others.

T: If that's the case, let's learn how it's possible to be strong in other people's eyes, without hurting them and without it harming you. For this to happen, we need to learn how to control ourselves, our thoughts, our emotions, and our behavior. We'll begin with an exercise that is connected to the book we read, *Grandfather Jamiko's Secret Jar*. Before we worked with a jar, now we will work with a magic shield, one that will help you feel safe and protected in unpleasant situations.

The Shield Exercise

As noted earlier, in *Grandfather Jamiko's Secret Jar* (Epel, 2003), the open system of self-control is expressed by a "secret jar," while the closed system of self-control is illustrated with the "magic shield." The purpose of the shield is to create a partition between aversive experiences and negative emotional arousals that are liable to be expressed, especially with impulsive children, as aggressive behavior. That is to say, the goal is to enable the child to face an unpleasant situation and be capable of moving in the "elevator" from the amygdala to the cortex (which was covered earlier), so the situation will not be perceived as a catastrophe and reactions will be regulated. The entire exercise is done with guided imagery, as we will illustrate here:

T: Yaniv, our mission now is to enable you to react to different social situations in a more effective manner for yourself, so that you will feel you are acting in accordance with the results that are important to you. In order to progress in that direction, I would like you to find a shield, and for this, I'd like us to go on a journey of the imagination. I'll be your guide for this journey. Is that all right?

   I will ask you to imagine all sorts of interesting things, and everything that comes up in your imagination is wonderful. In the imagination, there is no correct or incorrect. Let's start with you raising your arms high above your head, as high as you can. Just a little bit more. Now, all at once, drop your arms and notice how the blood flows into your torso. Now, close your eyes and take a deep breath, and simply begin to concentrate on the air coming in and going out. You're doing it very well.

Now imagine you are boarding a vehicle, real or imaginary, and you ride away to a place where you feel the most secure. In this place you are completely relaxed, and it's very nice for you there. Please notice whether you are alone in that place or if there are other people around. Notice exactly where you are in that place and what you are doing there. Let yourself feel the relaxation and the sense of calm in your special place. In a short while, we will go to another place, not as safe, so this is why I want you to think of some kind of shield, real or imaginary, that will help you feel safe even when you are in a less secure place. Imagine that your shield has a sort of switch, like an electric switch. When you turn it on, the shield will be activated and will completely guard you in the best possible way; it will give you a complete sense of protection. When you have a shield like this, nod "yes."

Yaniv nods "yes."

T: Excellent, now imagine a faraway storm is approaching…a very big storm. Activate the shield and check to see if it can protect you from the wind. If not, change the shield so that it can keep you safe. The wind is quickly getting nearer. This is a wild, raging storm that picks up everything along its path. Trees are ripped from the ground, pieces of branches are flying through the air. There's heavy hail and pounding rain, but nothing from the storm can penetrate your shield. You are completely protected from the storm. The storm has passed now…the sun is out…you can turn off your shield, fold it up very small, the size of a Ping-Pong ball, and put it away somewhere on your body that needs protecting. Starting today, every time you need that shield, you'll know where to pull it out from.

I will count to three and you can open your eyes.

How was it Yaniv?

Yaniv: It was so cool. I made a really cool shield.

T: Soon you can tell me all about the shield. It's important for me to hear about everything that appeared in your imagination. Let's start with the vehicle. What did you imagine?

Yaniv: I imagined I was riding a motorcycle.

T: And where did you go?

Yaniv: I rode to my room.

T: What did you do there?

Yaniv: I played computer games.

T: Were you alone or with other people?

Yaniv: I was alone.

T: So, I understand that being in your room, alone playing computer games, is the nicest place for you to be.

Yaniv: Another place also came to mind, a place where the whole family went for vacation, but in the end, I stayed in my room.

T: That is interesting, because for some people, the safest and nicest place to be is alone with themselves, while other people feel safer with people around them. So, both of these things appeared, and in the end, you decided to be alone with yourself. What sort of shield did you find?

Yaniv: It's like a clear, hard lid that comes up from behind my head.

T: Can you describe it to me or draw a picture of it?

Yaniv: Well, it's like a cake cover, only it covers all of me.

T: And what happened when the storm hit? How did you activate the shield? How did you operate it?

Yaniv: I put my hand behind my head (puts his hand on the nape of his neck). The shield opened up and covered me. When the wind came, I saw everything, but I was protected. It was cool. Like in a movie.

T: Does that mean you felt totally safe from the storm and even enjoyed it? Did I understand correctly?

Yaniv: Yes, it was cool to see everything flying around and know it couldn't hurt me.

T: And then the storm passed and the sun came out, and I asked you to turn off the shield, fold it up, and tuck it away inside your body. What did you imagine?

Yaniv: I touched the back of my head another time and it just went back in again.

T: So, the on and off switch for the shield is behind your head. It's important to me that you remember this.

        The shield you created will help you a lot. In our next session, instead of the wind, things that really make you angry will appear and we'll see how your shield handles them. Meanwhile, until our next session, whenever something angers you, try to activate the shield (by touching the nape of your neck), and look at whatever is making you angry the same way you watched the storm. You're protected, and you can look at what is happening without it hurting you. It's not an easy exercise. Next week, together, we'll see how it worked.

A few days later, Yaniv called on the phone and told me he had managed to activate the shield. He sounded very pleased with himself. I gave him some encouragement and told him that we would continue to work on the shield in our upcoming session, in a few days' time. In the next session, we moved along to the following phase of the exercise, which also includes similar guided imagery, only this time we activated the shield in a real and threatening situation. Instead of the wind, I asked Yaniv to imagine the boy who agitates him the most.

T: (After finding the correct vehicle and safe haven) Imagine the boy who irritates you the most is coming from far away; he's slowly, slowly getting closer. You have plenty of time to activate the shield. He's trying to make you angry, swearing and teasing, but the shield won't let anything he says penetrate, annoy, or aggravate you.

You are safe from his cursing and taunting. You can watch him fly by as if he were only a strong wind that can't get through your shield.

From this point, there were many situations where we activated the imaginary shield. In order to embed the activation of the shield in reality, we found a self-talk phrase, "Shield Up!" Then we moved on to another challenge for the shield, through a physical strength experience and exposure to aversive situations in the form of the "I'm a Mountain" exercise (Zetler-Rom & Epel, 2014).

"I'm A Mountain"

The aim of the exercise is to equip the child (or adult) with a classic conditioned response between self-talk and a sense of strength, empowerment, and self-efficacy. The exercise includes several phases.

Phase One

At the start of the exercise, I asked Yaniv to stand in a fixed position and imagine he is a mountain, with all that this implies.

T: Yaniv, I want you to make certain your feet are planted firmly on the floor, that your posture feels very strong. Now, close your eyes and imagine the most powerful mountain you can envision. Perhaps it's a mountain you've seen before or maybe even a mountain that exists only in the imagination. Can you see a mountain like that?

Yaniv: It's a mountain like the one I saw once in a movie. It's very big. It's covered with trees and it can make itself bigger whenever it wants.

T: Excellent, now imagine that you are that mountain and say out loud a few times, with a smile, "I'm a mountain." I'll say it with you to help. You've done great so far; now open your eyes. You are now ready for the next phase of the exercise.

Phase Two

You will be the mountain you envisioned and I will try to push you off balance. I will try to move your head, feet, hands, shoulders (from side to side, not backwards and forwards, so as not to accidently push him over), but you won't let me. Use all your strength, like a mountain, where nothing happens to it even when there are heavy winds all around, when there's raining and flooding. While I'm pushing on you, continually say to yourself, with a smile, (which helps with positive conditioning), "I'm a mountain." Excellent. You're a very strong mountain and you won't let me push you about. Good for you!

Phase Three

T: Now I will be the children you told me about and saw in your imagination. I'll tell you exactly what you told me they said, "Fatty," "Stupid," "You an idiot." I'll also make offensive gestures just like you showed me how they did it. Our goal is for you to feel strong when facing these kinds of bullying remarks – for you to be "above it." That these remarks won't tear you apart and you won't react by hitting, which is the reason you are always being punished. For the first step, you will say, "I'm a mountain," with a smile. During the exercise, I'll tell you when to say, "Up Shield!" and you will try to imagine your shield, which is supposed to give you a sense of complete protection. We will check when you feel the strongest and the most protected, okay? In addition, after the exposure to aversive stimuli, I will try to push you off balance.

It appears like this:

Yaniv: I'm a mountain. I'm safe. I'm a mountain. I'm safe. I'm a mountain. I'm safe (in repetition).

T: What sort of mountain are you, a weakling? You stupid idiot, you fatty…

Yaniv: "Up Shield!" – I'm safe; I'm safe; I'm safe (without pausing).

I try to push him off balance while he constantly repeats his self-talk. I continue to expose him to the words and gestures (like the "finger") he encounters in reality.

It is important to note that at this stage there are children and adults who will cry. This signifies that the exposure was precise and hit home. The message to them is, "If you are crying, then we are right on target. It hurts but we won't stop. Soon you will feel stronger. You are allowed to yell out your self-instruction phrase, if it helps."

Yaniv was exceedingly cooperative and succeeded in anchoring his self-talk with a sense of bodily strength. In general, children who place importance on social relations will cooperate, since their goal is to lessen aggression and injury to others. There will be problems with children who do not have pro-social aims. With them, we will first work on pro-social values, and only afterwards, work on increasing self-control, in the event they lack self-control (Epel, 2007).

In order to instill a sense of strength when faced with aversive situations, Yaniv also needed to learn how to verbally respond in a suitable manner so he would feel strong without feeling the need to harm anyone. Therefore, we practiced an exercise called "Expressing Yourself," whose purpose was to equip Yaniv with the ability to respond verbally in aversive situations.

"Expressing Yourself"

Purpose of the exercise: to enable a child to verbally express suitable replies in various social situations. Children like Yaniv are not accustomed to verbally expressing needs, thoughts, and emotions. Instead, they "behave" or act out the anger or vulnerability; they do not say it with words.

T: Do you remember how you told me the kids at school
        only understand your fists?
        Are there any kids in your class who never get teased
        or pestered?

Yaniv: Yes, the king of the class, everybody does what he
        wants, and two other kids. They're sort of the good
        kids but not jerks.

T: What do you think about those two? Are they strong
        or weak?

Yaniv: They're in the middle. They don't fight with anybody.

T: What happens when somebody starts to pick on them?

Yaniv: They don't pay any attention to it.

T: That means they give the impression they're "above
        that," just as we started to talk about in our last session.

Yaniv: Yes, as if they had their own natural shield.

T: Exactly so. I would like for us to try an exercise. You'll
        give the impression that you're "above that," but not in
        a snobbish way, not "I'm the best," but rather from a
        place where you don't give the kids who are annoying
        you the satisfaction of seeing you lose control. You will
        decide not to be offended, feel hurt, or get upset, and
        give them the impression that it doesn't bother you.
        This doesn't mean you'll ignore them, but rather cause
        the children around you to feel that on the one hand,
        you can take their nonsense, and on other hand, you're
        not affected by them. In addition to this, you'll learn to
        say things that will cause you to be seen as strong and
        not weak or like a sucker. For instance, say to me right
        now, "You fatty," and I'll answer in three different ways.
        You tell me which reply makes me seem the strongest.

Yaniv: "You're fat."

T: "Wow!" (with a small grin, then break eye contact)
   "Hey, good you noticed," (break eye contact)
   "It's great that it bothers you and not me," (then break
   eye contact)
Yaniv: I liked the first one best. Short and to the point.
T: Fantastic. Now we'll switch roles. You'll say to me,
   "Wow!" with a small grin and then break eye contact.

While we practiced the role playing game, we thought up more replies by brain-storming and then by trial and error. We put together three sentences that Yaniv could relate to on a verbal level, and some responses he could send out on a nonverbal level, which demands a great deal of work and practice (such as posture, eye contact, etc.).

"Wow!"

"Whatever,"

"Cool. If it makes you happy,"

We prepared for the possibility that some of the children would try to increase their teasing and taunting of Yaniv because they wouldn't understand his new attitude. We spoke about the importance of consistency when sending the new message and the need for practicing the words and the nonverbal messages again and again, even in front of a mirror. We talked about the importance of training with self-talk and self-instruction, which strengthens the sense of inner power ("I'm a mountain;" "I'm safe;" "I won't let them have the satisfaction of making me mad;" "I know who I am and what I'm worth, and nobody can change that"). We shared this with his parents and explained to them all about the process. We allowed them to be participants in the amazing process that Yaniv is going through.

Think Sea: An Example of Working with an Adolescent for Outbursts of Anger and Aggression

Na'ama was fifteen years old when she came to me for treatment. A young girl full of life and a wealth of good humor. The sort of girl who always wears a smile. At eight years old, Na'ama was diagnosed with having a severe attention disorder and significant learning impairments, and was enrolled in special education programs. She came for treatment of what her parents described as "harsh outbursts of anger, total loss of control, including situations of endangering herself and others." In the process of our working together, we tried to identify the automatic thoughts accompanying various events, which had caused her outbursts of anger, particularly with the other children in her class at school. The cognitive work with Na'ama was quite involved, apparently because of the attention disorder and learning deficiencies, which impaired a linear process of clarifying thoughts and their reactions. Despite these obstacles in the cognitive work, we managed to identify how most of the incidents, in which Na'ama displayed aggression at school, were related to the recurring thought that others were willfully acting to harm and hurt her. "They're evil," she would say.

This thought is consistent with the cognitive component linked to aggressive behavior – hostility. Hostility, which we mentioned earlier, is the constant negative thinking of an individual concerning their surroundings, which are perceived as threatening and wrongful (Buss, 1961). For a person who views the world as hostile, there is remarkably easy access to memories of negative and aggressive thoughts. The tendency to relate one hostile event to another is linked to the erroneous perception according to which the intentions of others is to do me harm (Dodge & Somberg, 1987) and is clearly related

----

to feelings of anger and to aggressive behavior (Epel, 2007; Berkowitz, 1990; Buss & Perry, 1992).

In light of the existing limitations when working on the cognitive sections, we made an attempt to work directly with the feelings of anger. Controlling the emotion of anger is achievable given the individual is able to identify the state of emotional arousal and translate it as anger. In other words, to comprehend, to define, and to evaluate the emotion one experiences (Zeman & Shipman, 1996), and then to express that anger in a manner that is effective for the individual (Dahlen & Deffenbacher, 2001; Southam-Gerow & Kendall, 2002).

In one of the sessions with Na'ama, I asked her to draw a picture of the emotion of anger. She then suggested that she do this at home, since at home she had special colored pencils and she also wanted to put plenty of time into the drawing. This attitude pleased me and surprised me at the same time, since some of Na'ama's personality characteristics included poor planning, high impulsivity, and lack of attention to detail. My reply to her was thus, "I really liked hearing what you said just now. Because this means that our work is very important to you and you are willing to invest your effort. Good for you!" A broad smile covered her face. She was not accustomed to positive reinforcement; the majority of her interaction with those around her was hostile and negative. In her realm of experience, she frequently disappointed herself and others. The reinforcement she received from me, throughout the treatment, empowered her and granted her an experience where she felt worthy. In a session with her parents, we worked on the "Warm" model, in order to increase Na'ama's positive experiences at home.

Na'ama returned for the following session and brought her "Picture of Anger," which she had worked very long and hard on preparing at home.

T: Wow….I can tell you spent a lot of time on this drawing.

Na'ama: Yes.

T: I'd like to understand the drawing. Would you explain to me what you drew?

Na'ama: On the top it's dark. That symbolizes the anger. The yellow and orange are flames that heat up the anger (in professional terms, we can relate to this as the process of rumination). The drop of blood from the eye symbolizes my vulnerability. As if they shot an arrow into my eye. Inside the eye the background is red. This symbolizes disappointment.

T: Why the eye in particular?

Na'ama: It means that I need help. Help me! I'm in a dark place. My eye feels anger, pain, and disappointment, and is asking for help. My eye is the window to the world. In eyes, we can see everything, and I can see others through the eyes, but it's also the most vulnerable place.

T: (My eyes are stinging from the tears I feel pooling in the corners of my eyes) Na'ama you've moved and touched me. You've been able to describe your feeling of anger in such an incredible way. It's so very clear to me what you feel. You have connected between your feeling of anger and your sense of vulnerability with such perfection. It's been a long time since I have seen such an ability to express a very complex feeling. Do you think there is anyone in the world who knows and understands what you feel?

Na'ama: No one really. Everyone thinks I'm problematic, crazy. Even my best friends are cautious of me.

T: Are your parents cautious around you as well?

Na'ama: Of course they are. They're even more cautious than everyone else. I disappoint them the most.

T: What do you think would happen if they could see what I see right now? If they could understand your feelings of anger?

Na'ama: (Crying) Maybe they would understand me better.

T: I think so, too. We judge people according to their behavior even though we're not aware of what goes on with them on the inside. One of the things we learn here is how to express emotions with words and not with behavior. When we are attacked, we become cautious; it's only natural. It's not pleasant to be attacked. This is why people are so cautious around you. They are afraid of your aggression. But they don't understand the aggression, and perhaps it is important we explain to the people closest to us what goes on behind your anger. When you explained the picture to me and what happens to you, not only was it very moving for me, you also let me feel very close to you. I think if we can explain this to your parents, it will bring you closer together. What do you think?

Na'ama: Okay.

T: How would you like us to do this? We have the option of inviting them here to show them the picture and explain it to them. There's the option that I meet with them. Then there's the possibility that you take the picture home with you and try to explain it to them yourself. What seems best to you?

Na'ama: I don't know.

T: If we invite them here, we can do more than explain the picture. We can explain why you feel the way you do. We can find out what they are feeling; we can understand their reactions at home and together try to find solutions. What do you think?

Na'ama: That sounds good to me.

The parents came and joined us for several sessions together with Na'ama. The positive atmosphere, the accepting attitude, and the openness of the parents and their collaboration brought about a definite improvement at home and in Na'ama's relationship with her parents. There remained the issue of lack of self-control and outbursts of anger at school for which Na'ama pays a heavy price. Particularly so when she feels that she ruins so much in her relationships with her friends and she's left with experiences of rejection and loneliness.

T: Na'ama, I've heard what happens to you at school, how hard it is for you to control your anger, and how much you would like your relations with friends to be different. I want us to talk about an idea that may help you. The idea appears in a book I wrote for children, even though it's an idea that suits all ages. If you are willing, I'd like us to read the first part of the book together, just so you can understand the idea, and afterwards, we'll work with the idea. Is that okay?

Na'ama happily agreed. It should be noted here that Na'ama was remarkably cooperative throughout the entire therapy treatment. Perhaps, for this reason, I felt comfortable suggesting to her that together we understand the metaphor of the jar, which appears in the book, *Grandfather Jamiko's Secret Jar*, originally intended for younger children.

We leafed through the first section of the book, although I lingered with her over the part of the metaphorical jar in order to ensure she had understood the concept. Afterwards, we discussed the more unpleasant items; the things that fill her jar. As expected, it became clear that anger filled a major portion of her jar. I asked her to draw a picture of her jar and in the drawing, to make a note of the material it was made from, what filled it, how it was filled, and what happens to the unpleasant things that get inside the jar. Following the success of her earlier drawing of anger, we decided that this time she would also make the drawing at home and bring it with her to our next session.

In the following session, Na'ama explained to me about the clay jar she had drawn:

"When the anger goes in, it's black. The black goes inside the jar, which is made of clay. The brown and red colors are evil (from people). The snails inside the jar make the anger build up more and more, like wheels that heat up the anger and make it bigger. When it's full, the clay breaks. All the rage and hate and vulnerability bursts out, and afterwards, I'm busy with putting the pieces back together again."

It happened to me once again. I looked at Na'ama, open-mouthed with wonder and amazement, just as her parents were left speechless when they saw the drawing and heard Na'ama's explanation for the "Anger Art" she had drawn. I could not have hoped for a more exact description of the rumination process and the "self-heating," which is linked to the process of anger. Especially touching for me was the part when she explained how her clay jar broke to pieces when it was full, and how much energy she had to muster in order to repair the damage and put herself back together again. The process of drawing the clay jar and the explanation Na'ama gave, stood in complete contrast to the therapy process in the session room. When we talked, she had great difficulty in focusing her attention. She would "flitter" between different topics from moment to moment, as in the manner of associations, which often made it difficult for me to understand her meanings, thoughts, and emotions. Now, when she attempted to express her emotions in a drawing, there was pure logic, sensible order, and cognitive and emotional depth, which was accessible to her only when she was requested to draw her feelings, as in the "Picture of Anger" and the "Picture of the Jar."

T: Na'ama, I so love to see the depth you achieve when you draw a picture of what goes on inside of you. Truthfully, it even astonishes me, how well you manage to express your thoughts and feelings when drawing. Drawing is a wonderful tool of expression for you and perhaps we should consider how to develop this talent.

Na'ama: How fun. I really love to draw.

T: Your parents are very supportive of you and they'll be happy to know that there's a subject that interests you and you want to invest effort in it. Would you like to speak with them about this? Would you prefer I spoke to them?

Na'ama: I'll talk to them.

T: Excellent. I trust you to do it well and if you have any concerns about how to talk with them about this, we can practice it here in the session room.

Na'ama decided to practice the conversation with her parents in the session room. Later on, she spoke with her parents and together they decided to sign Na'ama up for art lessons.

Over the next few sessions, we dealt with ways in which to empty the jar. The principle techniques were: learning to breath, relaxation, the use of guided imagery for finding a haven (the sea), and shield (enlarging a gold medallion that she wore on a chain), using self-instruction ("I'm learning to love myself," "When angry – think sea," "I'm expanding my jar"), and the application of "I'm a Mountain" (when coping with offensive words from me as someone who represents her negative thoughts, along with hurtful things she has heard from people in her nearby surroundings). Subsequent to this process, we dealt with building a new jar, a more suitable jar tailored to Na'ama's personal requirements.

T: Na'ama, let's assume we can build a new jar, one that will be more practical for you. What would it look like? What would it be made of?

Na'ama: I don't know. I have to think about it; it's complicated.

T: That's right. It does mean inventing something new that doesn't exist yet in your mind. I suggest you try to do it at home. We've already seen what you are capable of doing when you take an assignment home. I'm sure this time you'll also be able to handle my request in good form.

Na'ama returned for our next session with the following drawing and explanation:

"The new jar is made of gold with flowers, which means renewal and resilience. The blue color symbolizes positive thoughts and the ability to overcome vulnerability, disappointment, and stress. It is indestructible. There's more self-love. This jar can hold much more than the other jar could and it doesn't break apart as easily as the old clay one did."

T: Again, as usual, you move me...you've done an impressive job. It looks as though you've made significant progress since you have more positive thoughts and developed a sense of resilience and power. Good for you, Na'ama. I'm so proud of you. Do you think when anger, or any other negative emotion arises, you'll be able to imagine how the new jar will accommodate all of them?

Na'ama: I'll try. Actually, I feel a lot less angry. I think I have fewer angry outbursts than before.

T: That's a wonderful sign and it means we are headed in the right direction. Do you remember when we said that whenever we experience a wild storm, it's hard for us to use the upper part of our brain? The cooler part of the brain, the part that plans more, contains more? Now that the storm has subsided, this is a good time to activate the new jar for those times when you have fits of anger. Let's try to imagine the last outburst of anger you had.

Na'ama: It was a few days ago, in class. The guy who sits behind me, the one I told you teases me all the time and I hate him…he started to throw paper wads at my head. I told him to stop. I told the teacher, too. He stopped, but I could still feel how my wheels were heating up with anger, and when the teacher told me to be quiet, I exploded.

T: What did you do?

Na'ama: I screamed at her (the teacher), threw a chair, and ran out of the classroom.

T: Okay, I want you to close your eyes and imagine that situation, especially the part when you made yourself boil. Anyone would be angry if someone was throwing something at their head. The matter is that he stopped throwing the paper wads, and you remained with the anger, which began to fill up the jar, and then the wheels heated up and increased the anger even more. Now, close your eyes and try to re-enter that situation. What do you see?

Na'ama: I see myself getting hit with a ball of paper and I start to heat up. I turn around to him and ask him to stop, which is something I wouldn't have done before, and then he actually stopped.

T: What happened inside your body at that moment?

Na'ama: I felt all the nerves in my body, like a hot wave.

T: Take a deep breath and tell yourself that you can accommodate the anger. Imagine how it enters the new clay jar, not the one with the wheels that heat up the anger, but the one made of gold, with flowers. What is happening now?

Na'ama: The anger is very hot, like the heat wave I told you about, then when it touches the gold, which is a cold metal – it cools down. When it cools, it goes down to the bottom of the jar and takes up less space.

T: Excellent. Do you have any other ideas how the new container can help?

Na'ama: Maybe when I breathe deeply, I can imagine that I'm breathing the fragrance of the flowers that are on my jar.

T: Wonderful. And what about the positive thoughts that go into the jar?

Na'ama: Thinking about the sea really helps me.

T: I have an idea; you can think of the anger as an enormous wave in the sea, where you have to dive underneath it and let it pass over you. What do you think?

Na'ama: Yes, when I dive under the wave I'll be able to see what's underneath the water.

T: I understand. You are looking for a way to distract your mind from the anger and focus your attention on something else. Am I right?

Na'ama: If I continue thinking with the anger, it gets bigger.

T: Anger is a natural feeling. It's impossible not to feel anger sometimes. It's not reasonable to never be angry. But I don't want you to be frightened of anger. I want you to accommodate it, without hurting yourself or anyone else when you experience anger.

Na'ama: This week, I'll try to activate my new shield.

T: I also want to request something else. If you manage to activate the new shield, I'd be happy if you would draw the sensations you have after you've activated the shield. In our next session, Na'ama returned with this drawing:

Na'ama: I drew this after I activated the new shield two times. I think about the sea because it relaxes me. The sea creatures have to survive, too. They get hurt too and have to survive attacks by predators. Blue is my favorite color. It means that I'm not the only one who has problems. Even the sea animals have problems. The eye symbolizes calmness. It's as if I'm diving and I'm safe while the eye watches all the fish swimming around.

T: The difference between the eye in your first drawing and the eye in this drawing is quite impressive. In general, there's a vast difference between the first stormy drawing and this drawing, which is much more serene. It's fantastic to see. Can you tell me how you activated your new jar this week?

Na'ama: Actually, I found a new trick that really helps me. When I left the classroom angry, I turned up the music in my earphones and imagined the sea. It really calmed me down. All the time I say to myself, "When stressed – think sea."

T: Tell me exactly what happened and how the new jar helped you.

Na'ama: I had an incident with the linguistics teacher. I didn't scream at her. I simply left the classroom, but then I began to feel I was heating up and sensed a crack in the old clay jar, so I imagined that it was actually the new gold jar, which can cool down the anger. I turned on the music I like and sat down on a bench, and cried. A friend of mine came over and I talked to her and felt the crack in the jar disappear.

T: It's interesting how the old jar and the new jar are combined. That's very sensible. Many times, when we try to learn to think differently or to behave differently, there is a struggle between the familiar, the known and automatic, and the new and less familiar. The more you practice what you have learned here, the more you will be able to think in terms of the new jar. You've done a wonderful job and I believe you will succeed in overcoming your difficulties.

Na'ama: For years, I had the feeling that what happens to me couldn't be resolved. The most important thing that happened to me here was, that now I can tell myself that I can get over my problems.

3. "If Only I was" – Treating Social Rejection

The year is 1979. I am a student in the eighth grade. My social situation is not a simple one, to put it mildly. I had one good friend in my class besides the other ten girls who made fun of me, teased me, and ostracized me for almost a year. It's not clear to me even today, what the reason was. During that entire time, I felt I was being banished. Sometimes I felt worthless. My grades were adversely affected and so was my motivation to go to school. That said, that same year didn't leave a deep scar on my personality or on the social life I developed afterwards. For years I tried to clarify for myself how the fact that I experienced such a painful year in my young life did not cause me to develop, in contrast to many of my clients, traumatic experiences that significantly affected the course of my life. Where did I find the psychological resilience that contributed to my coping with such a complicated and disheartening situation? It seems to me that a number of factors enabled me to overcome the prolonged incident. The extroverted side of my personality contributed to my ability to share my feelings with my parents and other people around me. It could have been my sense of self-efficacy and my belief that I could create new friendships and somehow overcome those bad experiences. Then there was my positive thinking, which gave me the hope and faith that it would pass and matters would change for the better. Perhaps more than anything else, was the knowledge that my parents always loved me unconditionally and that nothing could ever diminish that feeling, not even a long-term boycott.

Research on the subject is less optimistic than my personal story and indicates there are direct damages as a result of social rejection upon the psychological well-being of children and adults. Significant social rejection is liable to lead to psychological distress and traumatic reactions, and sometimes even to post traumatic disorders. These can range from low self-esteem to as far as difficulty in creating social and intimate relations, from emotional disorders such as depression and anxiety, to high-risk hazards like dropping out of school, adjustment difficulties, anti-social behavior, addictions, vagrancy, and criminality (Asher & Coie, 1990; Dodge, Coie & Brakke, 1982; Dodge & Feldman, 1990). It is no coincidence, then, that the majority of referrals we receive at the institute where I direct, relate to difficulties with social integration linked to experiences of social rejection.

Creating Resiliency When Facing Situations of Rejection

We all want to make connections, to be accepted socially and avoid social rejection. This desire stands as the basis for one of mankind's most basic and primary motivations (Baumeister & Leary, 1995). Whenever I lecture before groups of parents, educators, and professional people on the subject of social rejection, I generally use a metaphor of fishes in the sea in order to illustrate our existential motivation to belong. Nature is clever. When a mother fish spawns little fingerlings, they arrange themselves behind her in a sort of thick cloud of swimmers. This "cloud" of fingerlings repels potential attackers and thus assures their survival. But what happens to the little fingerling who leaves the cloud? What happens to the little guy who is slower than the rest? Perhaps limited in his movements? Or doesn't know which way to swim? It's most likely that he would find it difficult to survive. Being part of a group, however small, even a dyad, satisfies a crucial existential and survivalist need. This sense of belonging not only creates resilience but also influences the manner in which a child perceives himself and the events surrounding him, and is most likely to be a determining factor in his ability to cope with an undesirable social situation (Ford & Collins, 2010). Research reveals that high self-esteem and self-efficacy comprise an element of resilience against cognitive, emotional, and behavioral implications of social rejection, ridicule, and humiliation (Leary et al., 1995; Nezlek et al., 1997; Strauss, 2000). When an individual actually experiences episodes of social rejection, this experience will be linked to a decrease in self-esteem (Leary et al., 1995), self-efficacy, and self-regulation (Baumeister et al., 2005). Moreover, it becomes apparent that an individual's negative self-perception is one of the important predictors of acceptance or rejection by his peers (Leary et al., 1995). Therefore, it becomes evident that there exists a multi-directional connection between social rejection, self-esteem, and psychological resilience. We can illustrate this connection graphically:

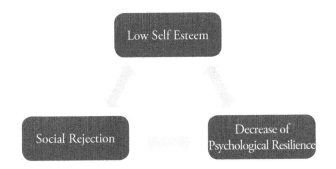

Experiencing social rejection is an integral part of our lives and we need to develop genuine psychological resilience in order to cope with this fact (Asher & Coie, 1990).

Yet, there is a difference between prolonged, or chronic

rejection, as experienced by approximately ten percent of children, as opposed to isolated incidences found with approximately fifty percent of all children. The fifty percent, at some point, encounter instances of exclusion, harassment, isolation, ostracism, degradation, and physical injury, which cause them to experience rejection (Asher & Coie, 1990). In their eminent book on social rejection among children, Asher and Coie (1990) claim that more than half of all children are involved in acts of rejecting others or in observing these types of episodes from the side, and are influenced by them. Therefore, it reveals that most children are involved in some act of social rejection, whether as instigators or as victims, as active or passive participants, either overtly or covertly.

Hence, more than the treatment of social rejection itself, whether it be chronic or isolated, we should aspire to provide every child who comes to us for treatment, with the ability to develop resilience and be capable of coping with undesirable social situations. When we work in child-direct therapy, we should equip the children with skills that will aid them in lessening such situations of social rejection (entering a social situation, initiative, assertiveness, self-control, and more). It's best to place our goal directly in front of the child's eyes; our goal to equip them with "super-skills," which will enable a child to deal with social rejection whenever it may occur.

The reasons for social rejection are many and varied. They include a lack of social expertise, personality characteristics, and cognitive, emotional, and behavioral traits in addition to environmental responses to social events. The upcoming table enumerates some of the reasons for social rejection while attempting to list the cause and possible consequential results on a social level:

Cause	Child's Behavior	Social Result
Child feels obligation to and shares with adults and not his peers	Informing, ingratiating	The children's experience is that this child "betrays" them, that he is not one of them
Difficulty with self-control and self-regulation	Over reaction, aggression	The children's experience is that this child is unpredictable, unpleasant, and threatening
Difficulty entering a social situation	Non-verbal introduction (sees, but is not seen), aggressive introduction	The group rejects the newcomer
Social learning deficiencies	Difficulty reading the social map, unsuitable responses	The children's experience is that this child is not understood and not socially suitable
Lack of humor, particularly self-humor	Child does not go with the flow, "heavy" social mannerisms	The children's experience is that it's not fun to be with this child. Sometimes seen as "old"
Low self-esteem and self-efficacy	The child relates social rejection to himself, and does not believe in his social competence and broadcasts weakness, passiveness, and subservience	Possible exploitation of the child at the hands of the more powerful children
Ineffective adult involvement (parents and teachers)	Aggression from the child's parents towards the offensive children	Distancing from the victim and increasing the hostility towards him

Social rejection is expressed differently among boys and girls. Boys tend to use more direct aggression (physical and verbal) than do girls, while girls tend to apply indirect social aggression more than the boys: gossip for instance, spreading rumors, slander, shunning, and ostracizing (Archer & Coyne, 2005). Apparently, factors such as social expectations and gender identity prevent them from expressing aggression directly (Eagly & Steffen, 1986; Egan & Perry, 2001). The girls may display aggressive behavior only if they receive social validation for their behavior (Owens, Slee & Shute, 2000). Some girls use indirect and implied aggression for the purpose of gaining a sense of belonging, closeness and intimacy, in order to reach the highest possible social status. On account of this difficulty in expressing aggression directly, girls are liable to turn natural emotions, such as anger, frustration, and retribution, into extremely hurtful social behavior, whose consequences are liable to become increasingly severe (Simmons, 2002).

The parents of eleven-year-old Gali met with me and told me of their situation:

Parents: Gali is a good girl. She is obedient and studies hard, but lately there's been some trouble, socially. She's miserable. She won't open up about it. Even though she has two other close girlfriends, because of some sort of misunderstanding, one of Gali's friends initiated a boycott on her. All the girls are against her. They stopped inviting her over; she's alone at school and in the afternoons. She's crying a lot and doesn't want to go to school.

T: How long has this been going on?

Parents: It's been going on for about two months. We approached the school faculty and they tried to help, but it didn't do much good.

T: What did they try to do?

Parents: They had a special meeting with the girls to talk with them about how they were treating Gali. Not only did it not work, it just made the problem worse.

A child's anguish, as a result of social rejection, often leaves parents feeling helpless to deal with their child's experience of exclusion. They feel the pain along with their child and try various ways to ease the distress. Unfortunately, in some instances, not only does the parents' and faculty's involvement not benefit, but it can aggravate the situation. Parents who are inclined to respond apprehensively, characterized by over protecting their children, are liable to send a verbal and nonverbal message of catastrophe, which amplifies their child's emotional distress. Even the imprecise actions taken by the educational staff are likely to increase the anguish of the rejected child. The intervention of the educational and parental systems in cases of social rejection must take into account the unique interaction that has been formed between the children involved. For instance, in Gali's case, the educational counselor met with the other girls without Gali being present. In this situation, not enough empathy can be generated, which will eventually lead to a change in the girls' behavior. Therefore, it is preferable to prepare the rejected child for a meeting with the children who are shunning them. In this case, there should be explicit preparation done with the rejected child concerning the messages they want to send out and how they can do this affectively by practicing with role playing exercises. It's important there be preparation for replying to the various reactions of the rejecting children, and how, for the rejected child, to best respond. This type of intervention gives the rejected child the experience of control and power. He will know exactly what the plan is, what is expected to happen, and how he must behave in different situations. He will feel that he has someone to turn to and someone to trust within the system. The goal here is to deal not only with the rejection. Children need to learn that they will not always be accepted. They need to learn to expect that sometimes, they will be rejected, so it is necessary to assist them in building up an "immunity" to rejection situations (Asher & Coie, 1990).

In my first session with Gali, she seemed completely dejected. Her curly hair was a bit neglected; her eyes were tired and listless. My smiling greeting did not suit the heavy mood Gali brought with her into the room. I told her a little about myself and asked her to tell me about herself. I felt as if I was conducting a monolog. Gali was huddled up inside herself, hardly glancing at me at all, and this caused me to feel uncomfortable, as if she was saying with her entire body, "Leave me alone." In order for me to help Gali, my first goal was to establish a connection with her and begin building a bond of trust.

There are a number of ways to build relations of trust with a child. However, when we are speaking of a child who expresses such a high verbal and nonverbal level of resistance to connection or therapy, I find it worthwhile to broach the issue directly, thereby providing the child with a sense that we both know the purpose of our meeting. This immediately forms the impression that I am understood and that my actions are aimed at aiding them with their problem. Following this, it is important to normalize the problem and present the psychoeducational explanation along with gaining the cooperation of the child, by their taking part in some measure, in the exchange.

T: Gali, your parents were here with me for a meeting and I understood from them that it has not been easy for you lately with your classmates. Have I understood correctly?

Gali: (Nods "yes" in agreement)

T: There are many children who face difficulties with

friendships, and it's a good thing you came here. Together, we will try to understand what the difficulty is with your friends and what we can do to change that. For us to understand these things together, I will ask you questions and we'll talk about what bothers you. Would you agree to that?

Gali: (Shrugs her shoulders and lowers her head as if to say: "If we have to, then all right...")

T: Can you try to describe to me in words, what I just saw in your response?

Gali: I don't like to talk about it.

T: You don't like talking in general or you don't like to talk about this in particular?

Gali: At all.

T: Yes, there are a lot of children, and adults, too, who don't like to talk very much. We call them "introverted" or "suppressed," which means everything remains inside and doesn't come out. Does this sound like something that characterizes you?

Gali: (Looks at me from the corner of her eye, finally a tiny smile creeps onto her lips) Seems like it.

T: Let's draw a line and on it mark where you are. At one end of the line are the very open children; we call them "extroverts." With them, everything is outward – they talk a lot, share what they are feeling, and tell about things that happened to them. Do you know any children like that?

Gali: Of course.

T: Who for example?

Gali: Tal and Stav.

T: And do you have a good friendship with them or not?

Gali: Not especially.

T: Would you like to have a better friendship with them?

Gali: (Nods her head "yes.")

T: On the other end of the line are the children who are more closed, introverted, and don't talk about what happens to them. I would like you to mark on the line where you feel you are today, and if you would like to be in a different place.

(It's also possible to suggest marking where the classmates are on the axis.)

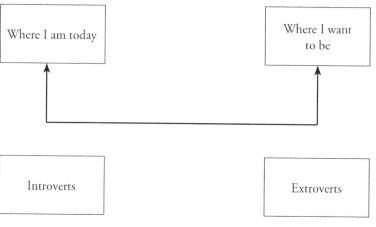

T: Let's imagine that you were extroverted, as you indicated on the graph. How would that be different?

Gali: I'd be popular.

T: What does that mean?

Gali: They would like me and I wouldn't have these kinds of problems.

T: What problems do you think you have right now?

Gali: The girls hate me; they won't talk to me.

T: What do you think the reason for that is?

Gali: I don't know. Tal and Stav used to be good friends with me, but now they hate me and because of them all of the other girls started to hate me, too.

T: What happened with Tal and Stav?

Gali: A while ago we decided to go to Tal's house after school. Tal started to go and Stav and I walked behind her and laughed about something. Tal thought we were laughing about her. She turned around and started to yell at me.

T: What did she yell at you?

Gali: You're horrible. Go home; you're not coming to my house. You'll never be my friend anymore…things like that.

T: What did you think at that moment?

Gali: I didn't understand what happened. We weren't laughing at her at all. I didn't understand why she was yelling at me.

T: And what happened after that?

Gali: Stav went off with Tal and left me there in the middle of the road.

T: Wow, that is a harsh experience.

Gali: (With tears in her eyes) And that's it. From that day on they won't talk to me. I don't understand what I did and the worst thing is they've got all the girls in the class to exclude me, too.

T: What you have told me is a very troubling experience, especially when we don't understand what we did, wrong. I want to address two things that seem to me, to be genuinely important. One, that you are at a very difficult age from a social standpoint. It's an age when many girls are not loyal to friendships. They mainly see only themselves and not the person standing in front of them, and this is the reason many girls of your age go through what you are going through. This is something very typical of this age. In a few years, it completely changes. The other thing that seems we should consider is, we should try and understand Tal's behavior.

The Social Antennae of Children with Rejection Sensitivity (RS)

T: You carry around the feeling that you've done something wrong, but I suppose that what you experienced is more likely linked to Tal's interpretation of things, and not so much tied to anything you did or didn't do. There are children, and adults, who are very sensitive to rejection (Downey et al., 1998). They have antennae, like an antenna (I lifted my finger up like an antenna above my head and Gali laughed), which is always busy picking up clues of rejection. Let's suppose you had antennae like that, all the time checking to see – are they rejecting me or not? What would happen if two friends of yours were walking behind you and laughing?

Gali: I'd think they were laughing at me.

T: And then…

Gali: I'd be mad.

T: Does it sound sensible to you that this might be what happened to Tal?

Gali: Yes, and it's not the first time she behaved like that. Every time we don't do what she wants, she gets irritated. But that's odd because she's a strong girl, so why would that happen to her?

T: What do you mean when you say she's strong?

Gali: She always decides when and where. Stav and I are sort of her servants.

T: We're not absolutely sure if she's sensitive to rejection, we can only presume. But, in general, there are any number of reasons that cause people to be sensitive to rejection. For instance, if you were rejected when you were younger, your relationship with your parents, and more. When they feel the slightest suggestion of rejection, even if they aren't actually being rejected, they react very angrily. Their friends don't understand what they've done wrong to make their friend react so angrily. Do you understand? It's as if they are in a movie of their own thoughts and emotions. We don't know what goes on through peoples' head or how they interpret things. You don't even know if Tal was inside her own movie, because you didn't do anything intentionally to hurt, harm, or even laugh at her. Still, she went inside her movie of feelings of rejection. What you saw was only the tail-end of the movie, the anger and aggression towards you, without even understanding how it was all connected.

Gali: (Leans back, looks at me for a long time) Now I understand.

T: What do you understand now?

Gali: Tal is sensitive to rejection, and that's why she thought I was laughing at her. She could have interpreted anything I do as if it was against her. Because of her sensitivity, she's always sure she's being rejected even when it's not intended.

T: Despite the fact that Tal seems like someone who gets everything easily, that's not exactly so is it? Perhaps it's exactly the opposite?

Gali: I never thought of it that way.

T: Children with difficulties behave in many different ways. Some of them even hurt others. Vindictiveness is one of the characteristics of sensitivity to rejection (Downey & Feldman, 1996). Maybe this is what happens to Tal. Maybe she is angry and vindictive. We don't know the whole truth. We can only conjecture. If my conjecture is correct and Tal is a girl who has difficulties, then perhaps she is also sensitive to rejection. What does this mean for you?

Gali: That I'm not to blame for what happened. (Silence) But now it doesn't help me. All the other girls have shut me out.

T: In our next session, we will discuss solutions and how you can cope with this complicated situation. For the moment, it's important for me to know how you are feeling after we tried to understand what happened between you and Tal.

Gali: I feel much better.

T: What helped you to feel better?

Gali: I understood why Tal yelled at me, and that it's not as easy for her as it seems. I understood that maybe I'm not to blame at all. I learned that at my age it can be very difficult socially, but it's something that will change.

In our next session, Gali entered with a smile and then sat down:

T: How are you Gali?

Gali: Better.

T: What's better?

Gali: My feelings.

T: What changed in your feelings?

Gali: I'm not as sad.

T: Have you had any more thoughts since our last session?

Gali: I thought that maybe Tal isn't a good sort of friend for me.

T: If she's not a good friend for you, what does that mean?

Gali: That maybe I need to find other friends. But still, all the other girls in my class aren't talking to me.

T: How much do you feel you have control over whether the other girls talk with you or not?

Gali: I don't have any control. Tal is the queen and she decides. And until she decides otherwise, the rest of the girls won't talk to me.

T: Could be that you are right. There are situations in life that happen to us and which we have no control over. We need to find a way to get along with them, even if it's very unpleasant. When I was a girl, the others banned me, too. I also have a lot of friends, who are already grown up, who were excluded, too. Today we all have families, jobs we enjoy, and friends we like to be with. I suggest we build a program that will help you through this rough period. I suggest that for the first stage we think of ways to help you feel stronger in light of the current situation. After that, we will both know you a little deeper: what characterizes you, what your needs are, and examine how you would like to cope with the reality you find yourself in. Does my plan sound all right to you?

I received Gali's consent and we began working on the ability to accommodate with the aid of the book, *Grandfather Jamiko's Secret Jar*. Gali molded a pitcher out of Plasticine and found a self-instruction phrase for herself, "Lots of kids go through rejection. It's not nice but I can take it." We also worked on her internal sense of protection with the help of a "magic shield," challenging the shield through guided imagery and confronting the taunting faces of the other girls. We challenged the self-instruction phrase by using the "I'm a Mountain" exercise, and the "Word of Mouth" exercise. All the while we worked on inner resilience, which included cognitive structuring and working with emotions. Gali cooperated extremely well, and when we began to work on the behavioral elements of "Word of Mouth," it proved to be very difficult for her.

T: Gali, I can see it's really hard for you to answer or even make eye contact when someone says mean things to you.

Gali: Yes, I already told you I don't like to talk.

T: You speak beautifully and explain yourself quite charmingly here in the session room. That's not what happens with your friends though is it? Or perhaps more correctly, it happens with your friends when they talk with you?

Gali: No. I don't usually talk very much and definitely don't answer when someone insults me.

T: If you answered them, what would happen?

Gali: It's just not me, and it seems to me it would be even worse.

T: That takes me back to our first session when we spoke about extroverts and introverts. Remember?

Gali: Yes, I'm an introvert.

T: I like it when you say that, because being an extrovert or an introvert is something we are born with. There are advantages to being an introvert and there are benefits to being an extrovert. You can't become an extrovert in the same way you marked on the line in our first session, but you can certainly learn some skills that will make relations with others easier. At the moment, it's important for me to check how difficult it is for you and if you avoid social activities because you are introverted. I'll give you a questionnaire to fill out that will help us understand this, all right?

In order to rule out any existing social anxieties, we filled out the anxiety questionnaire for children (SPAI-C), and the results were low (less than 18). According to these results, we then turned to dealing with Gali's introverted areas, while attempting to clarify what were the advantages and disadvantages of being an introverted person, and which of her social skills were in need of improvement.

T: I want us to understand more deeply what it means to be an introverted person, and what the differences are between introverted people and extroverted people. We'll try to do this through a story, and although it was written for children, we can still use it with adults.

The title of the book is *Zazee and Lalee Discover What Friendship Is All About* (Epel, 2013a).

Therapy work with the book, Zazee and Lalee Discover What Friendship is All About (Epel, 2013a)

In order to grasp the differences between the social skills of extroverted people and the social skills of introverted people, it is possible to use a metaphor of bees and beetles. In this book, we meet up with Zazee the Bee, who is extroverted and endowed with the ability to fly from one flower to the next and form social ties in a short matter of time. Conversely, Lalee the Beetle is introverted and likes to stick close to a single leaf, with whom she has a fond connection, and spends most of her time nearby her leaf (Epel, 2013a; Epel, 2013b).

For children and adults endowed with the social skills of a bee, it is easier to create social connections. They are extroverts, skilled in making direct contact and gifted with the ability to approach, to initiate, to ask and tell about themselves, to create eye contact, and communicate through body language and facial expression of desire to connect. Extroverts expend their energy on social connections, they are chatty, full of life, and tend to be impulsive. They require strong stimulus in order to arouse their brains' reward centers, and therefore, they respond well in a highly stimulating environment. They are less sensitive to pressures than introverts and their "immune" system is more durable (Eysenck, 1997). That said, they tend to be risk takers, are more likely to be involved in car accidents, and inclined to use drugs and alcohol more than introverts (Maddi, 1989).

In this day and age, western cultures place high value on personal achievement and admire those endowed with strong social skills (Cain, 2012). There are so many workshops and seminars given on topics such as, making money and getting into relationships, the purpose of which is to develop these kinds of social skills among shy or introverted people. Even so, the extrovert is liable to pay a psychological price. For example, he has the never ending need to be in the company of others and is afraid to be alone. When an individual seeks to be the center of attention and finds it difficult to accept situations where someone else is in the limelight, he finds it nearly impossible to create close and intimate relationships, such as romantic relationships.

Adults and children blessed with the gift of the beetle's social artistry are more introverted, preferring a quiet environment with few stimuli. Introverted people direct their energy inwardly. They may be more contemplative, cautious, quiet, and prefer to spend their time with themselves reading, on the computer, or enjoying their own imagination. Introverted people are the happiest when they are inside their inner world, a world of sensitivity and thoughts (Cain, 2012). The long term memory areas of the brain are very developed in introverts. The routing of messages in the brain is longer and slower, but much deeper. Introverts respond with high levels of arousal to stimuli, and therefore, find it difficult to cope with an environment full of action and excitement, for instance, noisy surroundings full of people. In a society that admires those who have strong social skills, introverted people often feel they are not well equipped to deal with social situations. (Eysenck, 1997)

Due to preferences for extroverted social skills, introverted people often feel they are not well adapted in the social sense (Cain, 2012). In the competitive world in which we live in, action is valued more than contemplation or attentiveness, conspicuousness is preferred over observation. Nevertheless, introverts have a rich internal world. They are very creative and have more academic success than extroverts. Their knowledge is broader than extroverts. They are more persevering in their missions and process information thoroughly and precisely. They are level-headed and are excellent listeners (Ackerman & Rolfhus, 1999). Due to their ability to be highly attentive, they are likely to be first-rate friends and have an admirable capacity for intimate relationships, more so than extroverts (Cain, 2012).

Moreover, introverted people are good leaders and great managers, since they are not motivated by any desire to standout, but rather by a more profound goal. They are not afraid to cast doubt and they take the time to think, so their choices are wiser. Maimonides, Charles Darwin, Mahatma Gandhi, and Albert Einstein are a few examples of introverts (Cain, 2012; Grant, Gino & Hofmann, 2009).

In the book, *Zazee and Lalee Discover What Friendship Is All About*, we learn to recognize the depths of Lalee the Beetle, and her close relationship with her leaf. With her leaf, she feels secure enough to be herself:

Lalee whispered revealing stories to the leaf.
Sometimes the stories were short and the leaf listened with curiosity, while other times the stories were long and the leaf would yawn, stretch his edges in the breeze, and then return to listen to Lalee.

T: Lalee feels very close to her leaf. She shares with him, listens to him, and they have a very intimate relationship. Have you ever felt like Lalee?

Gali: When Tal and I were friends, we would tell each other everything.

T: Would you talk more or did you listen more?

Gali: Listen more.

T: That's one of the wonderful advantages introverted people have. They are very good listeners. When we have a close relationship, listening to someone else is very important. It's fantastic that you know how to listen.

Gali: But Tal always said that she was the only one telling things and that I wasn't talking at all. But that's not true, because I told her all sorts of things.

T: How did you respond to her saying that?

Gali: I didn't say anything. How should I have responded?

T: If we understand that knowing how to listen is a very important skill, what can we say about listening?

Gali: That I'm better at listening than talking.

T: That's a wonderful response, Gali. To know how to listen is truly a gift. Let's continue reading and see if you have any more gifts like these.

Lalee watched in amazement as Zazee danced between the flowers. Sometimes Zazee sat on a flower, drank its sweet nectar, collected the flower's pollen, and then flew off to the next flower.
"Maybe she will come to my flower? Perhaps even to my leaf?" thought Lalee.

T: Has that ever happened when you looked at Tal, maybe at other friends too, from the side, and you see how they quickly make connections and you hoped they might come up to you?

Gali: All the time. I want to be like that, too.
        I'm not someone who starts up conversations.

319

I am more of the shy type. Sometimes I'm jealous of Tal. Everything is easy for her.

T: I'm not so sure that your assumption is completely true. There are studies that show how even the most popular children don't have such an easy time, as it might seem from the side. As it turns out, almost one third of the attempts of the popular children to merge into social situations – fail. I will explain. Let's assume that Tal wants everyone to play a certain game. According to the study (Putallaz & Gottman, 1981), approximately one time out of three, no one will actually listen to her, or necessarily do what she wants.

Gali: That can't be right. We always do what she wants.

T: Let's make our own study and check it for ourselves. Who are the three most popular girls in your class?

Gali: Tal, Stav, and Nofar.

T: It would be great if you could make some observations this week, of the three of them, and check how they mix into social situations. What happens when they join a group that is already together, and what happens when they suggest something. Write everything down and together we'll analyze what you saw. It's a good idea if you take a notebook. We'll have a lot more assignments. What would you like to call the notebook?

Gali: "The Beetles Book."

T: Fantastic. You'll do the research, and in our next session, we'll continue to read from the book, *Zazee and Lalee Discover What Friendship is All About*.

In our next session, we analyzed Gali's findings. She was very happy to discover that Stav suggested to the other girls to play dodgeball and they rejected the suggestion. Gali was very glad to find out that Nofar suggested to one of the girls to come over after school and she said she couldn't. But most of all, Gali was thrilled to notice that Tal, the instigator of the ban, the one who was her closest friend and who "everything was easy for her," asked Niv to be her friend, and he declined. How much pleasure there was in this experiment and the conclusion that was reached as a result; to be a member of a group demands an investment of energy also from the most popular kids. Until we looked very closely, we didn't fully understand that: nothing comes easy, as it seems, for anyone. We also looked over the responses of the others that were refused. "What did they do?" I asked. Stav and Nofar totally ignored the refusal and went on as usual, as if nothing happened. The group also continued as before, and the momentary rejection wasn't even noticed. Tal, on the other hand, was very upset and angry. She seemed to have been deeply offended by the rejection of her offer of friendship and was very aggressive towards everyone. We presumed this was linked to her sensitivity to rejection, which we spoke about in earlier sessions. We learned that when we, or our ideas, are rejected, it's best to move on as if nothing happened, not to be shocked, and not to shrink away. It's a natural and normal process that happens to everyone.

We continued to read from the book and got to know Zazee and Lalee better.

Once, Lalee heard a humming sound coming closer.
She raised her eyes and discovered Zazee right above her – sitting on a white flower petal.
Lalee hopped and skipped and her heart pounded like a thousand drums.
"Who are you?" Zazee asked Lalee, as she spun around twice in

*the air, "Uh…I'm…La…Lalee…" stammered Lalee, and was at
a loss for words.*
"I'm Zazee," said the bee, and then smiled.

T: This segment relates to the way we create initial
        connections. Zazee asks Lalee, "Who are you?" Has it
        ever happened that you turned to someone you didn't
        know and asked them something in order to make a
        connection?
Gali: Not really.
T: Let's pay attention to what Zazee did. She asked a
        question and also smiled. What do you think about
        that?
Gali: That it's good.
T: Why is it good?
Gali: I don't know how to explain.

Practicing How to Make a Connection

In order to make a connection, it is best to begin with a verbal
or nonverbal clue whose purpose is to send the message, "I'm
interested in a connection." This can be a question or a phrase.
When we smile, we give the other side a sense of ease and safety.

I suggested to Gali that we do an exercise and try to feel these
things. I left the room and re-entered in a number of different
ways. One time I spoke and another I did not; once I smiled
and the other time I didn't. I asked Gali to write down what
she thought of me each time I entered the room. What feeling
did she get and if it caused her to want to create a connection
with me.

I was several types of people:

The Manner in Which I Entered the Room	Gali's Thoughts and Feelings	Would Gali Want to Make a Connection with Me?
I entered the room, sat down, and didn't say anything.	Odd, uncomfortable, what am I supposed to do?	No.
I entered the room, looked at Gali, smiled, sat down, and said nothing	She's nice.	A little.
I entered the room and said, "Shalom, I'm Naomi," without smiling	I'm not sure if she's nice or not.	Not really.
I entered the room, looked into Gali's eyes, smiled, and said, "Shalom, I'm Naomi."	She's nice; she's not scary.	Yes, very much.

T:　　So, Gali, what is your conclusion from this exercise?

Gali:　That a smile is a good thing.

T:　　**A smile, eye contact, and saying hello**, these are the behaviors that draw us nearer to one another. There are behaviors that bring us closer and there are behaviors that distance us – exactly the way you felt during the exercise. Now, we'll switch roles. You'll be various people coming into the room and we'll see how you feel. I'll try to respond to you in a genuine and natural manner according to how I feel at the same moment. If it's pleasant for me, I'll smile, and if it's not pleasant for me, I won't smile.

Exercises for entering a room help to "design" our style of entry into a social situation that increases the desire to make a connection. It was easy for Gali to smile, although it was hard for her to make direct eye contact and say, "Shalom, I'm Gali." We tried it over and over again until Gali succeeded in entering the room with a smile, made eye contact, and introduce herself. Following this, we played a game where we walked around a little table I have in the session room, in the same direction. While we were walking round and round the table, at a certain moment, I turned around towards Gali, and we both looked each other in the eyes, smiled, and said hello. After this, she became the initiator. Gali was the one who turned to me, both of us making eye contact, and saying hello.

T: Gali, you did a fine job. You succeeded in looking me in the eye, smiling, and saying, "Hi." I'm very proud of you. I'd like you to try the exercise we practiced here at school this week, with one friend from your class or section. Is there someone who seems to you to be nice, and that you could do the exercise in front of her?

Gali: There's a girl that isn't involved in the ban, but she's not really popular.

T: Why do you think she's not popular?

Gali: Because she's even more introverted than I am. She's really closed; she hardly talks.

T: How do you think she would react to a gesture like that from you, a look, a smile, and you saying, "Hi"?

Gali: Seems to me that she'll wonder why I'm doing it.

T: And how do you think she will respond?

Gali: Don't know.

T: We all want a connection. Even that girl. For some of us it's harder to make connections than for others. Like we said, not everyone is Zazee, but everyone wants to connect. I imagine that she will smile at you in return. Are you willing to make an experiment and check it?

Gali: I've thought about her a lot lately. I thought that maybe she feels very lonely, like me. But I didn't know what the right thing to do was and how to even start a conversation with her. I guess I'll try, if I have the courage.

T: What has to happen for you to have courage?

Gali: Not to think too much. I should just do it.

T: Let's think of something you can say to yourself that will help you not to think too much and just do it. Do you have any ideas?

Gali: Maybe "Don't think – do."

T: That's an excellent phrase. Give it a try and when we meet again next week I'll hear what happened.

The very next week after that, Gali came into the room, looked me in the eye, smiled and, said, "Shalom."

T: That was a great entrance. It makes me happy when you come in like that. How was it this week? Did you try to make a connection with that girl, the one we talked about?

Gali: Yes, I smiled at Reut and quietly said, "hi," and she smiled back at me. All of a sudden, I noticed that she looks at me many times, so sometimes I smile and sometimes I pretend I didn't see she was looking over.

T: From what you describe, it seems that she wants a connection, but doesn't know how to do it. Let's learn from Zazee how to do it.

Zazee initiates connection. She suggests to Lalee to join her, invites her, asks her questions, and lets her understand that

Lalee's friendship is important to her. Zazee suggests they go for a walk together among the flowers (*"Perhaps you'll come for a walk with me between the flowers?" suggests Zazee*), and she proposes this again when they have a closer bond (*"I have an idea!" continued Zazee. "Tomorrow we'll have a picnic together, underneath your leaf... What do you think?" Lalee jumped for joy*).

T: Do you think you might ask Reut to join you, maybe initiate a conversation?

Gali: I'm not sure. I don't know if it's the right thing to do, because then I won't have any chance with Stav and Tal, who are the most popular. But even if I decide that I want to be friends with Reut, I'm not sure about the right way to do it. With Tal and Stav, I wasn't the one who was responsible for creating the connection. It was their initiative.

T: If so, this is a great opportunity to learn new skills you were lacking and that you can practice with Reut. We'll have to talk about the matter of belonging to Tal and Stav's group and what gains and losses there are for you when you try to reconnect with someone who, at the moment, doesn't want your friendship. I suggest that for now we try to learn how to make a first contact. Learn how you can make contact with Reut, or with any other girl you would like to. I'll be Reut and you try to tell or do something that seems like a good way to create a connection. Try to suggest something to me, ask me for something, tell me something, or maybe ask me a question. I'll help you and together we'll think of different ideas. After we write down the ideas, we'll rate them from one to ten, according to what you feel is best for you and what works for you.

Creating a First Contact	Gali's Rating Scale
Want to listen to a song on my I-phone?	2
I brought some chocolate. Want some?	4
Did you do the homework assignment?	1
To say, "What an annoying teacher."	6
Do you have the homework assignment for tomorrow? I didn't have time to write it down.	8

T: It is no coincidence that the last sentence got the highest mark. It's the most relevant. It reflects a point of connection, both of you are students in the same class. The other sentences don't reflect such a connection, and therefore, are perceived as less appropriate. Do you think you can say that sentence to Reut this week?

Gali: Yes. She's a good student and she really does write everything down, so it's appropriate.

A few days later, Gali's mother called and was excited to tell me that Reut had been over at their house one afternoon. It turns out that Gali initiated another step and invited Reut to come over to her house. A well-known characteristic of social rejection is the following heightening of motivation to make new bonds, even if they aren't genuine. Meanwhile, the individual is making an effort to create a positive impression and advance himself in new social circles (Maner et al., 2007).

During the next few sessions with Gali, we deepened our knowledge of her introverted side, through our familiarity with Lalee. We learned to appreciate Gali's ability to create a close, accepting, and accommodating bond. Furthermore, to appreciate Gali's ability to be alone, to imagine, to think, to contemplate, to write, to sing with the music on the I-phone, and also to dance alone in her room. We learned that sometimes it's not easy to be Zazee. Sometimes she doesn't even have a leaf to be with, despite her large number of friends:

"I want a leaf of my own, too," said Zazee.
"Really?" asked Lalee in wonder.
"Really," answered Zazee, "I float from flower to flower and dance with them, but sometimes I would like to rest on my very own leaf, and play games with him and tell only him stories and secrets."

We understood that something new was happening to Gali and her new friendship with Reut. We understood that Reut had become a sort of "leaf" for Gali. We understood that there was a mutual bond between them, close and intimate, which reminded us of Lalee and her leaf. Gali learned, through Zazee, to share her own experiences and not only to listen. She learned from Zazee additional social skills, such as, the skill of talking about feelings clearly and directly, to talk about herself and her preferences – what I like or don't like, to initiate social contacts, and much more. We discovered which of our behaviors draw people closer to us and which ones distance other people from us. In particular, we learned to tell ourselves, "Who I am is wonderful." Being Gali is fantastic. The bee doesn't turn into a beetle and the beetle doesn't become a bee. Being a bee is beautiful. Being a beetle is brilliant. But they can learn from one another the communication skills each one is lacking.

Bibliography

Ackerman, P. L., & Rolfhus, E. L. (1999). The locus of adult intelligence: Knowledge abilities, and non-ability traits. *Psychology and Aging, 14,* 314-330.

Alford, B., & Beck, A. T. (1997). *The Integrative Power of Cognitive Therapy.* New York: Guilford Press.

Anderson, C. A., & Bushman, B. J. (2002). Human aggression. *Annual Review of Psychology, 53,* 27-51.

Archer, J., & Coyne, S. (2005). An integrated review of indirect, relational, and social aggression. *Personality and Social Psychology Review, 9,* 212-230.

Asher, S. R., & Coie, J. D. (1990). *Peer Rejection in Childhood.* New York: Cambridge University Press.

Bandura, A. (1973). *Aggression: A Social Learning Analysis.* New Jersey: Prentice – Hall Inc.

Bandura, A. (1977). Self-efficacy: Toward a unifying theory of behavioral change. *Psychological Review, 84,* 191-215.

Bandura, A. (1994). Self-Efficacy. In V. S. Ramachaudran (Ed.), *Encyclopedia of Human Behavior* (Vol. 4, pp. 71-81). New York: Academic Press.

Bandura, A. (1997). *Self-Efficacy – The Exercise of Control.* New York: Freedman and Company.

Bandura, A., Caprara, G. V., Barbaranelli, C., & Regalia, C. (2001). Socio-cognitive self-regulatory mechanisms governing transgressive behavior. *Journal of Personality and Social Psychology, 8,* 125- 135.

Bandura, A., & Walters, R. H. (2010). Dependency conflict in aggressive delinquents. *Journal of Social Issues, 14*, 52-65.

Barkley, R. A. (1995). *Taking Charge of AD/HD: The Complete Authoritative Guide for Parents.* New York: Guilford Press.

Barkley, R. A. (2001). Executive functions and self-regulation: An evolutionary neuropsychological perspective. *Neuropsychology Review, 11*, 1–29.

Barlow, D. H. (2008). *Clinical Handbook of Psychological Disorders, Fourth Edition: A Step-by-Step Treatment Manual.* New York: Guilford Press.

Baumeister, R. F. (Ed.) (1999). *The Self in Social Psychology.* Philadelphia, PA: Psychology Press: Taylor & Francis.

Baumeister, R. F., Bushman, B., & Campbell, K. (2000). Self-esteem, narcissism, and aggression: Does violence result from low self-esteem or from threatened egotism? *Current Directions in Psychological Science, 9* (1), 26-29.

Baumeister, R. F., Campbell, J. D., Krueger, J. I., & Vohs, K. D. (2003). Does high self-esteem cause better performance, interpersonal success, happiness, or healthier lifestyles? *Psychological Science in the Public Interest, 4* (1), 1-44.

Baumeister, R. F., DeWall, C. N., Ciarocco, N. J., & Twenge, J. M. (2005). Social exclusion impairs self-regulation. *Journal of Personality and Social Psychology, 88*, 589-604.

Baumeister, R. F., & Leary, M. R. (1995). The need to belong: Desire for interpersonal attachments as a fundamental human motivation. *Psychological Bulletin, 117*, 497-529.

Baumeister, R. F., Smart, L., & Boden, J. M. (1996). Relation of threatened egotism to violence and aggression: The dark side of high self-esteem. *Psychological Review, 103*, 5-33.

Baumrind, D. (1966). Effects of authoritative parental control on child behavior. *Child Development, 37* (4), 887-907.

Baumrind, D. (1967). Child care practices anteceding three patterns of preschool behavior. *Genetic Psychology Monographs, 75* (1), 43-88.

Baumrind, D. (1971). Current patterns of parental authority. *Developmental Psychology Monograph, 4,* (1, Pt.2).

Beck, A. T. (1967). *Depression: Clinical, Experimental, and Theoretical Aspects.* New York, NY: Harper and Row.

Beck, A. T. (1976). *Cognitive Therapy and the Emotional Disorders.* New York: Meridian.

Beck, A. T. (1988). *Love is Never Enough.* New York: Harper & Row.

Beck, A. T., Emery, G., & Greenberg, R. L. (1985). *Anxiety Disorders and Phobias: A Cognitive Perspective.* New York: Basic Books.

Beck, J. S. (1995). *Cognitive Therapy: Basics and Beyond.* New York: Guilford Press.

Beck, J. S. (2011). *Cognitive Behavior Therapy: Basics and Beyond* (2nd ed.). New York: Guilford Press.

Beidel, D. C., Turner, S. M., & Morris, T. L. (1995). A new inventory to assess social anxiety and phobia: The social phobia and anxiety inventory for children. *Psychology Assessment, 7,* 73-79.

Bernstein, G. A., Layne, A. E., Egan, E. A., & Tennison, D. M. (2005). School-based interventions for anxious children. *Journal of the American Academy of Child and Adolescent Psychiatry, 44* (11), 1118-1127.

Berkowitz, L. (1990). On the formation and regulation of anger and aggression. *American Psychologist, 45,* 494-503.

Briesmeister, J. M., & Schaefer, C. E. (1998). *Handbook of Parent Training: Parents as Co-Therapists for Children's Behavior Problems.* New York: Wiley.

Broidy, L. M., Nagin, D. S., Tremblay, R. E., Bates, J. E., Brame, B., Dodge, K. A., Fergusson, D., Horwood, J. L., Loeber, R., Laird, R., Lynam, D., Moffitt, T. E., Pettit, G. S., & Vitaro, F. (2003). Developmental trajectories of childhood disruptive behaviors and adolescent delinquency: A six site, cross-national study. *Developmental Psychology, 39*, 222-245.

Brown, A. D. (2011). Children's self-esteem and parental influence. *Canadian Counseling and Psychotherapy Association.* Retrieved April 14, 2011.

Brown, J. D., & Dutton, K. A. (1995). The thrill of victory, the complexity of defeat: Self-esteem and people's emotional reactions to success and failure. *Journal of Personality and Social Psychology, 68* (4), 712-722.

Burns, D. D. (1980). *Feeling Good: The New Mood Therapy.* New York: Wm. Morrow and Co.

Bushman, B. J., Bonacci, A. M., Pedersen, W. C., Vasquez, E. A., & Miller, N. (2005). Chewing on it can chew you up: Effects of rumination on triggered displaced aggression. *Journal of Personality and Social Psychology, 88*, 969–983.

Buss, A. H. (1961). *The Psychology of Aggression.* New York: John Wiley & Son.

Buss, A. H., & Perry, M. (1992). The aggression questionnaire. *Journal of Personality and Social Psychology, 63*, 452-459.

Butler, A. C., Hokanson, J. E., & Flynn, H. A. (1994). A comparison of self-esteem lability and low trait self-esteem as vulnerability factors for depression. *Journal of Personality and Social Psychology, 66* (1), 166-177.

Cain, S. (2012). *Quiet: The Power of Introverts in a World That Can't Stop Talking.* New York: Crown Publishers.

Campbell, S. B., Spieker, S., Burchinal, M., & Poe, M. D. (2006). Trajectories of aggression from toddlerhood to age nine predict academic and social functioning through age twelve. *Journal of Child Psychology and Psychiatry and Allied Disciplines*, 47, 791-800.

Chadha, N., & Misra, G. (2004). Patterns of prosocial reasoning in Indian children. *Psychology & Developing Societies*, 16, 159-186.

Christie-Mizell, C. A., Ida, A. K., & Keith, V. M. (2010). African Americans and physical health: The consequences of self-esteem and happiness. *Journal of Black Studies, 40* (6), 1189-1211.

Cohen, E. (2006). Parental level of awareness: An organizing scheme of parents' belief systems as a guide in parent therapy. In C. Wachs & L. Jacobs (Eds.), *Parent-Focused Child Therapy: Attachment, Identification, and Reflective Functions* (pp. 39-64). Lanham, MD: Rowman & Littlefield.

Cohen, E., Chazan, S. E., Lerner, M., & Maimon, E. (2010). Post-traumatic play in young children exposed to terrorism: An empirical study. *Infant Mental Health Journal, 31* (2), 1-23.

Clarke, G. N., DeBar, L. L., & Lewinsohn, P. M. (2003). Cognitive–behavioral group treatment for adolescent depression. In A.E. Kazdin (Ed.), *Evidenced-Based Psychotherapies for Children and Adolescents* (pp. 120-134). New York: Guilford Press.

Crick, N. R., & Dodge, K. A. (1994). A review and reformulation of social information: processing mechanisms in children's social adjustment. *Psychological Bulletin, 115* ,74-101.

Crocker, J., & Wolfe, C. T. (2001). Contingencies of self-worth. *Psychological Review, 108*, 593-623.

Dahlen, E. R., & Deffenbacher, J. L. (2001). Anger management. In W. J. Lyddon & J. V. Jones (Eds.), *Empirically Supported Cognitive Therapies: Current and Future Applications* (pp. 163-181). New York: Springer Publishing Company.

Dattilio, F. (2010). *Cognitive–Behavioral Therapy with Couples and Families.* New York: Guilford Press.

Denson, T. F., Pedersen, W. C., & Miller, N. (2006). The displaced aggression questionnaire. *Journal of Personality and Social Psychology, 90*, 1032-1051.

Dodge, K. A., & Coie, J. D. (1987). Social information processing factors in reactive and proactive aggression in children's peer groups. *Journal of Personality and Social Psychology, 53*, 1146-1158.

Dodge, K. A., Coie, J. D., & Brakke, N. P. (1982). Behavior patterns of socially rejected and neglected preadolescents: The roles of social approach and aggression. *Journal of Abnormal Child Psychology, 10*, 389-410.

Dodge, K. A., & Feldman, E. (1990). Issues in social cognition and sociometric status. In S. R. Asher & J. D. Coie (Eds.), *Peer Rejection in Childhood* (pp.119-155). New York: Cambridge University Press.

Dodge, K. A., Laird, R., Lochman, J. E., & Zelli, A. (2002). Multidimensional latent-construct analysis of children's social information processing patterns: correlations with aggressive behavior problems. *Psychological Assessment, 14* (1), 60-73.

Dodge, K. A., & Somberg, D. (1987). Hostile attributional biases among aggressive boys are exacerbated under conditions of threats to the self. *Child Development, 58,* 213-224.

Donnellan, B., Trzesniewski, K., Robins, R. W., Moffitt, T. E., & Caspi, A. (2005). Low self-esteem is related to aggression, antisocial behavior, and delinquency. *Psychological Science, 16* (4), 328-335.

Downey, G., & Feldman, S. I. (1996). Implications of rejection sensitivity for intimate relationships. *Journal of Personality and Social Psychology, 70,* 1327-1343.

Downey, G., Lebolt, A., Rincon, C., & Freitas, A. L. (1998). Rejection sensitivity and children's interpersonal difficulties. *Child Development, 69,* 1072-1089.

Dryden, W. (2009). *Rational Emotive Behavior Therapy: Distinctive Features.* London: Routledge.

Dummett, N. (2010). Cognitive–behavioral therapy with children, young people, and families: From individual to systemic therapy. *Advances in Psychiatric Treatment, 16* (1), 23-36.

Dweck, C. S. (2006). *Mindset: The New Psychology of Success.* New York: Random House.

Eagly, A. H., & Steffen, V. J. (1986). Gender and aggressive behavior: A meta-analytic review of the social psychological literature. *Psychological Bulletin, 100,* 309-330.

Egan, S. K., & Perry, D. G. (2001). Gender identity: A multi-dimensional analysis with implications for psychosocial adjustment. *Developmental Psychology, 37,* 451-463.

Eisenberg, N. (2006). Social, emotional, and personality development. In *Handbook of Child Psychology* (6th ed.). Hoboken, NJ: Wiley.

Eisenberg, N., & Fabes, R. A. (1992). Emotion, regulation, and the development of social competence. In M. S. Clark

(Ed.), *Emotion and Social Behavior: Review of Personality and Social Psychology* (pp. 119-150). Newbury Park, CA: Sage.

Ellis, A. (1979). The basic clinical theory of rational-emotive therapy. In A. Ellis & J. M. Whiteley (Eds.), *Theoretical and Empirical Foundations of Rational-Emotive Therapy* (pp. 61-100). Monterey, CA: Brooks/Cole.

Ellis, A., & Dryden, W. (1987). *The Practice of Rational Emotive Therapy.* New York, Springer.

Emler, N. (2001). *Self-Esteem: The Costs and Causes of Low Self- Worth.* New York: York Publishing Services.

Epel, N. (2003). *Grandfather Jamiko's Secret Jar.* Tel-Aviv University, Ramot Publishing.

Epel, N. (2007). *Aggressive Behavior: The Moderating Role of Self-Control Skills and Their Pro-Social Values.* Dissertation for Doctorate of Philosophy Degree, Tel-Aviv University.

Epel, N. (2011). *Grandfather Jamiko's Light Switch.* Kiryat Bialik, Ach Publishing.

Epel, N. (2012). "Then Came the Fist" on childhood aggression [electronic version]. Derived on October 5, 2014, from the Hebrew Psychology website: http://www. hebpsy.net/articles.asp?id=2897

Epel, N. (2013a). *Zazee and Lalee Discover What Friendship Is All About.* Kiryat Bialik, Ach Publishing.

Epel, N. (2013b). *About Bees, Beetles, and Creating Social Ties* [electronic version]. Derived on November 2, 2014, from the Hebrew Psychology website: http://www.hebpsy.net/ articles.asp?id=2980

Eysenck, H. J. (1997). *Dimensions of Personality.* New Jersey: Transaction Publishers.

Field, T. M. (1998). Massage therapy effects. *American Psychologist, 53* (12), 1270-1281.

Field, A. P. (2006). I don't like it because it eats sprouts: Conditioning preferences in children. *Behaviour Research and Therapy, 44*, 439-455.

Ford, M. B., & Collins, N. L. (2010). Self-esteem moderates neuroendocrine and psychological responses to interpersonal rejection. *Journal of Personality and Social Psychology, 98*, 405-419.

Fredrickson, B. L. (2001). The role of positive emotions in positive psychology: The broaden-and-build theory of positive emotions. *American Psychologist, 56*, 218-226.

Friedberg, R. D., & McClure, J. M. (2002). *Clinical Practice of Cognitive Therapy with Children and Adolescents: The Nuts and Bolts*. New York: Guilford Press.

Friedberg, R. D., McClure, J. M., & Garcia, J. H. (2009). *Cognitive Therapy Techniques for Children and Adolescents*. New York: Guilford Press.

Ginsburg, G. S., Grover, R. L., & Ialongo, N. (2004). Parenting behaviors among anxious and non-anxious mothers: Relation with concurrent and long-term child outcomes. *Child and Family Behavior Therapy, 26* (4), 23-41.

Goleman, D. J. (2006). *Social Intelligence: The New Science of Social Relationships*. New York: Random House/Bantam Books.

Grant, A., Gino, F., & Hofmann, D. (2009). The hidden advantages of quiet bosses. *Harvard Business Review, 28*.

Hamlyn. D, W. (1983). *Perception, Learning and the Self: Essays in the Philosophy of Psychology*. London; Boston: Routledge & K. Paul.

Hastings, P. D., Zhan-Waxler, C., Robinson, J., Usher, B., & Bridges, D. (2000). The development of concern for others in children with behavior problems. *Development Psychology, 36,* 531-546.

Hendrix, H. (1988). *Getting the Love You Want.* Melbourne, Victoria: Schwartz Wilkinson.

Hewitt, J. P. (2009). *Oxford Handbook of Positive Psychology.* Oxford University Press. pp. 217-224.

Hubbard, J. A., Dodge, K. A., Cillessen, A. H. N., Coie, J. D., & Schwartz, D. (2001). The dyadic nature of social information processing in boys' reactive and proactive aggression. *Journal of Personality and Social Psychology, 80,* 268-280.

Hudson, J. L., Lyneham, H. J., & Rapee, R. M. (2008). Social anxiety. In A. Eisen (Ed.), *Clinical Handbook of Childhood Behavioral Problems: Case Formulation and Step-by-Step Treatment Programs* (pp. 53-101). New York: Guildford Press.

Joireman, J., Anderson, J., & Strathman, A. (2003). The aggression paradox: Understanding links among aggression, sensation seeking, and the consideration of future consequences. *Journal of Personality and Social Psychology, 84,* 1287-1302.

Judge, T. A., & Bono, J. E. (2001). Relationship of core self-evaluations traits – self-esteem, generalized self-efficacy, locus of control, and emotional stability – with job satisfaction and job performance: A meta-analysis. *Journal of Applied Psychology, 86* (1), 80-92.

Kazdin, A. E. (1984). *Conduct Disorder in Childhood and Adolescence.* Newbury Park, CA: Sage.

Kazdin, A. E. (2003). Problem solving skills training and parent management training for conduct disorder. In A. E. Kazdin, & J. R. Weisz (Eds.), *Evidence-Based*

Psychotherapies for Children and Adolescents (pp. 241-262). New York: Guilford.

Kendall, P. C. (2006). *Child and Adolescent Therapy*. New York: Guilford Press.

Kendall, P. C., Choudhury, M., Hudson, J., & Webb, A. (2002). *The CAT Project Manual*. Ardmore, PA: Workbook Publishing.

Kendall, P. C., & Hedtke, K. (2006a). *Cognitive-Behavioral Therapy for Anxious Children: Therapist Manual* (3rd ed.). Ardmore, PA: Workbook Publishing.

Kendall, P. C., & Hedtke, K. (2006b). *Coping Cat Workbook* (2nd ed.). Ardmore, PA: Workbook Publishing.

Kendall, P. C., & Suveg, C. (2006). Treating anxiety disorders in youth. In P. C. Kendall (Ed.), *Child and Adolescent Therapy* (pp. 243-294). New York: The Guilford Press.

Koeppen, A. S. (1974). Relaxation training for children. *Elementary School Guidance and Counseling, 9*, 14-21.

Kushnir, J., & Sadeh, A. (2012). Assessment of brief interventions for nighttime fears in preschool children. *European Journal of Pediatrics, 171*, 67-75.

Kuster, F., Orth, U., & Meier, L. L. (2012). Rumination mediates the prospective effect of low self-esteem on depression: A five-wave longitudinal study. *Personality and Social Psychology Bulletin, 38*, 747-759.

Lane, J., Lane, A. M., & Kyprianou, A. (2004). Self-efficacy, self-esteem, and their impact on academic performance. *Social Behavior and Personality, 32* (3), 247-256.

Leary, M. R., Tambor, E. S., Terdal, S. K., & Downs, D. L. (1995). Self-esteem as an interpersonal monitor: The sociometer hypothesis. *Journal of Personality and Social Psychology, 68* (3), 518-530.

Levin, N. (2004). *The Behavior of Silence Among Children with Selective Muteness*. A dissertation paper for Certified Psychology Degree, Tel-Aviv University.

Linehan, M. M. (1993). *Cognitive Behavioral Treatment of Borderline Personality Disorder*. New York: Guilford Press.

Ludwig, K. B., & Pittman, J. F. (1999). Adolescent prosocial values and self-efficacy in relation to delinquency, risky sexual behavior, and drug use. *Youth & Society, 30,* 461-482.

Luthar, S. S., Barkin, S. H., & Crossman, E. J. (2013). "I can, therefore I must": Fragility in the upper-middle classes. *Development and Psychopathology, 25,* 1529-1549.

Lyneham, H. J., & Rapee, R. M. (2005). Evaluation and treatment of anxiety disorders in the general pediatric population: A clinician's guide. *Child and Adolescent Psychiatric Clinics of North America, 14* (4), 845-862.

Maddi, S. R. (1989). *Personality Theories: A Comparative Analysis* (5th ed.). Chicago: Dorsey Press.

Maner, J. K., DeWall, C. N., Baumeister, R. F., & Schaller, M. (2007). Does social exclusion motivate interpersonal reconnection? Resolving the "porcupine problem." *Journal of Personality and Social Psychology, 92* (1), 42-55.

Meichenbaum, D. H. (1977). *Cognitive Behavior Modification: An Integrative Approach*. New York: Plenum.

Meyers, J. (2012). *Problem Solving as a Treatment Method for Children*. Kiryat Bialik, Ach Publishing.

Muris, P. (2007). *Normal and Abnormal Fear and Anxiety in Children*. Elsevier Inc.

Muris, P., Merckelbach, H., Ollendick, T. H., King, N. J., & Bogie, N. (2001). Children's nighttime fears: Parent-child ratings of frequency, content, origins, coping behaviors, and severity. *Behavior Research and Therapy, 39* (1), 13-28.

Nezlek, J. B., Kowalski, R. M., Leary, M. R., Blevins, T., & Holgate, S. (1997). Personality moderators of reactions to interpersonal rejection: Depression and trait self-esteem. *Personality & Social Psychology Bulletin, 23* (12), 1235-1244.

Omer, H. (2002*). The Struggle Against Childhood Violence: Non Violent Resistance.* Ben Shemen: Modan.

Owens, L. D., Slee, P., & Shute, R. (2000). Guess what I just heard: Indirect aggression among teenage girls in Australia. *Aggressive Behavior, 26,* 67-83.

Padesky, C. A. (1993). Socratic Questioning: Changing Minds or Guiding Discovery? A keynote address delivered at the *European Congress of Behavioral and Cognitive Therapies,* London, September 24th.

Poulin, F., & Boivin, M. (2000). The role of proactive and reactive aggression in development of boys' friendships. *Developmental Psychology, 36,* 233-240.

Putallaz, M., & Gottman, J. M. (1981). Social skills and group acceptance. In S. R. Asher, & J. M. Gottman (Eds.), *The Development of Children's Friendships.* New York: Cambridge, University Press.

Ramsey, R. D. (1994). *501 Ways to Boost Your Child's Self-Esteem.* McGraw-Hill Professional Publishing.

Ronen, T. (1992). *Self-Control and Learned Resourcefulness: Planning, Application, and Preparation for Intervention.* Tel-Aviv: Papyrus, Published by the School for Social Work.

Ronen, T. (1994). *More Than Anything – Love: The Art and Expertise of Children's Therapy.* Tel-Aviv University, Ramot.

Ronen, T. (1994). Imparting self-control in the school setting. *Child and Family Behavior Therapy, 16,* 1-20.

Ronen, T. (2003). *Cognitive Constructivist Psychotherapy with Children: Theory, Techniques, and Case Studies*. New York: Kluwer/ Plenum.

Ronen, T. (2005). Students' evidence-based practice intervention for children with oppositional defiant disorder. *Research in Social Work Practice, 15*, 165-179.

Ronen, T., Rahav, G., & Moldawsky, A. (2007). Aggressive behavior among Israeli elementary school students and associated emotional/behavioral problems and self-control. *School Psychology Quarterly, 22* (3), 407-431.

Ronen, T., & Rosenbaum, M. (2001). Helping children to help themselves: A case study of enuresis and nail biting. *Research on Social Work Practice, 11*, 338-356.

Rosenbaum, M. (1980). A schedule for assessing self-control behaviors: Preliminary findings. *Behavior Therapy, 11*, 109-121.

Rosenbaum, M. (1990). The role of learned resourcefulness in the self-control of health behavior. In M. Rosenbaum (Ed.), *Learned Resourcefulness: On Coping Skills, Self-Control, and Adaptive Behavior* (pp. 3-30). New York: Springer.

Rosenbaum, M. (1998). Opening versus closing strategies in controlling one's responses to experience. In M. Kofta, G. Weary, & G. Sedek (Eds.), *Personal Control in Action: Cognitive and Motivational Mechanisms* (pp. 61-84). New York: Plenum.

Rosenbaum, M. (2000). The self-regulation of experience: Openness and construction. In P. Dewe, M. Leiter, & T. Cox (Eds.), *Coping, Health and Organizations* (pp.51-67). London: Taylor & Francis.

Rosenberg, M., Schooler, C., Schoenback, C., & Rosenberg,

F. (1995). Global self-esteem and specific self-esteem: Different concepts, different outcomes. *American Sociological Review, 60,* 141-156.

Satir, V. (1985). *The Modern Family.* Sifriat Poalim Publishing Group, Tel-Aviv.

Seligman, M. (2010). *Flourish: A Visionary New Understanding of Happiness and Well-being.* New York: Free Press.

Simmons, R. (2002). *Odd Girl Out: The Hidden Culture of Aggression in Girls.* New York: Harcourt.

Skinner, E., Johnson, S., & Snyder, T. (2005). Six dimensions of parenting: A motivational model. *Parenting: Science and Practice, 5* (2), 175-235.

Southam-Gerow, M. A., & Kendall, P. C. (2002). Emotion regulation and understanding: Implications for child psychopathology and therapy. *Clinical Psychology Review, 22,* 189-222.

Speirs Neumeister, K. L., & Finch, W. H. (2006). Perfectionism in high ability students: Relational precursors and implications for achievement. *Gifted Child Quarterly, 50,* 238-251.

Spielberger, C. D., Crane, R. S., Kearns, W. D., Pellegrin, K. L., Rickman, R. L., & Johnson, E. H. (1991). Anger and anxiety in essential hypertension. In C. D Spielberger, I. G. Sarason, Z. Kulcsar, & G. L. Van Heck (Eds.), *Stress and Emotion* (pp. 265-283). New York: Hemisphere/Taylor & Francis.

Strauss, R. S. (2000). Childhood obesity and self-esteem. *Pediatrics, 105* (1), 15-20.

Tremblay, R. E. (1999). When children's social development fails. In D. Keating & C. Hertzman (Eds.), *Developmental Health and The Wealth of Nations: Social, Biological, and*

Educational dynamics (pp. 55-71). New York: Guilford Press.

Twenge, J. M. (2000). The age of anxiety? Birth cohort change in anxiety and neuroticism. *Journal of Personality and Social Psychology, 79* (6), 1007-1021.

Tyson, P. D. (1998). Physiological arousal, reactive aggression, and the induction of an incompatible relaxation response. *Aggression and Violent Behavior, 3,* 143-158.

Uzonwanne, F. C., & Uzonwanne, G. C. (2014). Prevalence of self-efficacy and self-esteem among bankers in select southwest states in Nigeria. *Journal Of Humanities And Social Science, 19* (8), 110-119.

Vohs, K. D., Bardone, A. M., Joiner, T. E., & Abramson, L. Y. (1999). Perfectionism, perceived weight status, and self-esteem interact to predict bulimic symptoms: A model of bulimic symptom development. *Journal of Abnormal Psychology, 108* (4), 695-700.

Wolpe, J. (1958). *Psychotherapy by Reciprocal Inhibition.* California: Stanford University Press.

Wolpe, J., & Lazarus, A. (1996). *Behavior Therapy Techniques.* Oxford: Pergamon Press Ltd.

Wolpe, J., & Wolpe, D. (1981). *Our Useless Fears.* Boston: Houghton Mifflin Company.

Zeman, J., & Shipman, K. L. (1996). Children's expression of negative affect: Reasons and methods. *Developmental Psychology, 32,* 842-849.

Zetler-Rom, T., & Epel, N. (2014). Cognitive behavior therapy for Trichotillomania: Case analysis. *Conversations, 2,* 192-198.

Made in the USA
Middletown, DE
21 January 2020